Living Inside Our Hope

Also by Staughton Lynd

*Anti-Federalism in Dutchess County, New York: A Study of
    Democracy and Class Conflict in the Revolutionary Era*
The Other Side (with Tom Hayden)
Class Conflict, Slavery, and the United States Constitution
The Resistance (with Michael Ferber)
*Strategy and Program: Two Essays Toward a New American
    Socialism* (with Gar Alperovitz)
Intellectual Origins of American Radicalism
*The Fight Against Shutdowns: Youngstown's Steel Mill
    Closings*
*Solidarity Unionism: Rebuilding the Labor Movement from
    Below*
*Labor Law for the Rank and Filer; or, Building Solidarity
    While Staying Clear of the Law*

Edited by Staughton Lynd

American Labor Radicalism: Testimonies and Interpretations
*Rank and File: Personal Histories by Working-Class
    Organizers* (with Alice Lynd)
Homeland: Oral Histories of Palestine and Palestinians
    (with Alice Lynd and Sam Bahour)
Nonviolence in America: A Documentary History (with
    Alice Lynd)
*"We Are All Leaders": The Alternative Unionism of the Early
    1930s*

Living Inside Our Hope

A Steadfast Radical's Thoughts on Rebuilding the Movement

Staughton Lynd

ILR PRESS
An imprint of Cornell University Press
Ithaca and London

First published 1997 by Cornell University Press
First printing, Cornell Paperbacks, 1997

Printed in the United States of America

Library of Congress Cataloging-in-Publication Data

Lynd, Staughton.
    Living inside our hope : a steadfast radical's thoughts on rebuilding the movement / Staughton Lynd.
        p.   cm.
    Includes bibliographical references and index.
        ISBN 0-8014-3363-0 (alk. paper). — ISBN 0-8014-8402-2 (pbk. : alk. paper)
        1. New Left—United States.   2. Radicalism—United States. I. Title.
    HN90.R3L93   1997
320.53—dc21   96-39270

TCF This book is printed on Lyons Falls Turin Book, a paper that is totally chlorine-free and acid-free.

Cloth printing   10 9 8 7 6 5 4 3 2 1
Paperback printing 10 9 8 7 6 5 4 3 2 1

Codi, here's what I've decided: the very least you can do in your life is to figure out what you hope for. And the most you can do is live inside that hope. Not admire it from a distance but live right in it, under its roof.

—Barbara Kingsolver, *Animal Dreams*

Contents

Preface

In thinking about and writing these essays, I have been "accompanied" by many members of my immediate family. The reader of Essays 1, 3, 4, and 6 will come to understand the particular nature of some of these debts. Above all and always, my wife, Alice, has both nurtured and clarified what I try to say here. Alice and I are co-authors of Essay 4, "Liberation Theology for Quakers," which offers an overview of our journey together. I also thank my cousin David Hartley, the first Quaker and first conscientious objector I ever knew.

To make a publishable book out of essays written over a period of . twenty-five years for very different audiences I needed other kinds of help.

I first met Frances Goldin in 1958. She ran a weekly clinic for tenants at the University Settlement House on New York City's Lower East Side, where I was employed as a community organizer. Later she became a literary agent. Reading Barbara Kingsolver's *Animal Dreams* (from which the title of this book is taken), I noticed that Frances had been Kingsolver's agent in finding a publisher for that wonderful novel. A minimalist definition of a literary agent is a person willing to send a manuscript to a publisher after rejection by another publisher more times than any author would have the chutzpah to contemplate. Without Frances Goldin, this volume would not have seen the light of day.

During the months in which I drafted the Introduction to these essays, Alice and I had the opportunity to make a new friend, Margaret Randall. Margaret Randall spent most of the 1960s in Mexico, the 1970s in Cuba, and the early 1980s in Nicaragua. She produced remarkable collections of oral histories, especially of women in these revolutionary societies. Then she successfully did battle with the Immigration and Naturalization Service to return to the United States. Her comments about my draft Introduction were detailed, incisive, and consistently useful.

Finally, it has been a pleasure to work with Frances Benson, Andrea Fleck Clardy, Susan Kuc, Teresa Jesionowski, and their colleagues at Cornell University Press. Perhaps I have given some of these co-workers an opportunity to relive their own experience of the 1960s. What I know for sure is that they are editors and marketing staff with whom I have laughed more often than I have struggled.

All but two of the following essays have previously appeared in print and are included in this volume by permission of the publishers. There have been minor editorial changes in some of these essays, and in some cases notes have been added.

"The Internationalization of Capital and Labor's Response" is an unpublished talk to the Second Annual Conference on Workers' Self-Organization in May 1990. David Roediger encouraged me to expand it into a small book with the title *Solidarity Unionism,* published by Charles H. Kerr.

"The Webbs, Lenin, Rosa Luxemburg" is an unpublished paper delivered at the North American Labor History Conference in October 1995. Elizabeth Faue supported me in this project and chaired the session at which I presented the paper.

During that session I asked Elizabeth whether she thought (as I do) that feminism is associated with values of horizontal decision making and nonviolence. In response, she indicated that these were values likely to be espoused by any person in a marginalized social position, and described "feminism" as including the belief that every person should have a voice in decisions affecting his or her life. Margaret Randall used almost the identical words in defining "feminism" a few months later, adding: "But I think we must have *more* than a voice. We must also have the *power* to effect change. For me, this is what feminism is really about: an equitable distribution of power. There are so many places where women do have a voice, but then that voice is drowned out by (largely male) structures of power." If "feminism" can be thus defined and understood, then these are feminist essays.

This book is the work not only of someone who has been both an academic and an activist but of someone who has been both a lawyer and a historian. I ask practitioners of both disciplines to understand my attempt to create a consistent style of notes that will be reasonably intelligible to the lay reader.

The conventional way to cite a legal decision is to indicate the parties in the manner that they appear in the complaint, then to set forth the volume of the legal series in which the decision appears followed by the abbreviation designating the series and the number of the page on which the decision begins, followed by an abbreviated designation of the court and the year of the decision, in parentheses. Thus the most significant case in which I have been involved is conventionally cited as *Local 1330, United Steel Workers of America v. United States Steel Corporation*, 631 F.2d 1264 (6th Cir. 1980).

I have followed this form. However, when the citation is to a certain page or pages within the decision I have inserted "p." or "pp." for the convenience of the lay reader. Hence in referring to material that appears on pages 1279–80 of this decision, I use the form, *Local 1330*, 631 F.2d, pp. 1279–80. In citing a law, I similarly begin with the volume number of the series, then the name of the series, and finally the section or sections of the law to which the reader's attention is directed with the word "section" spelled out: thus, 29 United States Code sections 1361–62.

So as to be consistent, I have also put the volume number first in citing both legal and historical periodicals. Thus, 62 *Texas Law Review* refers to volume 62 of the *Texas Law Review*, and 74 *Journal of American History* to volume 74 of that periodical.

To historians and others concerned to write the history of the 1960s, or to write memoirs that implicate the history of the 1960s, I also direct a concern. This book is neither a history of the 1960s nor a memoir. Some of the struggles in which I took part personally, such as resistance to the closing of steel mills in Youngstown and Pittsburgh, are documented in conventional scholarly fashion. But in some of the pieces, and in the Introduction, I have relied on memory, and in doing so, have encountered problems about which I must say a few words.

Participants in movements of the 1960s have found the first histories of those years to be riddled with factual errors. One such protagonist says, "When I get one of these books I look in the Index for my own name. I turn to the pages indicated, and if what is said is simply wrong I have a hard time reading further." Let me give an example from the Introduction as to how this kind of problem can arise.

My draft of the Introduction began as follows:

In June 1965 a friend and I went to the steps of the Pentagon to picket against the war in Vietnam. Within moments of our arrival, we were surrounded by military policemen incredulous that two individuals would undertake so obviously ineffectual an action. "You don't understand," I replied with all the dignity I could muster, "we are just the first of thousands." (As it turned out, we were.)

Then I went to a gathering of veterans of the 1960s and encountered Bill Hartzog, whom I had not seen for thirty years. "Staughton," Bill said, "remember when five of us picketed at the Pentagon in June 1965? That was the first protest at the Pentagon against the Vietnam War."

After some conversation with Bill about who he thought had been present with us (his memory was quite vague on this point), I telephoned the friend with whom I remembered picketing, Bill Davidon. I hadn't talked with him in thirty years, either. He had no memory at all of such picketing. I said it happened just after a meeting in Washington, D.C., to plan the Assembly of Unrepresented People which occurred later that summer. Bill said he remembered the meeting, but he didn't recall the picketing. His earliest recollection of protesting at the Pentagon involved members of A Quaker Action Group who attempted to plant a small tree there, sometime later than June 1965.

It is very unlikely that there is a document somewhere which can clarify how many people picketed. If there is such a document in some Pentagon archive, I don't know how to find it. Moreover, that archival entry—if it exists—would probably not resolve who the picketers were, since we were not arrested, and the MPs would have had no way to learn our names. But picketing *did* occur, and I am certain that I said the words I quote myself as saying. I re-drafted my paragraph to say that I had been one of a very small group who picketed at the Pentagon in June 1965, that is, to say what Bill Hartzog and I both remember to be true and Bill Davidon does not refute. (It seems relevant, too, that I knew neither Bill Hartzog or Bill Davidon intimately. My best guess at the moment is that I was there with Hartzog, not Davidon.)

I offer this as a humble example of how we who took part in the struggles of the 1960s can contribute to writing its history. There are some things that we can do better than can any scholar who comes along after the events. For instance, how would such a person know to talk to Staughton Lynd and Bill Hartzog about an event that hardly made headlines? How would that scholar know what I had said, or what the occasion *meant* to those who took part? But as to details about which we're not sure, let's say, "To the best of my recollection . . ." and if it is the case, suggest in a footnote that others remember it differently.

S. L.

Living Inside Our Hope

The Once and
Future Movement

I n June 1965 a very small group went to the steps of the Pentagon to
picket against the war in Vietnam. Within moments of our arrival, we
were surrounded by military policemen incredulous that a handful of
people would undertake so obviously ineffectual an action. "You don't
understand," I replied with all the dignity I could muster, "we are just
the first of thousands." (As it turned out, we were.)

At the time, I was thirty-five years old and an assistant professor of
history at Yale. From 1961 to 1964 my wife, Alice, our two small children,
and I had lived in Atlanta, where I had taught at a college for black
women. In the summer of 1964 I directed the Freedom School component of the Mississippi Summer Project. In 1967 we would move to
Chicago, and in 1976 to Youngstown, Ohio. As Legal Services lawyers in
Youngstown during the years when all the steel mills closed, we have represented rank-and-file workers at odds with both company *and* union
bureaucrats.

The essays in this book were written after the collapse of the leading
organizations of the Movement of the 1960s—the Student Nonviolent
Coordinating Committee (SNCC) and Students for a Democratic Soci-

ety (SDS). During the quarter century in which the essays were composed, many societies around the globe that called themselves "socialist" abandoned that project.

Nevertheless I write as an unrepentant New Leftist and socialist. In 1988, Alice and I attended an SDS reunion. At the opening session all of us sat in a big circle. Each one said a few words about his or her life in recent decades. When it was my turn, I said I felt like the Japanese soldiers who were found on Pacific islands years after 1945 and did not know that World War II was over. I said that if a letter had gone out to tell us that the Movement was at an end, I had not received it. Since the late 1960s, I concluded, I had been on assignment for the Movement and I was looking for someone to whom I could make my report.

This book is that report.

A Mindful Activism

The theme that more than any other underlies these essays is the project of connecting theory with practice. In the 1960s we called this "putting your body where your mouth is" or "walking your talk."

It is an old idea, of course. The youthful Karl Marx wrote in his *Theses on Feuerbach:* "The philosophers have only interpreted the world. The thing, however, is to change it."

I have tried to take seriously this notion of deeds, not words. The essays that follow reflect life choices that often departed from the counsel of friends and parents: setting aside plans for a career in regional planning to join a commune in the 1950s; seeking a teaching job at a Southern college for black students during the early years of the civil rights movement; moving to Youngstown, Ohio, to practice law in association with rank-and-file workers whom we found profoundly congenial. (Didn't I know, asked a well-meaning friend on the Left, that everything important happens in Los Angeles, Chicago, Boston, or New York?)

Precisely because 1960s activists placed so high a value on practice, on activity, we were sometimes accused of "mindless activism" or "anti-intellectualism."

I think this criticism is wrong. As Helen Garvy, a Movement veteran, recently wrote to me, much depends on how one defines the word "intellectual." True, we avoided traditional intellectual terms, whether derived from Marxism or from the discourse of academic disciplines.

But if it is an intellectual pursuit to talk about values and goals, and how to reach them, we were endlessly intellectual. We didn't just act blindly; we tried things, based sometimes on gut feelings but more often on theories that we viewed as hypotheses. Then we evaluated and adjusted what we were doing, just as a scientist reformulates a hypothesis in the light of experimental results. Helen Garvy asserts, and I agree with her: "I think that our use of our own experience in figuring things out was a whole lot smarter (and more 'intellectual') than bullshitting about other people's theories, which might have little or no relevance to our situation. . . . The anti-intellectual argument has been used to marginalize not just the New Left, but also women and community people."[1]

Surely Paul Goodman, William Appleman Williams, Herbert Marcuse, and Barbara Deming were acting as intellectuals when they set forth their new ideas about "growing up absurd," "corporate liberalism," "repressive tolerance," and the "two hands" of nonviolence.[2] I also recall the brilliant speeches of SDS presidents Paul Potter and Carl Oglesby at antiwar rallies in Washington, D.C., in April and November 1965. Paul spoke of "naming that system" which causes imperialist wars, and Carl asked how Franklin or Jefferson would have reacted to what America was doing in Vietnam. These were all intellectuals using the tools of the mind to comprehend new forms of oppression and liberation.

SNCC, too, was heir to a "complex intellectual legacy."[3] As Charles Payne has explained, SNCC organizers learned from older persons such as Ella Baker, Septima Clark, and Myles Horton. These three "were all radical democrats, insistent on the right of people to have a voice in the decisions affecting their lives, confident in the potential of ordinary men and women to develop the capacity to do that effectively, skeptical of top-down organizations, the people who led them, and the egotism that leadership frequently engendered."[4]

Nevertheless, Paul Potter did not actually name the system "capitalism," although that is what he meant. Likewise it took some years before antiwar protesters felt comfortable calling the Vietnam War "imperialist." And while many, perhaps most, SNCC and SDS organizers were "socialists," we rarely used that word. All these words—"capitalism," "imperialism," "socialism"—had been used in such hackneyed and dogmatic ways by the Old Left that we shied away from repeating them.

So it *is* true that some of our ideas were implicit, acted out in practice but not fully articulated. This book seeks to articulate more fully some of the ideas in our practice.

Radical Ideas

In no particular order, some of the things we believed in the 1960s and that I still find to be true are as follows.

1. *Nonviolence.* The SNCC founding statement adopted in April 1960 reads in part:

> We affirm the philosophical or religious ideal of nonviolence. . . . Nonviolence as it grows from Judaic-Christian traditions seeks a social order of justice permeated by love. . . .
> Through nonviolence, courage displaces fear; love transforms hate. . . . Love is the central motif of nonviolence. . . .
> By appealing to conscience and standing on the moral nature of human existence, nonviolence nurtures the atmosphere in which reconciliation and justice become actual possibilities.[5]

In the tradition of Protestant conscientious objection to war, "nonviolence" is an individual's refusal to kill. The SNCC statement, like Latin American practice of nonviolence, suggests additional dimensions. Liberation theologian Leonardo Boff of Brazil visualizes nonviolence not as a boundary but as a core of passionate love. "Not being violent—in and of itself—is not the key to the praxis of Christ. The key is the capacity to love, which in turn means to be in solidarity with the socially and religiously marginalized."[6] And in Latin America, there is much more consciousness than traditionally in the United States that nonviolence must challenge the unjust *structures* of society: the institutionalized violence of class oppression.

Some persons in and out of the Movement concluded in the late 1960s that "nonviolence doesn't work." The years since then suggest otherwise. During the period 1968–1986, nonviolent movements associated with Lech Wałęsa in Poland, Nelson Mandela and Desmond Tutu in South Africa, Oscar Romero in El Salvador, and Corazon Aquino in the Philippines made headlines worldwide. In the late 1980s, masses of unarmed demonstrators carrying candles brought down Communist regimes throughout eastern Europe.

2. *Participatory democracy.* Participatory democracy was the key phrase in the SDS founding document, *The Port Huron Statement,* adopted in

1962. This polysyllabic commandment was generally understood to mean that "people should participate in the decisions that affect their lives." More briefly, our buttons read: "Let The People Decide."

Although SDS provided the term, SNCC developed the richest practice of participatory democracy. SNCC organizers believed in learning from the people whom they organized. They shared "a faith that ordinary people who learn to believe in themselves are capable of extraordinary acts, or better, of acts that seem extraordinary to us precisely because we have such an impoverished sense of the capabilities of ordinary people."[7] The culture of SNCC, shaped both by the intellectuals who influenced SNCC and by local leaders encountered in the Deep South, committed organizers "to participatory political forms because people develop by participating, not by being lectured to or told what to do."[8]

The women's movement that emerged from the Movement of the 1960s likewise insisted that no one should undertake to represent the feelings or beliefs of another, that each person should speak with his or her own voice. This, too, was an aspect of participatory democracy. Mary King, co-author with Casey Hayden of "The Position of Women in SNCC," believes that it "was from immersion in SNCC's profoundly democratic ideology during the years 1960 through 1965 that the activist branch of the modern women's movement awakened." On the one hand, the civil rights movement like the rest of U.S. society at that time "reflected entrenched patterns of the diminishment of women." But on the other hand,

> the civil rights movement gave training, experience, seasoning, and proficiencies to the women who participated in it. In many instances it provided the very first nurturing of leadership skills for girls and women. Ideologically, it was profoundly committed to female participation in the struggle. It was localized, decentralized, and organized around the specific needs of different communities. There was no "women's wing" or women's auxiliary in this movement. And when . . . the Mississippi Freedom Democratic Party in the autumn of 1964 decided to mount a challenge to the Congress, they put up Fannie Lou Hamer in the 2nd Congressional District, Annie Devine in the 3rd District, and Victoria Jackson Gray in the 5th.[9]

3. *An experiential approach to learning.* Learning theory is another area that the Movement of the 1960s explored in practice, without fully articulating a theory at that time. In planning for the Freedom Schools of the

Mississippi Summer Project, for instance, there were both an incredible richness of empirical materials and an implicit assumption that learning had to grow from "the conditions affecting black life," but little in the way of explicit pedagogical theory.[10]

Yet to a degree that many of those involved hardly realized, the educational praxis of the freedom schools drew on the work of citizenship schools that Highlander Folk School and the Southern Christian Leadership Conference had pioneered. We taught literacy with documents required for daily life, such as the voter registration form; we emphasized that students could teach each other; we helped students learn to *read* by encouraging them to *write* about experiences that mattered to them.[11]

Later, Paulo Freire found words for what we had done. Traditional pedagogy, Freire wrote, considered students to be empty vessels that the teacher filled with a predetermined content. A liberating pedagogy would begin with the needs and desires of the students, and with the practical problems that the students needed to overcome in the immediate future. Charged words and concepts would emerge from that existential context, teaching the instructor what needed to be taught.[12]

4. *Accompaniment.* A political theory that empowered ordinary people to speak for themselves, a pedagogy in which the student helped define what should be learned, inevitably meant that Movement "organizing" was something quite different from the organizing practiced then and now by AFL-CIO trade unions or by community organizers trained in the tradition of Saul Alinsky.

SNCC and SDS organizers went to live with the people. They ate what was set before them in the homes of their hosts, and drew on the cultural traditions—such as the singing in Southern churches—of those among whom they worked. If they felt strongly that a certain kind of action was called for, they tried to exemplify it: to do it themselves before asking others to join in. The organizer tried to create community organizations in which everyone could speak and be involved, and to encourage ordinary people to recognize their strengths and expertise, to become leaders and run for office. Mississippi Freedom Democratic Party and Newark Community Union Project folks who got involved in local politics and War on Poverty local boards are good examples.[13] In this style of organizing, success meant that the organizer had made himself or herself no longer necessary.

The best term I know for this style of organizing, again a term that came into use only after the 1960s ended, is "accompaniment." In his last Pastoral Letter, Archbishop Oscar Romero asserted that the advocate of nonviolence must take sides in the struggle between rich and poor. Such an advocate should *prefer* the poor and choose to stand at their side. So situated, however, the advocate of nonviolence should not pretend to be anything he or she is not. The advocate should listen to the voice of conscience, despite pressure from popular organizations to give uncritical support to revolutionary projects. The essential task of the nonviolent advocate is to be present: to "accompany" the poor, and with them seek appropriate means for social transformation.[14]

5. *Anti-capitalism and anti-imperialism.* In the 1960s we considered that capitalism produces poverty, racism, and imperialist exploitation.

Domestically, the analysis of SDS's Economic Research and Action Project (ERAP) was that because of automation a sizable part of the work force would become unnecessary to the existing economic system and would be laid off or never hired to begin with. ERAP therefore projected the possibility of an interracial movement of the unemployed that would demand "Jobs or Income Now." In the short run, this analysis was overlaid by the inflationary effects of the Vietnam War. But beginning in the early 1970s real wages began their downward slide, and as I write in 1996 amid corporate downsizing, the export of jobs to low-wage economies overseas, and "normal" unemployment of over 5 percent, the tasks ahead seem very much like those that ERAP set forth a generation ago.

As for the overseas impact of United States capitalism, and resistance to it, Howard Zinn and Noam Chomsky found (and are still finding) fresh words to describe them. In the 1960s we observed that the United States was greatly increasing its export of capital, just as Lenin had predicted in *Imperialism,* and also took note of a new organizational form: the multinational corporation. I recall an experience of my own that brought anti-imperialism suddenly to life. In December 1965 I had occasion to visit Moscow on the way to Vietnam, and to speak with Dang Quang Minh, the North Vietnamese ambassador to the Soviet Union. He was a slight, elderly man, who spoke very softly. Some remark of mine alerted him to my assumption that the United States had the military power to destroy the Vietnamese guerrilla movement. "You don't understand, professor," I recall him saying. "We're going to win. The United

States has two choices. One, you can withdraw from our country immediately, which of course we would prefer. Two, you can send more American soldiers, in which case we will also win, because for every United States soldier who lands in Vietnam one more Vietnamese will come to the National Liberation Front."

Marxism

Unrepentant New Leftists cannot avoid explicitly dealing with Marxism, if only because it was Marxist sects—authoritarian, secretive, and dogmatic—that invaded SNCC and SDS and helped destroy the Movement.

I think of Marxism as an indispensable background. At the aforementioned SDS reunion, I sat under a tree with one of my oldest friends in SDS. I said, "Of course, we still believe in a transition from capitalism to socialism, perhaps centuries long, perhaps with false starts and bastardized variants, but basically inevitable." He said, "No, Staughton, I don't believe in that any more. I believe in doing what I can for single causes: the movement against nuclear weapons, civil liberties, preservation of the environment."

Living in Youngstown during the years when the steel mills closed I (in contrast to my friend) became *more* persuaded by Marxist analysis and *more* convinced of the need for a publicly owned economy. The collapse of the steel industry in Youngstown and Pittsburgh was traumatic, but also stimulated new ideas. Worker ownership appeared as an option in the American heartland. When the first big shutdown was announced in Youngstown, the question was asked at a community meeting: "Why don't we buy the damn place?" A movement developed based on the strategy of taking over, by use of the government's "eminent domain" power, facilities that private enterprise no longer wished to operate.

The eminent domain strategy drew on certain strands in radical Catholic thought as well as on traditions of the labor movement. U.S. Steel's conduct—closing its Youngstown mills after promising to keep them open, buying the Marathon Oil Company instead of modernizing its mills in Pittsburgh—dramatized the concept that in disinvesting from steel, capitalist corporations were solely motivated by their desire to maximize profits. The threat of using eminent domain helped to prevent the departure from Pittsburgh of a major Nabisco plant.

More than a dozen municipalities in the Pittsburgh area, including the City of Pittsburgh, now participate in a Steel Valley Authority empowered to acquire abandoned industrial property by means of the eminent domain power. Intellectually, these communities have achieved a major breakthrough, concluding that when private industry no longer finds it profitable to run a socially needed enterprise, the community should step in and do the job itself.[15]

Experience in Youngstown reinforced conclusions I had reached in research as a historian. Again in no particular order, here is a list of Marxist concepts that I find indispensable in forming a background picture of the world.

1. History is driven forward by classes defined by their ownership and control (or lack of ownership and control) of the means of production.[16]

2. Classes generate distinctive outlooks on the world, or ideologies, that reflect their economic interests.

3. Government, despite its ostensible neutrality, tends to express the interests of dominant classes.

4. Despite the apparent worldwide triumph of neo-liberalism, capitalism is *unstable* and still subject to what Marx called the "contradictions of capitalism."

5. Trade unions serve as "centres of organization of the working class, as the medieval municipalities and communes did for the middle class."[17] But unions have an interest in preserving the existing system, and will predictably be slow to respond to unorganized, minority, female, and Third World workers who need basic change.

6. Humanity needs a society in which enterprises are publicly owned, and operated to meet social needs rather than to maximize profit.

I consider that for almost twenty years I have experienced as a Legal Services lawyer the possibility of a humane, participatorily democratic, decentralized socialism, a "socialism with a human face." We Legal Services lawyers offer good representation to the poor in civil cases without picking their pockets in the process. Funds for Legal Services are provided by national and state legislatures. About 95 percent of those moneys are distributed to field offices such as the one for which I work on the basis of the number of persons in these various areas who fall below the federal "poverty line." Federal law requires each field office to be

managed by lawyers and representatives of the poor in designated proportions. From time to time, a monitoring team visits to assess the compliance of our local office with the guidelines set forth in national law
and regulations. It is a system that works, and could work for the provision of a variety of other goods and services.[18]

Indispensable as Marxist analysis may be to frame the background of
our politics, Marxism is *not* a scientific "guide to action." The Marxist vanguard parties who set themselves up as sole custodians of scientific truth,
and as unique exemplars of the "correct" way to act politically, are profoundly destructive to the Movement as a whole. All this is incisively set
forth by Simone Weil and Rosa Luxemburg in Essays 5 and 12. I think that
we need to combine Marxist analysis with an ethical (in my case, a
Quaker) approach to how to act.

The Vietnam War

The Lynds' first venture in accompaniment was a response to the
Southern civil rights movement. Alice and I describe this experience in
Essay 4, "Liberation Theology for Quakers," and I add some thoughts
about Mississippi Freedom Summer in Essay 2.

The Vietnam War presented a different kind of challenge. Those
being set on fire by jellied gasoline (napalm) dropped from United
States planes were on the other side of the world and spoke a foreign
language. (In my own case, since I did not speak French, they spoke
more than one unknown language.) What could accompaniment mean
in such circumstances?

In Mississippi, during the summer of 1964, I attended a memorial
service for James Chaney, Michael Schwerner, and Andrew Goodman.
The service was held at the site of a burned church in Philadelphia, Mississippi, that had been offered for use as a freedom school and was
burned for that reason. Chaney, Schwerner, and Goodman died because
they went to Philadelphia to seek another location for the school. Speaking at the memorial service, Bob Moses of SNCC emphasized that the
bodies of the three men were found at almost the same time that President Johnson used the Tonkin Bay incident to obtain authorization for
undefined escalation of the Vietnam War.

Moses spelled out the connection more fully at the Berkeley Teach-
In against the Vietnam War in May 1965.

> Before the summer project last summer we watched five Negroes murdered in two counties of Mississippi with no reaction from the country. We couldn't get the news out. Then we saw that when the three civil rights workers were killed [Chaney, Schwerner, and Goodman], and two of them were white, the whole country reacted, went into motion. There's a deep problem behind that, and I think that if you can begin to understand what that problem is—why you don't move when a Negro is killed the same way you move when a white person is killed—then maybe you can begin to understand this country in relation to Vietnam and the third world, the Congo and Santo Domingo.[19]

I also spoke at the Berkeley Teach-In, calling for civil disobedience so massive that President Johnson and his advisers would be forced to resign. I was particularly concerned that during the summer of 1965, when students were away from campus, so many United States soldiers would be sent to Vietnam that by fall it would be impossible to dissent.

In early August 1965, on the twentieth anniversaries of the bombing of Hiroshima and Nagasaki, an Assembly of Unrepresented People convened in Washington. After two days of workshops (in the course of which Alice decided to become a counselor for conscientious objectors),[20] we sought to march to the steps of the Capitol to declare peace with the people of Vietnam. I was in the front row flanked by Bob Moses and David Dellinger. Red paint was thrown on the three of us as we proceeded slowly from the Washington Monument toward the Capitol. (See the picture in the photo section.) There we encountered several lines of police, and were arrested.

In December 1965 I took part in what turned out to be my most publicized act of accompaniment during the war. Herbert Aptheker, a fellow historian and a member of the Communist Party of the United States, Tom Hayden and I made a trip to Hanoi.[21] One result of the venture was that I could no longer find full-time work as a teacher of American history.

In January 1966, SNCC publicly stated its support for refusing induction into the armed services. During the months that followed, I worked with a number of young men who had been in Mississippi to develop a draft resistance movement. We shared the Movement concept of "putting your body in the way" and sought a strategy to act in that spirit against the Vietnam War.[22]

Others took accompaniment much further. In November 1965, Norman Morrison went to the steps of the Pentagon, set his small daughter a safe distance to one side, poured kerosene over himself, and burned himself to death. Norman, a Quaker, was employed by the Stony Run (Baltimore) Friends Meeting where Alice and I had been married. We knew him slightly, and Alice's parents knew him well: he drove to the Pentagon in a car owned by Alice's mother. When Aptheker, Hayden, and I arrived in Hanoi a few weeks after Norman's death, we found that he was a national hero there.

Norman Morrison's legacy was passed on to Brian Willson, who had known Norman in high school. In 1987, Brian acted out accompaniment by sitting in the path of a train carrying munitions for El Salvador and Nicaragua, and lost both his legs.[23]

Solidarity Unionism

The most long-lasting and fundamental project of accompaniment Alice and I have undertaken has been our move to Youngstown, Ohio, and our subsequent experience as lawyers for rank-and-file workers. Essay 10, on our work to try to stop the closing of the mills, and the first section of Essay 11, tell something of the story of our twenty years in Youngstown (where we still live).[24]

The ideas I came to call "solidarity unionism" are not ideas that were in my head when I began to work with rank-and-file union members. When I was growing up, the Congress of Industrial Organizations (CIO) was considered the most progressive social force in the United States. There were books in our home about the CIO with titles like *Labor on the March*. My mother belonged to the executive board of the New York City teachers' union. The first picket line I ever joined was at the General Motors offices in New York City during the 1946 UAW strike. I remember the happiness in my father's face and voice when he came home after speaking to a UAW educational conference in 1949. He had advocated a labor party.

I still had much the same attitudes toward the labor movement when Alice and I moved to Chicago in 1967. These conventional liberal ideas changed only after I came to know a series of remarkable worker-intellectuals: Marty Glaberman, John Sargent, Ed Mann, and Stan Weir.

Marty Glaberman was an auto worker associated with the West Indian Marxist, C. L. R. James, and with a group that called itself Facing Reality. Marty argued that in a shop where the collective bargaining agreement contains a no-strike clause, the shop steward becomes a cop for the boss. That is, under such circumstances union representatives are obliged to enforce contractual prohibitions *against* rank-and-file workers who engage in direct action.[25]

John Sargent lived in Gary and worked at Inland Steel in nearby East Chicago, Indiana. In the 1930s he had been the first president of the 18,000-member Inland Steel local union, and was reelected in 1943, 1944, and 1946. He and I became friends just after John had served another term as local union president, in 1964–1967, and then had returned to his work in the mill as an electrician.

John Sargent contended that steelworkers were better off after they had organized themselves but *before* they had collective bargaining agreements (see Essay 11).[26] John told me that after Inland Steel accepted collective bargaining, if the entire local union negotiating committee voted against a contract, the international union would put it into effect anyway.

Ed Mann too was a local union president in the Steelworkers union, at the Brier Hill mill of Youngstown Sheet & Tube from 1973 to 1980. In January 1980, after U.S. Steel announced the closing of all its facilities in Youngstown, Ed led an occupation of the U.S. Steel administration building.[27] Like Marty Glaberman and John Sargent, Ed advocated direct action rather than filing grievances.

I think we've got too much contract. You hate to be the guy who talks about the good old days, but I think the IWW had a darn good idea when they said, "Well, we'll settle these things as they arise."

I believe in direct action. Once a problem is put on paper and gets into the grievance procedure, you might as well kiss that paper goodbye. When the corporations started recognizing unions, they saw this. They coopted the unions with the grievance procedure and the dues check-off. They quit dealing with the rank and file and started dealing with the people who wanted to be bosses like them, the union bosses.

We were the troublemakers. We'd have a wildcat strike. The International would say, "Either you get back to work or you're fired." It wasn't the company saying this. It was the union.[28]

Last among those who influenced me was Stan Weir, seaman, longshoreman, auto worker, teamster, labor educator, and co-founder of a small publishing house, Singlejack Books. In an interview with Alice and me, Stan described how he slowly came to recognize that the real authority in places where he worked was "the informal work group." Such groups might in turn create plant-wide committees made up of delegates from each department, and city-wide committees (parallel central labor unions, as it were) composed of delegates from each plant.[29] Stan has also written about how he was instructed in "unions with leaders who stay on the job" by veterans of the 1934 general strike in San Francisco, but had to learn their most important lessons from his own experience.[30]

Like Stan Weir, I have had to learn not only from older strugglers but also from experience. Marty Glaberman, John Sargent, Ed Mann, and Stan Weir revolutionized my view of the labor movement. But what cemented these ideas into place in my mind were many bitter experiences over a period of twenty years in representing rank-and-file workers.

There have been exhilarating experiences also. I have concluded that middle-class radicals like myself do not need to learn a new language to communicate with industrial workers. "Participatory democracy" makes sense to workers who have no voice in decisions about closing a plant or changing a medical insurance plan, just as it did to students and disfranchised blacks thirty years ago.

I have also concluded that workers are important not because the working class is destined to overthrow capitalism, but because their solidarity prefigures a better society.[31] As with anything human, that solidarity comes in fits and starts, and is far stronger in some persons and places than in others. But I have found more practice of community among rank-and-file workers, who have much more to lose, than among radical intellectuals or academics.

A Word to My Daughter Martha and Other Young People

You've told me that it would be nice to have words of encouragement from someone a little older in the struggle. Let me start by summarizing what I've said so far.

What I mean by "accompaniment" is that radicals prepared to offer a useful professional service, over a long period of time in a particular place, should have no difficulty in relating with integrity to poor and working-class people. My identity as a lawyer has made it possible for me to be part of the life of a working-class community. If I am at a meeting and someone asks, "Who is that guy?" the answer is, "He's our lawyer."

I remain, as I have been since age fourteen, a socialist. I think I have experienced as a Legal Services lawyer the possibility of a "socialism with a human face." Because the essays in this book often use words that are common in the radical and labor movements but that I do not adequately explain, I have provided a Glossary (just before the Index).

As to "solidarity unionism," the institutionalized labor movement strikes me as self-centered and incredibly undemocratic. The labor movement in a broader sense—including the unorganized and unemployed, women and minorities, as well as the workers of other countries oppressed by United States imperialism—still seems to me to offer great hope to the world. And I am cautiously optimistic that as more women enter the labor force, and increasingly refuse to let male trade union leaders speak for them, the values of nonviolence, horizontal decision making, and an experiential approach to learning, will come more to the fore.

I would also like to say to you: Don't worry that it takes so long to find a way to make a living consistent with your values. Don't give up hoping for a life's companion who shares your ideals. Try to be a long-distance runner.

Martha, you wanted to be sure I knew that you weren't "just political." As you'll see if you struggle through these pages, I believe that Marxist analysis is not enough, that socialism without "spirit" is likely to be bureaucratic, lifeless, inefficient, and repressive.

Here is the plan of the book. First I say a few words about my father, and how I've tried to carry on from a summer he spent in a Rockefeller oil camp, and about you, Martha, and how your weeks in a Guatemalan Indian village went beyond small beginnings by your mother and me. The rest of the book radiates out from these experiences.

I apologize that so much of what follows is about me: what I think about this or that, what happened to me then or there. I once read a novel by Victor Serge in which a character reflects that he has had a certain unique combination of experiences, which he feels the need to pass on. In a similar way I recall that in the mid-1930s a young man later killed in Spain carried me on his shoulders in a May Day parade; that as part of a "commune" in Georgia I got up at five o'clock every morning to milk the cows; that one of my students at Spelman College was the future Pulitzer Prize winner, Alice Walker; that I directed freedom schools in Mississippi and chaired the first march against the Vietnam War in April 1965; and so on. Perhaps the thoughts that these experiences have left behind amount to an ideological magpie's nest, an eclectic mishmash. On the other hand, perhaps these experiences give me the opportunity to help you and others your age in weaving the fabric of a new New Left.

I think there may be young people who would like to pick up the work of the 1960s and carry it forward, if only they had a way of finding out more about what we believed. In these essays I try to address such questions as: To what analysis and values might members of a revived Movement in the United States subscribe? What will enable us to be long-distance runners?

It may seem bizarre to you that I refer to the quarter century 1970–1995 as a time of "living inside our hope." The Reagan and Gingrich years were hardly hopeful nationwide. Locally, though, many seeds have been planted.

Let me offer a different metaphor drawn from another feminist author. In *The Mists of Avalon*, Marion Zimmer Bradley tells the story of King Arthur and his companions from the point of view of the women in the tale. At the end, Arthur lies dying in the arms of his sister Morgaine. He asks whether all that he attempted—his time with Merlin, the Knights of the Round Table, the quest for the Holy Grail—amounted to failure. Morgaine replies: "You did not fail, my brother, my love, my child. . . . You held back the darkness for a whole generation." Later she reflects:

> No, we did not fail. What I said to comfort Arthur in his dying, it was all true. I did the Mother's work in Avalon until at last those who came after us might bring her into this world. I did not fail. I did what she had given me to do. It was not she but I in my pride who thought I should have done more.[32]

Tlahuitoltepec, Oaxaca, Mexico
Youngstown, Ohio

PART I

Accompaniment

1

Father and Son: Intellectual Work Outside the University

I spent a lot of my adolescence and young manhood trying not to be what my father wanted me to become. What he wanted was not entirely clear, but two elements of the job description stayed in my mind: I was to be an American Lenin and a tenured professor at an Ivy League university.

I was born just after publication of the first *Middletown* book in the late 1920s. There was no time in my life when my father was not a famous writer and a tenured professor of sociology at Columbia. (Two interesting facts about his appointment are: 1. He had never taken a sociology course; and 2. The department required my mother to go through *Middletown*—which, of course, she had co-authored—and line out every sentence she had written, so that the altered manuscript could serve as my Dad's dissertation.)

As a boy, I hardly understood or thought about my father's eminence. Instead I relished the companion who took me hiking in Harriman State Park on winter Sundays; who hauled me up Mount Washing-

Originally published in *Social Policy* (Spring 1993). Reprinted by permission.

ton when I was six years old; who, during the academic year, bicycled around Central Park with me every morning before breakfast, helping me count the squirrels we saw; and who hit fungoes to me in front of the New Hampshire farm house where our family spent summers.

My co-conspirator on these occasions was a jolly person who laughed and sang a lot. He had many friends and the knack of getting on intimate terms, after only a few minutes, with almost anyone he met for the first time.

By the time I went away to college (at age 16) in 1946, I had begun to know another side of my father. However it may have been for him in the 1930s, after World War II my Dad seemed desperately unhappy as a professor. He thought the new emphasis on heavy statistical analysis in doing sociology trivialized his discipline, and in any case he couldn't do it: awkward circumstances, since Paul Lazarsfeld and Robert Merton—two major proponents of the new approach—were Columbia colleagues. His classes grew gradually smaller. He had a series of heart attacks. He developed a writing block. He would sit hunched over his desk like a small boy doing homework, smoke one cigarette after another, and clip the business press in perpetual preparation for the book on power that was never written. (The introduction my father wrote to Robert Brady's *Business as a System of Power* gives some indication of what he had in mind.)

I tried to help, ineffectually, but most of all I was frightened, and concerned not to fall into the same trap.

There developed also a sharp political difference between my father and myself. His style was progressive, managerial, centralizing. He thought that those who knew the most should make the decisions. Somewhat like Sidney and Beatrice Webb, authors of *Soviet Communism,* he admired the Soviet Union while at the same time—unlike the Webbs—he stubbornly criticized what he viewed as the Soviet Union's errors and excesses, and he remained a political independent. Contrapuntally, I became a premature New Leftist: I admired Rosa Luxemburg, Ignazio Silone's *Bread and Wine,* Trotsky; I advocated decentralization, nonviolence, democracy, direct action, and, above all, the unity of theory and practice.

Nothing I later experienced in academia caused me to revise my first impressions. Academic life is so mean-spirited. I have often felt that its practitioners fall into two groups: those grimly competing for tenure, and those worried that they may be over the hill. Despite grand talk of a "community of scholars," historians I have known guard their research findings as so much private property, and, therefore, when they are together, tend to talk about trivia. Ordinary working people risk their jobs frequently to protest an injustice done to a colleague, but I have only once—at Spelman College, not at Yale or Harvard—known a fellow academic to take such risks. Academic life in my experience nurtures middle-class selfishness, not solidarity. There are very few academics like Howard Zinn, who steadily understood his audience not to be other academics, who testified as an expert witness on civil disobedience while colleagues attended scholarly conclaves, who cut short his last lecture before retirement from Boston University to join a campus picket line.

I

It took me forever to begin to imagine an alternative to academia. I dropped out of Harvard in 1948, after reading Trotsky's *Literature and Revolution*. ("We shall all become Aristotles and Goethes, and beyond these new peaks will rise"—or words to that effect.) I took a train to the West Coast, fell in love, and hitchhiked back east. For a time I attended Columbia.

One evening I went to a movie about the life of Saint Vincent de Paul. According to the film, as a young man Vincent was chaplain to the French king, who liked to stage galley races in which the slaves in the king's galley raced with the galley slaves in the boats of his courtiers. The movie portrayed one such race. As the race progressed, the owners of the competing galleys stepped up the beat. Awkwardly at first, then with more feeling, Vincent began to protest the effect on the rowers. The king brushed away his concern. "They aren't like you and me. They enjoy it," the king said. Suddenly, standing with members of the court in the high rear of the king's galley, Vincent saw one of the rowers faint at his oar. He clambered down into the hold where the slaves were rowing, and picked up the oar.

I left college again the next day.

Another foreshadowing came in the winter of 1953–1954, when I was in the Army. I told my draft board that I was conscientiously opposed to killing, but I thought I should expose myself to the same dangers as other young men my age. I asked to be a noncombatant medic, classification 1-A-O. They gave it to me.

During the day or two after my induction, before we were issued uniforms, I found myself painting certain structures white. (No doubt each successive wave of draftees repainted them.) I dropped some paint on the toe of one of my civilian shoes. Thereafter, whenever we had inspections, I would be reprimanded and sometimes disciplined for the paint spot on my shoe.

Accordingly, one fall afternoon I was confined to the company area and given the task of raking leaves. As I raked, I had a sort of vision: to throw in one's lot with poor and working people, it was not necessary to sell all one had or give it away, and try to become like the people one wished to help. Another way to do it might be to acquire some useful skill like doctoring, and then live in a working-class community without pretending to be a steelworker or a meatpacker. St. Vincent's was one way, I began to perceive, but this might be another. Indeed, as a doctor or a lawyer one would in fact be a certain kind of skilled craftsperson, and without disguising the years of higher education during which the skill was acquired.

I loved the idea. Thirty years later, when my wife, Alice, and I went to Nicaragua and were told about "liberation theology"—priests and nuns going to live in particular villages and barrios for years at a time, but without ceasing to be priests and nuns—I had the reaction, "Oh, so that's what they call it."

II

From 1954 to 1967, I made a living (some of the time) milking cows in a community in Georgia, and as an activist historian.

I came to feel that my Dad was not opposed to my project or, at least, that even if he opposed it, I could take comfort from his life and see my own life as continuing his. Sadly, this became clear to me only in the early 1970s, after his death.

I had always known vaguely that in the early 1920s my father went to the Union Theological Seminary and, while he was there, spent a summer as a volunteer preacher in a Rockefeller oil camp called Elk Basin, Wyoming. He often sang songs that he learned that summer. One of them went:

> I'm off to Montana, the land of the free,
> The home of the bedbug, the grayback, the flea,
> Oh sing loud its praises, and sing loud its fame,
> I'm starving to death on my government claim.

Another began:

> When the Good Lord made the copper ore,
> He said I'll put you away to store,
> Where man won't find you any more,
> Unless he's a human bold.

> But he reckoned without the miner man,
> Who isn't built on the regular plan,
> So ever since the world began,
> It's the miner who digs the hole.

That was about all I knew. Somehow, after Dad died, I came across a manila envelope marked: "Stau [one of the names he called me], save these." Inside were crumbling copies of his first three published articles: "But Why Preach?," explaining why he gave up a job in publishing and went to theological school; and two articles about his summer in Elk Basin, "Crude-Oil Religion," published in *Harpers* in September 1922, and "Done in Oil," published in November 1922 in the *Survey Graphic*, with a response by John D. Rockefeller, Jr.

Elk Basin, my father wrote, was a "hole in the ground, gouged out of the naked clay and sandstone, a mile wide, three miles long, and perhaps three hundred feet deep." About 500 people lived there in slate-colored company barracks, tar-paper shacks, and tents. There was nothing green to be seen.

My father arrived by stagecoach. Necessarily, his first project was to find a house in which to spend the night (very much as with Mississippi Freedom School teachers when they got off the bus in the summer of 1964). Then came the most important decision of the summer. "I learned at the supper table," he writes, "that the men did not like the idea of my calling on their womenfolk while they were off in the field." After supper he made the rounds of the foremen and was hired as a roustabout by the Standard Oil subsidiary. He slept in a seven-by-nine-foot cubicle in the company bunkhouse, ate at the company cook shack, and made $4.05 a day for a six-and-a-half-day week.

"Crude-Oil Religion" tells the story of the summer in anecdotal style. "Done in Oil" is an entirely different kind of piece. It documents the fact, obfuscated by Standard Oil, that Rockefeller interests owned 87.5

percent of the crude-oil production of Elk Basin. The isolation and lone-liness of Elk Basin women are set forth at length. Bureau of Labor Statistics numbers are displayed to prove that, whereas in the East a majority of oil workers labored six days a week, in western fields like Elk Basin the seven-day week was typical.

The article ends by listing six demands:

1. A six-day week, with Sunday work only in real emergencies;
2. Abolition of the twelve-hour day and substitution of three eight-hour shifts;
3. Provision of a community center [the story at our family kitchen table was that my father asked John D. Rockefeller, Jr. for a contribution to build a community center, and Rockefeller wrote back that Standard Oil had had a bad year, and couldn't afford to give anything];
4. Recognition of labor's right to organize;
5. Better housing for 50 to 80 percent of Elk Basin's families;
6. Extra pay for overtime work.

The exchange with John D. Rockefeller, Jr. had a sequel, which scholars are still untangling, and I am still trying to understand. The Rockefellers offered my father a job. More precisely, the Rockefeller Foundation's Institute of Social and Religious Research wanted someone to do a study of the religious life of a typical American city, and my Dad got to do it, and the study became *Middletown.*

As I see it now, the boss was dealing with an outspoken shop-floor militant by making the man a foreman; at least, that was what the Rockefellers tried to do. My father resisted, and insisted on continuing the study until it satisfied him. My mother, in her own oral history, *Possibilities,* tells what happened next:

> Bob asked the Institute people if they would allow him to publish the manuscript if he could find a publisher. They owned it. It was their property. I think the only reason that they said he could was because they were sure he couldn't. They told him so.

Of course, he did find a publisher, Harcourt, Brace—the first publisher he approached; *Middletown* became a classic, and my Dad became a tenured professor.

But lately I have wondered, who won? My Dad won because he and my mother wrote the book they wanted to write, and it was a spectacular success. But Rockefeller also won, because he did get my father off the shop floor: my Dad became a professor.

III

I see my own life as a lawyer in a working-class community as a continuation of my father's summer at Elk Basin. This is what children do, it seems to me: they take a beginning that their parents were only able to sketch or to do for a short time or left undeveloped while the parents focused on other things, and build a whole life on that beginning. What my Dad did for one summer I have tried to make into a way of life.

I've become addicted to the notion that the once and future Movement requires us to be long-distance runners. My heroes are those who stayed active, like Hollis Watkins who 30 years later is still registering voters in Mississippi.

Alice and I moved to Chicago in 1967. She was successful in finding part-time work for the Movement as a trainer of draft counselors. I, however, was offered a job by the history departments at five Chicago-area institutions (Northern Illinois University, University of Illinois Circle Campus, Roosevelt University, Loyola University, and Chicago State College), only to have the appointments vetoed by the five administrations. For several years I pieced together part of a family income from a job at Saul Alinsky's school for organizers, and as an organizer for the Institute for Policy Studies, helping workers to use the just-enacted Occupational Safety and Health Act.

Meantime, Alice and I put together three books of oral history. She edited *We Won't Go: Personal Accounts of War Objectors,* working over the manuscript as she nursed our third child. Michael Ferber and I wrote *The Resistance,* which drew on group interviews with the Boston Draft Resistance Group, Palo Alto Resistance, Chicago Area Draft Resistance, and other protest communities. We wrote to draft resistance groups all over the country and asked them, when they closed their offices, to send their papers to us.

Alice and I also jointly collected the material for *Rank and File,* oral histories by working-class organizers. Our approach was that we were not collecting material to use in academic publications (which Alice had never done and I was doing no longer). Rather, we were arranging occasions when men and women who had fought to form unions in the 1930s could share their experience with younger persons in the same communities who wanted to try the same thing. Thus there came about a three-part forum at a local community college in Hammond, Indiana, on "Labor History from the Standpoint of the Rank and File," and smaller sessions at a writers' workshop in Gary where individuals told their oral histories. A byproduct was the movie "Union Maids," based on the accounts of three women in *Rank and File.*

Another byproduct was that Alice and I decided to become lawyers. Doing *Rank and File,* we would sit at someone's kitchen table, encouraging him or her to go back to the beginning and tell the whole story. After we finished, the interviewee would ask, "Have I done what you wanted?" "Yes," we would assure him (I am thinking of a particular man in Gary). "OK," came the response, "now you can help me." And he would go into a back room, emerging with a box full of papers arising from some current conflict with both the company and the union. "We're sorry," we had to say, "we aren't lawyers." We had a frustrating time trying to find lawyers who knew something about labor law but were not working for either a corporation or a union. Finally, we decided it would be simpler to become lawyers ourselves.

Over a period of 13 years, Alice and I took turns going to law school, one of us working while the other one studied. In 1976 we moved to Youngstown and in 1978, having been fired by the town's leading labor-law firm (for excessive sympathy with the rank and file), I went to work at Legal Services. The National Legal Services Corporation is funded by Congress to provide legal assistance to the poor. Almost all the money is sent to local offices like the one where I work. It's good work, and would not change that much in a socialist society. Off the clock, I do things that Legal Services regulations don't allow, like helping unions.

I still feel I'm a historian. I've written a book about the closing of Youngstown's steel mills (*The Fight Against Shutdowns*), and a pamphlet on labor law (*Labor Law for the Rank and Filer*). I helped Brian Willson, the Vietnam vet whose legs were cut off in 1987 when he sat down on a track to block a munitions train, write an autobiography (*Third World Legs*). Together with a group of younger historians, I'm putting together a book on the decentralized unionism of the early 1930s, before the CIO. And Alice and I have just finished a book of oral histories by Palestinians.

It isn't true that you must make your living as a university teacher in order to do intellectual work.

2 Freedom Summer: A Tragedy, Not a Melodrama

I was director of Freedom Schools in the 1964 Mississippi Summer Project. This gives me no special claim to insight. I was in Mississippi only about two months. I "directed" by traveling around the state rather than sitting at a telephone in Jackson, but inevitably my perspective was to some extent from above, not from below. Finally, I was white, male, and at thirty-four somewhat older than the typical summer volunteer or Student Nonviolent Coordinating Committee (SNCC) field secretary.

With all these caveats, I want to offer an analysis of Freedom Summer that I have not seen elsewhere. Media and historical treatment of the Mississippi Summer Project has been nostalgic, romantic, oversimplified. The dominant image is that of black and white young heroes engaged in melodramatic struggle with the dragon of Mississippi racism. I see things a little differently. The analysis I offer is based on facts that I think we all know, but there are some significant differences about details that I have tried to indicate. I hope others will respond and carry the analysis further.

Originally published in *Freedom Is a Constant Struggle: An Anthology of the Mississippi Civil Rights Movement*, a project of the Cultural Center for Social Change (Montgomery, Ala.: Black Belt Press, 1997). Reprinted by permission.

There was a long and serious debate among civil rights workers in Mississippi during late 1963 and early 1964 about whether Freedom Summer was a good idea. One position was that in more than two years SNCC had succeeded in registering very few black voters in Mississippi; that black Mississippians who had responded to SNCC's call had been killed (Herbert Lee), injured, imprisoned, expelled from school, and otherwise harmed, without a great deal to show for their sacrifices; and that if white volunteers were to come to the Magnolia State in large numbers, the nation's attention would be drawn to Mississippi, and helpful intervention by the federal government might follow.

The opposing position was that SNCC activity in southwest Mississippi and the Delta from 1961 to 1963, while it might not have registered many voters, had begun to build an indigenous black movement. Older leaders consulted by Bob Moses when he came to the state, like Amzie Moore, had been joined by younger leaders: Fannie Lou Hamer, Curtis Hayes, Brenda Travis, and countless others. The concern of those opposing Freedom Summer was that a flood of articulate, white, middle-class Northerners would cause these new leaders of the black community to become unsure of their skills in organizing, public speaking, and writing; that in the presence of the volunteers these local black leaders might revert to deference to white folks; and that, whatever the short-run gains, Freedom Summer might disorient and even destroy the self-organization of the Mississippi black community.

White students from Stanford and Yale took part in Mississippi "freedom votes"—occasions when disfranchised blacks cast ballots for their own candidates at alternative or parallel polling places—in the summer and fall of 1963. The idea presented itself, Why not bring an even larger number of students into the state the following summer? This proposal was discussed at a SNCC staff meeting in Greenville in November 1963; by the SNCC executive committee on December 30, 1963; and at a Council of Federated Organizations (COFO) meeting at the end of January 1964.

Howard Zinn was at the Greenville meeting. He reports that "the coming of sizable numbers of white students to Mississippi to help with the ... Freedom Ballot in October had led to much grumbling among Negro staff members that some of the white students had rushed into leadership positions, they had come quickly, gotten publicity, and left."[1] Notes taken by Mendy Samstein (a white graduate student who had dropped out of Atlanta University to work full-time for SNCC) are to the

same effect, but also suggest why many SNCC staff still felt that Freedom
Summer was a good idea:

> Considerable time was spent at Greenville discussing whether to invite a mas-
> sive number of Northern whites into Mississippi for the summer. It was clear
> from the nature of the publicity derived from the Freedom Vote campaign
> that the press would respond to the beating of a Yale student as it simply
> would not do to the beating of a local Negro. The *New York Times* headlined
> its stories about the campaign with the news that Yale and Stanford students
> were working "for a Negro gubernatorial candidate in Mississippi." During
> the Freedom Rally in Jackson which concluded the campaign, TV men from
> N.B.C. spent most of their time shooting film of the Yalies and seemed
> hardly aware of the local people and full-time SNCC workers. While it was
> agreed by all that this was a sorry state of affairs, many contended that such
> publicity was essential for awakening the national conscience and preparing
> a climate for greater federal involvement in Mississippi. . . . It was argued
> that by flooding Mississippi with Northern whites, the entire country would
> be made dramatically aware of the denial of freedom which existed in the
> state and that the federal government would be inevitably faced with a crisis
> of sufficient magnitude that it would have to act.[2]

Initially, most SNCC and CORE staff opposed the Freedom Summer
idea. Charles Payne states that MacArthur Cotton, Charlie Cobb, Ivan-
hoe Donaldson, Hollis Watkins, Willie Peacock, and Sam Block opposed
the idea at the Greenville meeting in November. Clayborne Carson indicates that Charlie Cobb and Charles Sherrod opposed at least the idea
of bringing hundreds of students to the state at the SNCC executive
committee meeting in December. John Lewis, Jim Forman, Marion
Barry, Lawrence Guyot, and Fannie Lou Hamer, as well as Dave Dennis,
coordinator of CORE work in Mississippi, are said to have supported the
Summer Project.[3]

There is disagreement about the role played by Bob Moses, the coordinator of SNCC work in Mississippi. Payne includes Moses in his list of
"proponents" of the Summer Project idea. Carson states that Moses
"proposed" the Summer Project, and that at Greenville the project was
"Moses' plan." At the SNCC executive committee meeting in December,
however, according to Carson, Moses played a "cautious role, repeating
the reasons that led him to support the plan while also attempting fairly
to represent the views of those on his staff who opposed it."[4]

Moses' own recollection, as related to Taylor Branch in 1984, is quite different. "Across weeks of raw debate," Branch writes, "Moses himself refused to express a firm opinion for or against the summer project. Always opposed to fiat by leaders, he added that this idea also carried special responsibilities. White volunteers would be beaten severely or killed, he said, and their race and status would magnify the national reaction. To the extent that SNCC consciously used the students as white lambs of sacrifice, they must bear the burden of that moral and political choice."[5]

I am inclined to credit Moses' recollection as paraphrased by Branch. Any one who knew Bob Moses then will recall the self-effacing style that he habitually assumed. If asked to speak, he would stand in place rather than come to the front of a room. Rather than lay out his own ideas he tended to ask questions. His characteristic manner was that of one who facilitates the empowerment of others. So it was, apparently, at the beginning of SNCC's internal debate on the proposed Summer Project.

All sources agree that the murder of Louis Allen on January 31, 1964, transformed the situation. Allen had witnessed the murder of Herbert Lee. Now he had himself been killed to prevent him from testifying against Lee's murderer. A messenger interrupted one of the marathon debates on the Summer Project to bring this news. Bob Moses immediately went to see Mrs. Allen. On returning to the meeting, Bob said, "We can't protect our own people," and threw his moral authority behind the Summer Project.[6]

In 1967 I had a conversation with Dave Dennis. Dave said that at the climactic meeting—it can only have been the COFO meeting at the end of January 1964—SNCC and CORE workers took a vote defeating the Summer Project proposal. He added that Bob Moses (with, as I understood it, Dave's support and assistance) then insisted on a second vote, and obtained a different outcome. The Summer Project went forward. But Charles Payne comments: "The way in which Moses and Dennis forced the issue was a long-term source of anger within COFO precisely because it was the opposite of SNCC's usual consensual style."[7]

I went to Mississippi to get a feel for the situation in the spring of 1964. I recall being told that there were two particularly dangerous areas: southwest Mississippi, the area around McComb, and east central Mississippi near Meridian and Philadelphia. I also made an effort to find a black co-director, because even in those days before Black Power it seemed to me that it would be odd for a white person to be solely in charge of a program for black teenagers. My eye lit on Harold Bardonille, who had been part of the sit-in movement in Orangeburg, South Carolina. In 1963–64 he was a graduate student in sociology at Atlanta University, and an occasional tennis partner. I asked Harold, and Harold said he would check it out. He went to Mississippi, came back, and said that people were going to get killed; he politely declined to be co-director of the Freedom Schools.

I heard John Lewis, then chairperson of SNCC, respond to such fear at a meeting of SNCC staff persons in Atlanta just before the Summer Project got under way.

The meeting was a somber one. People talked about the likelihood that there would be deaths that summer. At the end of the meeting, we stood in a circle, held hands, and sang "We Shall Overcome." We sang all the verses that we knew or could make up. Then—something I had never experienced before, and would never experience again—we hummed the tune, over and over, while John Lewis spoke over the humming. He told about the time in 1961 when Freedom Riders sought to integrate interstate bus travel by riding buses into the Deep South, black and white together.

When the buses reached Birmingham there was terrible violence. The organizations sponsoring the Freedom Ride decided to call it off. They thought that the point had been made and that to press on into Mississippi would risk too much. John Lewis was then a student at Fisk University in Nashville. He and his friends felt the ride should continue. They went to Birmingham, where they were arrested, loaded into police cars, and conveyed by Birmingham police chief "Bull" Connor to the Alabama–Tennessee state line. There they were left by the side of the road in the middle of the night.

"We didn't know what to do," John told us as we hummed. Any strategy that had existed was in shambles. They had no transportation. If they somehow got back to Birmingham, they would presumably again be arrested. "The only thing we knew," John said, "was that we should start back toward Birmingham."

Earlier that spring, I had gone to New York City for a conference on the proposed Freedom School curriculum. Alice and I reproduced those curricula on a hectograph machine in our Atlanta apartment, and in mid-June I carried them to the Summer Project orientation at Oxford, Ohio, in the trunk of our Rambler. The collected paper was so heavy that by the time we arrived the wheels of the car required realignment. Also in that car were three Spelman College students who were going to Mississippi too: Barbara Simon, Gwen Robinson (now Zaharah Simmons), and Barbara Walker.

The orientation session in Oxford was in two parts. The young people who were to work on voter registration had already been there for a week and left a few hours after we arrived. The Freedom School teachers were to be in Oxford for a second week.

Those who left to do voter registration included Mickey Schwerner, James Chaney, and Andrew Goodman. They drove to Meridian, arriving early on a Sunday morning. They decided to go to Philadelphia, where a church intended to be used for a freedom school had been burned down, and look for another freedom school site. In Philadelphia their car had a flat tire. As it was being fixed, they were arrested. (A month and a half later their bodies were found. They had been released from jail in the middle of the night, stopped at a roadblock, beaten, and killed.)

By Monday morning all of us in Oxford knew that three of our people had disappeared. Schwerner and Goodman were white. Chaney was a black Mississipian. Bob Moses, the leader of the Summer Project, called a meeting. We were all asked to telephone or wire our Congressmen, urging immediate investigation by the FBI. That evening we met again. I was in and out of the room, because I was counseling individual teachers who were wondering whether they should give up going to Mississippi. Inside the room Bob was talking about the same thing. He said that being a leader was like being Frodo in *The Lord of the Rings* trilogy (books I had never heard of before). A leader became attracted to power in the same way that Frodo, in the end, found it hard to give up the Ring of Power. Nevertheless, Bob went on, speaking very quietly and slowly with long pauses between the words, he felt that we should continue the Summer Project.[8]

That night I recall Rita Schwerner, Mickey Schwerner's wife, walking about the halls of the buildings unable to sleep.

It must have been the next day that, as Freedom School director, I was asked to attend a small meeting just of SNCC staff. We sang "Kumbaya, Lord," verse after verse. "Someone's missing Lord, Kumbaya." "We all need you Lord, Kumbaya." At the end of the meeting Bob Zellner, a white SNCC worker from Alabama, volunteered to go to Philadelphia and go through the woods at night, speaking to black families to see if they knew anything about the missing men.

While at Oxford I met a young man named Tom Wahman. His wife, Susan, needed to be in Jackson, Mississippi, the state capital and the headquarters of the Summer Project, in order to rehearse with a freedom theater group. Tom had volunteered to be a Freedom School teacher, but I asked him if he would answer the phone in Jackson so that I could spend my time visiting the schools. He agreed.

There were well over two thousand Freedom School students in as many as forty freedom schools. (It depended on how you counted: Hattiesburg, for instance, had a veritable system of freedom schools.) The typical school was in a church basement. Teachers lived with black families brave enough to take them in. The paper curriculum that Alice and I had produced was for the most part set aside as teachers improvised: writing school newspapers, typing, French, and poetry were among the most popular subjects.

I went to McComb where the "freedom house," the building where the SNCC workers slept, had been bombed. There was a meeting in the evening on the lawn outside the building. Bob Moses suggested the verse to "I'm on My Way": "If you can't go, let your children go."

One of the SNCC workers who most impressed me was Ralph Featherstone, later killed in a mysterious car bombing. I remember Ralph arriving in Jackson with a bad cold, and my sleeping on the floor of my little apartment while Ralph slept in the bed. Ralph kept volunteering for dangerous assignments. He had transferred from Holly Springs to McComb. Then he had the idea that we should try to start a freedom school in Philadelphia, where the three men had been killed looking for a freedom school site. But since it was too dangerous to have a stationary school, Ralph thought we should have a mobile school that taught in one place for as long as possible, and then, when the situation got too hot, took off. We actually spent some time remodeling a pickup truck for the purpose but finally decided even this would be too dangerous.

The Freedom School teachers and I decided to have a "Freedom School convention." It was held in Meridian, in a decrepit old high school or seminary building. Each freedom school elected delegates. The young people broke up into workshops to decide what they wished to propose about different problems. For instance, we had a discussion about whether freedom schools should try to continue through the winter. At the end of the convention, one student said: "I move that our resolutions should be sent to the United Nations and to the Library of Congress for its permanent records."

(Later, I learned that black public school students in Philadelphia went to class that fall wearing buttons that said "SNCC" and "One Man, One Vote." A court decision upholding their right to do so in turn became a precedent for a decision of the United States Supreme Court, affirming the right of a white high school student in Iowa to wear a black arm band to school in protest against the Vietnam War.)

The hard questions that need answering are: Who was right in the internal SNCC and CORE debate? Was the Summer Project a good thing or a bad thing?

My conclusion is: *Both* sides were right; the Summer Project was *both* good and bad. It was therefore a tragedy, in the classical Greek sense, wherein the tragic flaw in a good thing produces a bad thing as well.

On the one hand, it cannot be doubted that the Summer Project helped to bring about the passage of the 1964 Civil Rights Act and the 1965 Voting Rights Act, and played a major part in creating a South in which black persons can vote. This might or might not have been true had James Chaney, Mickey Schwerner, and Andrew Goodman not been killed. And no one expected the Freedom Democratic Party's bid to be seated at the Democratic Party convention in Atlantic City in August 1964 to be so nearly successful. The fact is that a voter registration strategy based on the Summer Project succeeded after the failure of a voter registration strategy based on years of sacrificial organizing by SNCC cadre.

But on the other hand, can there be any question that the Summer Project helped to break up the interracial civil rights movement that SNCC was until 1964?

There were whites in SNCC before 1964, among them Bob Zellner, Mary King, Casey Hayden, Howard Zinn, Jane Stembridge, Betty Garman, and Jack Minnis. They were a minority in the organization and took direction from black leaders like Jim Forman, Julian Bond, and Bob Moses. The summer of 1964 created a new situation. Unexpectedly, many volunteers decided to remain in Mississippi. Thus one white Freedom School director (myself) was succeeded by another (Liz Fusco). More important, after the Atlantic City events white Northern lawyers continued to make or try to make fundamental decisions about long-term SNCC strategy.

Perhaps the SNCC opposition to Freedom Summer was wrong in one respect. Perhaps it was not so much indigenous black Mississippians who resented the white volunteers from the North as it was SNCC organizers, SNCC *staff*.[9] (This had a sexual aspect that I have been chastised for trying to discuss. There was a great deal of sex between black male SNCC and CORE staff and white female volunteers during the summer of 1964. Sex happened, as Doug McAdam's book recounts, despite constant public pronouncements that it should *not* happen because it would endanger the Summer Project. A great deal of personal confusion and disorientation happened along with it.)[10]

Sometime in the 1970s I had a conversation about all this with a former student of mine at Spelman, Gwen Robinson, now Zaharah Simmons. After volunteering for the Summer Project, Zaharah dropped out of college and became a full-time SNCC organizer. She worked in the Vine Street project in Atlanta. This group drafted the first Black Power statement by members of SNCC early in 1966.[11] Zaharah sent me a copy.

When I saw Zaharah in the 1970s, I asked, "What was Black Power all about?" Her immediate answer was that Black Power responded to the fact that after the summer of 1964 decisions about SNCC strategy began to be made by white people in the North. Zaharah pointed to the fact that after Freedom Summer, SNCC came to have a much larger budget, including, for example, a fleet of rental cars. A larger fund-raising operation in the North, and greater dependence on that operation, resulted. Moreover, after Freedom Summer local organizing languished as attention focused on the effort to seat Freedom Democrats in Congress. This too was an effort headquartered in the North rather than in the South.

Cause and effect in these developments may be difficult to untangle. I hope I am not understood to be pointing a finger of blame at anyone. We were all protagonists in the play. I am not even blaming myself: as I explain above, after I was asked to be Freedom School director, I tried very hard to find a black person to share the job with me, but failed.

No, my thesis is that the Mississippi Summer Project was a tragedy, not a simple contest of good guys and gals on the one side, and bad guys on the other. The Summer Project was a tragedy because a strategy effective in winning the right to vote also disempowered blacks at the same time. Both sides in the Movement debate about whether to have a Summer Project were proved correct. The casualties of the summer included not only the individuals who died, but the idea of an interracial movement for fundamental social change.

3 Oral History from Below

Twenty-five years ago, Jesse Lemisch, I, and other New Left historians called for history to be written from below, from the bottom up. Jesse Lemisch argued that history was too often written as the history of "great white men." We said that there was needed a history of "the inarticulate," by which of course was meant, not persons who did not speak, but persons who did not write: persons who did not leave behind a trail of documents.

Inevitably the proposal for a history from below led to a great deal of oral history. The way to find out about people who talk but do not write is, obviously, to talk to them. However, while history from below requires oral history, oral history is not necessarily history from below. There can be an oral history of Great White Men; witness the Columbia University Oral History Project, at least as it was in the 1960s.

Keynote speech to the 1992 annual meeting of the Oral History Association. Originally published in 21 *Oral History Review*, no. 1 (Spring 1993), pp. 1–8. Reprinted by permission.

Accordingly it may be useful to talk about the particular kind of oral history appropriate to doing history from below. I want to talk about oral history as part of a life style that in nineteenth century Russia was called "going to the people," and in contemporary Latin America has been described as a "preferential option for the poor." I want to talk about oral history as a project, not just to observe and record poor people, but also to empower them.

There is a Spanish verb *acompañar,* "to accompany." As used for example by Archbishop Oscar Romero in his last pastoral letter, accompaniment does *not* mean to disguise one's identity, nor to give up one's independent judgment and conscience. The priest or nun remains a priest or nun, not a *campesino* or a steel worker. The teacher still teaches, the lawyer is more needed than ever as an advocate. To accompany another person is to walk beside that person; to become a companion; to be present. In accompanying, the professionally trained person chooses the world of poor and working people as a theater of action. By offering to tape-record the experience of poor and working people, we are implicitly saying: "Your life is important. It's worth my time to talk to you. It may be worth your time to talk to me. People like me need to know what people like you have learned."

Here are aspects of oral history from below as accompaniment:

1. *Interviewer and interviewee, historian and historical protagonist, meet as equals.*

Before my wife and I began to do oral history together, Alice had formulated this idea in the context of draft counseling. "When I do draft counseling," she said, "there are two experts in the room. I am an expert in certain regulations and procedures, and the person whom I counsel is an expert on his life, and what he wants to do with it."

Last spring our youngest daughter lived for a month in an Indian village in Guatemala. No one apart from Martha spoke English. Only a few persons spoke Spanish. The villagers spoke Quiche, which Martha did not speak or understand. She and they communicated partly through weaving. The villagers taught Martha backstrap weaving, and she managed to have constructed the wider upright loom familiar in North America, and to begin to demonstrate how to use it. In her journal Martha wrote in part as follows:

> I feel that a lot of researchers, anthropologists, etc., do not find this equalizing way to relate. I decided that I wanted to get to know the women in the

weaving group, and that gaining their trust was more important to me than actively looking for answers to my own questions about them. I made a decision that I would learn whatever they felt like sharing with me. I did not want to "use them" for research purposes. I chose not to ask a lot of sensitive questions about politics, the history of their community, massacres, about male/female relationships, etc. I did not conduct any formal interviews with anyone. However, once the family I lived with and members of the group knew me better, they voluntarily shared with me about several aspects of their lives.

2. *Transcription of the interview for use in the historian's written presentations to an academic audience is not the only purpose of an interview, and perhaps not the most important.*
When Alice and I came to do our book *Rank and File,* about half of the so-called interviews were actually presentations at community forums, or at smaller workshops, where young people in the community could receive an oral tradition from persons further along life's path. We said in a preface to the second edition:

> In working-class communities, even relatively recent history often becomes lost to the young people growing up there. In *Rank and File* we sought to provide occasions for older persons—as it were, the elders of the tribe—to recall their personal histories in the presence of the community. Thus, the purpose of the interviews reported in *Rank and File* was emphatically not to provide raw material for conventional academic history by ourselves or anyone else. Instead, the idea was to get beyond a situation in which one group of people (workers) experiences history, and another group of people (professional historians) interprets the experience for them. We wanted to see those who make history also analyze and record it.

Partly for this reason, "oral history" seems a more appropriate term than "interview," and I shall use it in the remainder of these remarks.

3. *Those who provide oral histories can themselves help to verify and correct the information provided.*
Oral historians are frequently criticized for the inaccuracy of their informants. It is suggested that we should pay more heed to the recollections of the rich and powerful, and to documents.
It is true that oral histories are often inaccurate as to dates and durations. This summer three men who took part in a hunger strike in Jneid

prison in the occupied West Bank five years ago told us about it in three separate conversations. Each thought the strike lasted a different number of days.

As to other matters, those who provide oral histories are often remarkably precise. Moreover, the things they remember frequently cannot be verified by the rich and powerful, because the rich and powerful were not present; and cannot be checked against documents which either don't exist or, like Israeli records of prison hunger strikes, will not be accessible for years to come.

One precaution is to do what any lawyer does in preparing a witness for trial: to ask, "Did you see that yourself or did someone else tell you about it?" Sometimes the answer will be, "My father told me." But sometimes the answer will not only confirm that the witness was present but trigger a torrent of new detail. "I was here (pointing) and the woman who was killed was there (pointing across the room). I can still hear the screaming of the people: 'Bring the ambulance! Bring the cars! There is a woman killed!'"

Another precaution, which likewise will not merely verify but enrich, is to convene a group of persons who shared the same experience. I recall the Boston Draft Resistance Group, circa 1969, sitting in a circle with the tape recorder on the floor in the middle. After getting the conversation started I simply listened to members of the group correcting and fine-tuning each other's statements. "But it was in the afternoon, don't you remember?" "That guy with the funny name was there; what did he call himself?" And then when someone finds just the right words, or remembers a telling detail, a long pause, finally punctuated by a muttered, "Yeah," or, "You got that right." It is time to prime the pump again with a few follow-up questions, or to turn off the recorder.

4. *In a history that reflects the reality of life for poor and working people, the ultimate subject of that history is likely to be not the individual, but the group.*

Far be it from me even to seem to suggest that poor and working people are somehow more uniform or monolithic than people who are not poor. The last thing one should want to do is to mute or obscure the way in which—all around the globe—women, who have been part of a group of silent listeners while the men talked, are stepping forward from the margins of the conversation as variegated individuals.

My point is simply that we who are relatively individualistic, who tend to live and move and have our being in nuclear families, not extended families, may misperceive the texture of communities in which we do oral history. Palestinians whom my wife and I interviewed spoke of how, when their parents' home in the Ein El Hilweh refugee camp was twice destroyed by the Israeli army, family members from all over the world sent money to rebuild the house "because that's part of our culture." The Guatemalan Indians with whom my daughter lived asked her why she was not at home, helping her elderly parents.

Was it interviewer or interviewee who chose the title, *I, Rigoberta Menchú?*[1] Probably the interviewer, for the interviewee says, in the first sentences of her oral history: "I'd like to stress that it's not only *my* life, it's also the testimony of my people. . . . The important thing is that what has happened to me has happened to many other people too. My story is the story of all poor Guatemalans." It's also interesting that the interviewing took place during a week in Paris at the interviewer's home, a scenario that in itself divorced one person's oral history from its natural collective background.

Here is a final example of the group content of oral history from below. My wife and I together with our friend Sam Bahour began to do oral histories with Palestinians just after the Gulf War, in spring 1991. A year after we began, I was asked to review a book by Donald Katz called *Home Fires.*[2] The book is a wonderful oral history of the members of a family that Katz, mistakenly I think, calls "middle-class." All four children in this family became rebels in the Sixties. In each case this required a dramatic break from family values.

I have always been judgmental, not to say self-righteous, about the fact that so many participants in the Movement of the Sixties proved to be sprinters rather than long-distance runners. Reading *Home Fires,* I was struck by the contrast between the young people it describes and the Palestinians whose oral histories we had been recording. No wonder it was so hard for young Americans to persevere politically, to be long-distance runners. There was typically very little support from their family culture. Palestinian fathers and mothers, too, like fathers and mothers everywhere, fear for the welfare of their children. But when those children come into harm's way, when they are arrested, interrogated, indefinitely detained, Palestinian parents, grandparents, aunts and uncles, and younger siblings, stand behind the vulnerable member of the family because the cause is one to which the family has been committed since before the child was born. Our collection of oral histories, which had begun as a chronicle of heroic individuals, came to be in part a story of the persistence of families.

5. *It is their story, not our story: they not we are those who do oral history.*
Studs Terkel said in an interview with the *New York Times*, May 6, 1992:

> It's like prospecting. The transcripts are the ore. I've got to get to the gold dust. It's got to be the person's truth, highlighted. It's not just putting down what people say.

The metaphor is terrific, and yet the oral history described falls short of accompaniment. I would vary it by saying to the person telling his or her history: "Let me hold the screen. Sift the dirt through and tell me when you see gold." Here are two little examples.

Early in the 1980s I found myself recording an oral history with a Youngstown steelworker, Gerald Dickey. When Youngstown's steel mills closed, Gerald was the person who first suggested that they should be reopened under worker-community ownership. "Where did you get the idea?" I asked. We were using an old reel-to-reel tape recorder. All through the first reel, Gerald fumbled with the answer. The tape stopped. I turned it over. Suddenly Brother Dickey's face brightened: "*Now* I remember. . . ." We were off and running. I felt that had I come twenty-four hours later, the memory might have been gone forever, and there would have been nothing I could do about it.

I have recently come to know a man named Brian Willson, who on September 1, 1987, sat down on the track at the Concord Naval Weapons Station near Oakland to block a train carrying munitions to dockside for shipment to Central America. The train didn't stop. Brian's legs were cut off, but miraculously he survived. He wanted me to help him tell his story in a book.

We collected transcripts of speeches, articles, published interviews. There was a mass of material. One publisher rejected it. Brian took off for South America.

I decided to start over, using Brian's own words about his life that had appeared here and there in the many pages of political argument and explanation. A statue emerged from the marble. Brian was an all-American boy who had grown up near the Chautauqua Institute in western New York State. Brian's father, an often-unemployed salesman, was virulently Christian and racist; he listened to Fulton Lewis, Jr., and made lists of suspected Communists in the State Department. Brian himself, when he graduated from high school, wanted to be an FBI agent.

Then came Vietnam, where it was Brian Willson's task to inspect the effectiveness of United States air strikes on Vietnamese villages. One day, he writes,

> I looked at the face of a young mother on the ground whose eyes appeared to be open as she had two children in one arm, another child in the other. Upon closer examination I realized she and her children had been killed by bomb fragments. Napalm had apparently burned much of her face, including her eyelids. I stared into her eyes from a close distance, leaning over to do so. Tears streamed down my face. . . .
>
> I looked at that mother's face, what was left of it, and it flashed at that point in my mind that the whole idea of the threat of Communism was ridiculous. Somehow I couldn't see Communism on her face. I remember looking at that woman's face and thinking, "I wonder what a Communist looks like?" All I saw was the face of a mother no older than twenty holding her children. All of them were dead. I said, "My God, this bombing, this war, is a lie. I've been living a lie. What does all this mean? These people are just persons, just human beings. . . ."
>
> The Vietnamese lieutenant accompanying me asked why I was crying. I stood straight up and turned to him and replied, "Because she is my sister, and these are my children, too." I have no idea from where that feeling and response came. . . .

The book has since been published under the title *On Third World Legs*.[3]

Summing up: In accompanying, one does not pretend to be the same as the person beside whom one travels. Nor does one romanticize that person, projecting virtues that are not there or condoning evils that are all too real. One expresses a preferential option for the poor and marginalized in deciding to live amongst them for a time, and to assist, if possible, in articulating and transmitting their collective experience.

"Oral history from below" requires the historian to enter into the lives of poor and working people who are that history's protagonists. Of necessity it exposes the historian's own class and cultural limitations to the light of common day. It is painful. It requires personal, not just intellectual, risktaking. Perhaps it will seem worthwhile only to intellectuals whose political and/or religious project is the remaking of society through the agency of the poor.

During the years 1978–1980, when Oscar Romero was Archbishop of El Salvador and the formation of Christian base communities in urban slums and villages went on apace, a group of pastoral workers and their constituents collectively produced a liturgy called the Salvadoran Popular Mass. Here are the words which begin the recessional to the Salvadoran Popular Mass:

> Cuando el pobre crea en el pobre,
> Ya podremos cantar libertad

> [When the poor come to believe in the poor,
> Then indeed we will be able to sing of freedom]

May our oral history be measured by that standard.

4

Liberation Theology
for Quakers

Alice and Staughton Lynd

W̶e are Quakers. We have faith that there is a potential for good in
every person and that this "inner light" needs no mediation by
priest or church. We believe in treating people as equals. We believe in
nonviolence and forgiveness. We disavow retaliation or retribution. We
try to practice direct speaking, speaking truth to power, and living consistently with our values. We follow a simple way of life and try to be
responsible stewards of the earth and its resources. We think these are
Quaker beliefs.

At the very opposite end of the spectrum of Christian belief, it might
seem, stands the Roman Catholic Church. Hierarchy, ritual, a prescribed liturgy, a fixed creed are sharply at odds with Friends' practice of
a gathered silent meeting in which any person present can become the
channel through which a message, unpredictable in advance, may be
voiced.

Originally published as a Pendle Hill pamphlet in April 1996. Alice Lynd and Staughton
Lynd, *Liberation Theology for Quakers*, no. 326 (Wallingford, Pa.: Pendle Hill, A Quaker Center for Study and Contemplation, 1996). 1-800-742-3150. Reprinted by permission.

Yet our most powerful spiritual experiences in recent years have been among Roman Catholics in Nicaragua who belonged to what they call the popular Church, that is, the segment of the Catholic community influenced by liberation theology and "the preferential option for the poor."

We urge Friends to reflect on the teachings of liberation theology. As a stimulus, we offer here a record of our own joint effort to live out our Quaker convictions, our own experiments in truth.

Liberation Theology

What is liberation theology? What is meant by "the preferential option for the poor"? In our experience, at least the following four things:

First, liberation theology is motivated by the conviction that God does not want anyone to be poor and oppressed and that the Kingdom of God should be lived out here on earth. The spokespersons of this approach refer to *institutional violence* and *structural injustice*, meaning that the institutions and structures of society that allow some persons to oppress others must be confronted and changed.

Second, the "preferential option for the poor," or, in plain English, *the choice to stand on the side of the poor*, refers to two kinds of choice.

For those who believe in a personal god (as we do not), there is God's choice of the poor, shown by the evidence that God chose to deliver his message through someone born in a cow stall, who was a carpenter (or whose father was a carpenter), who found his followers among fishermen, and who was executed in the humiliating manner used to silence slaves and rebels.

Next there is the choice for service to the poor that may be made by persons like ourselves: persons born into the middle class, or educated to a degree that offers access to a middle-class style of life. The preferential option for the poor led Sister Helen Prejean to St. Thomas, a housing project in New Orleans, and later to her work against capital punishment:

> I came to St. Thomas as part of a reform movement in the Catholic Church, seeking to harness religious faith to social justice. . . .
>
> In 1980 my religious community, the Sisters of St. Joseph of Medaille, had made a commitment to "stand on the side of the poor," and I had

assented, but reluctantly. I resisted this recasting of the faith of my childhood, where what counted was a personal relationship with God, inner
peace, kindness to others, and heaven when this life was done. I didn't want
to struggle with politics and economics. We were nuns, after all, not social
workers, and some realities in life were, for better or worse, rather fixed—
like the gap between rich and poor.

She recalls a meeting in June 1980 when Sister Marie Augusta Neal, a
sociologist, spoke:

[S]he described the glaring inequities in the world: two thirds of the peoples
of the world live at or below subsistence level while one third live in afflu-
ence. . . . I found myself mentally pitting my arguments against her challenge—*we were nuns, not social workers, not political.* But it's as if she knew what
I was thinking. She pointed out that to claim to be apolitical or neutral in
the face of such injustices would be, in actuality, to uphold the status quo—
a very political position to take, and on the side of the oppressors. . . .

"The Gospels record that Jesus preached good news to the poor," she
said, "and an essential part of that good news was that they were to be poor
no longer." Which meant they were not to meekly accept their poverty and
suffering as God's will, but, instead, struggle to obtain the necessities of life
which were rightfully theirs.[1]

In that moment, Sister Prejean says, she realized that her spiritual life
was too disconnected. She left the meeting and began to seek out the
poor.

We think that acting not just for, but with, the poor and oppressed,
and then living out the unforeseen consequences of that choice, is what
Archbishop Oscar Romero meant by "accompaniment."

Third, the *dignity and self-activity of poor and working people* is another
cardinal belief of liberation theology. All over the world, very much
including the United States, poor and working people are constantly
being told that they are dumb, that they are unworthy, and that they cannot solve their own problems. They tend to internalize the oppressor's
image of themselves.

Liberation theology responds that everyone has his or her own dignity, and together we can find a path ahead. In Latin America pastoral
agents of the new Catholicism teach the poor that they must not be passive victims, that they can and should "see, judge, and act." These words

were spread among Guatemalan workers in the 1950s and 1960s by European priests affiliated with the Young Catholic Worker organization.[2] These same words were the guiding principles of a base community we visited in a remote village in Matagalpa, Nicaragua, in 1987.

Finally, liberation theology promotes the institution of the *base community*. The essence of a base community as it exists in Latin America is for men and women (and inevitably children) in a neighborhood or village to meet regularly, read the Gospel, and try to apply it in their own life situation.[3]

The results can be startling. Here is a base community in Nicaragua reflecting on the story of the Good Samaritan, Luke 10:30–37:

> For us it is necessary to journey on the road,
> Like the man who was traveling to Jericho [and was set upon by thieves].
> We have to go to work, and to our homes.
> We are not able to stop using the road.
> What shall we do?
>
> And they conclude:
> This traveler was assaulted
> Because he was going by himself.
> He was alone,
> And for this reason
> The robbers were able to assault him
> And to leave him half dead.
>
> We must travel very much together.
> We must be well organized.
> That is: We must organize ourselves
> And do all things as a community.
> So that what happened to the traveler to Jericho
> Won't happen to us.[4]

Early Friends

Many of these same themes were exemplified in the lives of early Friends.

The early Quakers were "made up out of the dregs of the common people,"[5] and the original leaders of the Quakers were almost exclusively farmers and craftsmen.

Like radical Catholics in Latin America today, the early Quakers stressed institutional rather than individual sin.

It has been suggested that certain Quaker practices preserved in a kind of underground tradition the communal way of life of the medieval peasantry. In a village, "only one form of cultivation was possible at one time in the common fields. . . . The Quaker 'sense of the meeting' carried over into the modern world something of the desire for unanimity which meant so much to the medieval communities."[6]

The first Friends in the North American colonies expressed a thoroughgoing social and religious radicalism. There was nothing respectable about Quakerism then. Mary Dyer and other Friends were executed before Quakers were permitted to worship undisturbed in Boston.

Today, Quakers in North America are "overwhelmingly white, suburban and well-heeled," and our "meetings consist of well-educated and relatively wealthy enclaves of white people."[7] It is an open question whether Friends might once more, as in their beginnings, become a group that serves the poor directly and is at least in part made up of people who work with their hands, a group that seeks passionately to create a new society in which there will be no great disparities between rich and poor.[8]

Our Formation: Macedonia Cooperative Community

When asked by a Friend, "What motivated Alice and Staughton?" our immediate answer was "Macedonia." Nuns with whom we stayed in Nicaragua spoke of their "formation." The three years we spent at the Macedonia Cooperative Community, 1954–1957, were the period of our formation, establishing values and teaching us ways of living in community which we vowed to live by for the rest of our lives.

During the summer of 1954, we went for a two-week vacation to visit the Macedonia Cooperative Community in the hills of Northeast Georgia. As we approached, we saw a barefoot woman with a torn shirt carrying a young child. She, we learned later, was a neighbor who visited the community from time to time. Members of the community were better off but lived in "voluntary poverty." This was a poor area, inhabited by people whose children lacked shoes in winter, on poor land that was suitable for little but pastures and forests. The community earned a meager living from a dairy and from Community Playthings, which made and sold blocks and other wooden play equipment for use in kindergartens and Sunday Schools.

We soon noticed how people at Macedonia listened to each other. There might be a meeting in someone's living room. Someone spoke. Then a pause. Another observation. Another pause. The speaking was, as Quakers say, "out of the silence." We fell in love with what we experienced at Macedonia.

Staughton gave up his scholarship at the University of Chicago where he was studying regional planning, and Alice gave up her job as secretary of the Education Department at Roosevelt University. We returned to Macedonia, arriving on November 1, 1954. Our first child was born there in September 1955, and we became full members of the community in December 1955.

Decisions were by consensus, not voting. Consensus decision making, as practiced at Macedonia, was both a means of finding truth and a means of building community. We presumed that every human being is endowed with a conscience, and that we need to use this conscience, to listen and be guided by it: to keep our hearts open. We need each other because none of us can see the whole truth.

At Macedonia we felt that any one of us might notice something that the rest of us were missing. We treasured a particular member who often said at the end of a long discussion, "There's something off, something just doesn't ring true"—whereupon, no matter how few the hours before the morning milking, the discussion began all over again.

Each person spoke with his or her own voice. We tried not to represent what we thought someone else was thinking. We would say, let's ask that person.

We also practiced what we called "direct speaking," not "gossiping" or speaking behind someone's back in a way you would not say directly to that person. If you were irritated by what another person did, you went to that person and tried to work it out. If you needed help, you asked a third person to join the conversation.

Alice: Another woman and I had a personality clash that expressed itself in different approaches to the children in the kindergarten. I remember dragging myself to a meeting with this woman and a third member. That meeting was a turning point. I liked the routines of working with two-year-olds. The other woman liked to come up with something new every day for the older children. We came to appreciate our differences, each valuing what the other one could do.

The New Testament speaks of clearing up differences with a brother before going to the altar (Matthew 5:23). At Macedonia, we were living together, not just going to church together. We thought it equally important to straighten things out with someone before a business meeting, or on the way to work together at the cowbarn.

We also learned at Macedonia an experiential way of understanding the search for truth. We said that there was a common religious experience that different persons might use quite different words to describe.

We left Macedonia in 1957 when the community decided to merge with the Society of Brothers (or Bruderhof).

Why did our three years at Macedonia mean so much to us? Because it showed us that people could live together in a manner *qualitatively* different from the dog-eat-dog ambience of capitalist society. The qualitatively different atmosphere of human relationships that we encountered at Macedonia has been our objective ever since. We found it again, to some extent, in the Southern civil rights movement, which sometimes called itself "a band of brothers and sisters standing in a circle of love"; in the practice of solidarity by rank-and-file workers; and in Latin American notions about "accompanying" one another in the search for "el reino de Dios," the kingdom of God on earth. We found it in these other places because we were looking for it; because, after Macedonia, we knew it could happen.

Accompaniment: The Southern Civil Rights Movement

When the sit-ins began in early 1960, we cast about for a way to move South. Staughton was then a graduate student in history at Columbia University in New York. The mother of one of the black children in a kindergarten attended by our daughter suggested teaching in a Southern black (or, as they were then called, Negro) college. Staughton was offered a job at Spelman College in Atlanta. His meager salary would be supplemented by a free apartment on campus.

Alice: I viewed the situation as a "live-in." I do not like to participate in picketing, sit-ins, and the like. But, despite my fears that someone would put a bomb in our car, I felt that we could live in the situation.

Good things flowed from that modest preferential option. Spelman students proved full of life. One of them was Alice Walker, future author of *The Color Purple*. Also, we became convinced Friends. Atlanta schools were beginning to desegregate, starting with the upper grades of high school. The only space in Atlanta where black and white youngsters could meet one another socially before facing the common ordeal of the school year was Quaker House, then managed by John and June Yungblut. We began to attend regularly with our two children, aged six and three. We felt that our children, and the children of other families who believed in integration, needed one another and found support at Quaker House.

When our son had just turned five, he fell from a second-floor window of Quaker House and almost died. After the operation, the days and nights of hospital attendance, and Lee's miraculous recovery of his mind and spirit (he is now a professor of environmental engineering)— all of which we lived through with the Atlanta Meeting—we found that we were Friends; formally joining the Meeting seemed an acknowledgment of what we had already experienced.

In the autumn of 1962 came the Cuban missile crisis. The mayor of Atlanta wired President Kennedy that all Atlantans supported him (in going to the brink of nuclear war). That could not be permitted to pass, and so a handful of Spelman faculty members together with staff of the Student Nonviolent Coordinating Committee (SNCC) set up a picket line in downtown Atlanta.

Staughton: My picture appeared in the Atlanta Constitution *along with a colleague wrongly identified as Alice. As a result, Alice was forced out of her job as a daycare teacher.*

But something good came of it, too. As the picket line was breaking up, a young black man asked me if he could stay with us overnight until he got his field assignment from SNCC. Of course I said, Yes. It was ten days or two weeks before John got his assignment and in the meantime we got to know him well. A year later it was John who called from Mississippi to offer me the position of Freedom School director in the Mississippi Summer Project of 1964.

Accompaniment: Draft Counseling

Staughton: During the summer of 1965, I was involved in anti-war protests. I was arrested at the Assembly of Unrepresented People that met in Washington, D.C., on August 6th through 9th (Hiroshima and Nagasaki Days), to declare peace with the people of Vietnam.

Alice: I was asking myself what I could do about the war and still be responsible as a mother and nursery school teacher. Many groups held workshops on the grassy mall between the Capitol and the Washington Monument during the Assembly of Unrepresented People. I went from one to another, ending up in a tent where a representative of the Central Committee for Conscientious Objectors (CCCO) was selling handbooks and talking about the need for draft counselors. At the end of the meeting I asked the workshop leader whether I could become a draft counselor. He replied: "Well, I guess so, if you could get anyone to come to you. There is one female draft counselor." (That female was a Quaker, Honey Knopp.)

We lived just a few blocks from Yale University at that time, and students frequently came to our home. I put up a little sign that students would see as they entered our apartment saying they could ask questions about the draft, and some of them did. A group of divinity students asked to meet with us on a weekly basis to discuss what they should do about the draft.

During one such discussion, a young woman mentioned someone we knew who had gone to prison as a noncooperator. She said she thought he now regretted that action. I asked myself what that man would say if he were present. After the meeting, I said to Staughton, "Your next book should be a book of interviews with people who have refused military service, what happened to them, and what they would say to others who are considering it." "Why me?" Staughton replied. So I collected and edited a book of personal accounts of war objectors.[9] It was only because we were close to young people who were faced with the draft and military service that it became possible to do that book; and the book, in turn, became a way for war resisters to show family and friends that others were struggling with the same dilemmas.

I loved draft counseling. Sometimes my first reaction to a counselee was dismay at his appearance, but within an hour I had a deep respect for how he saw life, his relations to his family, and his hopes for the future. I talked with many young men who had grown up with religious training, who took religious values seriously, and who had left their churches because they did not see the members or leaders of the church acting consistently with what was being preached. I felt privileged to touch others at this moment when they were struggling with decisions that involved the whole meaning of their lives.

Because I was not a lawyer at that time, I could not give legal advice. More important, draft counselors knew that the counselee was going to have to live with the consequences of his decision, so the decision had better be his. Draft counselors didn't want to engage in "mindbending."

Former counselees who refused induction often had lawyers to defend them. They frequently reported that the lawyers would argue their own theories, rather than presenting the reasons that were at the heart of the matter for the refuser. It was as if the refuser were being tried not on his own grounds but to test some lawyer's theory. There seemed to be a difference between lawyers, who would take a case into their own hands, and counselors who would not.

I developed a conceptual model. The counselee and the counselor are both experts. The counselor knows about the regulations and what steps to take once the counselee has chosen a particular course of action, but the counselee knows more than the counselor can ever know about the counselee: what he thinks, his family situation, and what he is prepared to do. They work together as partners.

Years later, we both became lawyers. We carried Alice's counseling model with us into the law. Our labor law clients knew more about what went on in the shop than we could ever know, but we could find out the facts that were necessary to prove a claim, and we could present a legal theory that accurately reflected what our clients believed the problem to be.

Accompaniment: Moving to Youngstown

By the early 1970s we were in our early forties. Staughton could no longer find work as a university teacher because of his well-publicized civil disobedience against the Vietnam War. The federal monies that had made possible Alice's work in early childhood education were drying up. We needed a new means of livelihood.

Also, the Movement of the 1960s was at an end. Blacks told whites to leave the civil rights movement and organize in white working-class communities. The Nixon administration decided to carry on the Vietnam War with less use of the draft.

We felt that the Movement had come to grief partly because of class. Student activists in universities who protested rather than getting a formal education seemed irresponsible to working-class parents watching from afar. Sensing a lack of support off campus, student radicals tried to make up for it by escalating their tactics. This only increased the alienation of "hard hats" and others whose support students needed to bring about fundamental social change.

We resolved to try to strike up a conversation with industrial workers. The question was, how? In the 1970s, as in the 1930s, many middle-class radicals went to work in factories.

Staughton: There is strong biblical authority for sharing the situation of the person you are trying to help. Jesus often asked the rich to become poor. He told the rich young ruler to "sell all that thou hast, and distribute unto the poor" (Luke 18:22; Matthew 19:21). I once left college after seeing a film about the life of St. Vincent de Paul. Vincent was chaplain to the King of France. Watching from the high poop of the king's galley a race between galleys rowed by slaves, Vincent saw a slave faint at the oar. He clambered down to the bench, and took the oar into his own hands. He took the place of *the stricken rower.*[10]

But when I talked with friends who had gone to work in steel mills, I was told that I would always seem to fellow workers to be exactly what I was: a product of the upper middle class with advanced degrees. "You could be there twenty years, and people would say, Let's go ask the Professor," was one comment. So we resolved to offer what we hoped would be useful skills, but not to pretend to be other than what we were. Later, it seemed to us that this is also what priests and nuns do in Latin America, when they move to some rural hamlet or city barrio but continue to function as pastoral agents, often in clerical garb.

We began as oral historians. Led from one person to the next, we tape-recorded recollections of rank-and-file workers and put them together in a book.[11]

Staughton: In the summer of 1971, when the industry-wide Basic Steel Contract was under negotiation, I helped to draft an imaginary steel contract made up of the most radical demands of the many competing union caucuses in the Gary-Chicago area where we then lived. Someone gave us the address of a group in Youngstown, Ohio, called the Rank and File Team (RAFT). We put a copy of the pamphlet in the mail.

A few days later, as we were sitting at supper, the phone rang. "Hello!" bellowed a mighty voice. "This is Litch from Youngstown. What mill do you work in?" I confessed that I was only a historian. "That's all right," the big voice said. "We like your pamphlet." (Later we learned that Bill Litch talked so loudly because he had been partly deafened from years of work in the mill.)

It turned out that RAFT was planning to picket at the opening round of union-management negotiations in Washington, D.C., and that I would be in Washington that same day. It was arranged to meet at the picket line.

We met, and after a respectable period of picketing, we adjourned to a nearby coffee shop and got to know each other. The picketers included John Barbero and Ed Mann. John and Ed were advocates of racial equality as well as civil liberties. Former Marines, each had opposed not only the Vietnam War, but the Korean War as well; each had belonged to the Akron-based United Labor Party after World War II; they considered themselves socialists, although they didn't often use that word. We had never met workers like these, who believed all (or nearly all) the things that we believed.

Five years later, after acquiring credentials as lawyer and paralegal, we moved to the outskirts of Youngstown.

Using One's Pain

Alice: I was hired to work on workers' compensation cases but very soon found myself assigned to work primarily on Social Security disability cases. It was not like draft counseling. The most I could get for any client was money, and the disabled needed far more than money. Staughton mentioned my troubled feelings about this caseload to a colleague who unexpectedly replied, "Feed my sheep" (John 21:16).

I knew what it was like to be disabled. I had been disabled, unable to work for more than two years after surgery that did not heal properly. I had sometimes been desperate with pain and unable to cope with the needs of our children. I remembered our son's friend coming to the house and asking our son, "Is your ma crying again?" So I knew that physical hardship affects your mind and spirit.

I began to love the infinite ways people found to cope with disability: a person who lacked the use of her hand could slide a tray onto her forearm; another who couldn't lift much would fill a large pot on the stove with a small pot, carrying just a little water at one time. I heard about how people had found their personhood in their work. One man had figured out exactly how fast the machine could be set so that the maximum number of bread loaves came down the line without any of them touching each other; the foreman, so he said, would tell the other workers not to make any adjustments after this worker had regulated the machine.

Preparing disability cases became for me a way of expressing love to people. My clients told me that I listened to them as no doctor, nurse, or social worker had done. Because I had to learn about their work history and the activities they could no longer do, I would glimpse the person behind the mask of disability.

Nicaragua

Alice: One evening, perhaps in December 1983, I suddenly stopped what I was doing to give my full attention to what was on the TV. A Quaker woman was going to Nicaragua with a group called Witness for Peace. They were going to go into areas of conflict and stand between the warring parties as a deterrent. I thought, Wow, that's what nonviolent advocates have talked about for years, but here are people who are going to do it!

Staughton: A nonviolent dimension to the Nicaraguan revolution itself also caught our attention. I read in the New York Times *that when the Sandinistas took power in 1979 they did not execute Somoza's soldiers who fell into their hands. Those who were found to have committed crimes were jailed. All others were released.*

We also read of an encounter between Tomás Borge, the only surviving member of the group that founded the FSLN (Sandinista Front for National Liberation), and a man who had tortured him in prison. Borge let the torturer go.

Alice: So when our son suggested that we rent a cabin on a lake for a summer vacation, I responded, "I'd rather go to Nicaragua!"

We did go to Nicaragua, not with Witness for Peace, but with IFCO, the Inter-religious Foundation for Community Organization, which had ties to CEPAD, an interdenominational Protestant relief organization.

It was six years since the Sandinista revolution when we arrived in Nicaragua for the first time. Miskito Indians in northeastern Nicaragua had been evacuated from their homes on the Rio Coco River but now, in a reversal of policy, were being helped to return. We went to Puerto Cabezas on the Atlantic Coast. With the help of a friend who knew English and Spanish and an Indian who knew Spanish and Miskito, we conversed from Miskito to Spanish to English and back to Miskito. Norman Bent, a Moravian minister, told us about the "Fourth World" of indigenous people. We listened to Ray Hooker retell the Exodus story in modern Nicaraguan form, and heard him speak of his hopes for "the new woman, the new man." We had the opportunity to tape-record a discussion with Father Miguel D'Escoto, a Catholic priest who served as Foreign Minister and had not long before ended a thirty-day fast protesting U.S. support for the Contras.

D'Escoto told us that when the FSLN first invited him to join their effort, he had told them he was nonviolent. "And they said [according to our tape recording], We know that; we know what you believe, you have written about it; and that's one of the reasons why we want you. We would like for you to inject that dimension also in our revolution."

St. Mary of the Angels. St. Mary of the Angels is the neighborhood church in Barrio Riguero in Managua. During three of our five short visits to Nicaragua in the years 1985–1990 (we used our summer vacations of two or three weeks), we stayed in the home of a family only a few blocks from St. Mary's.

The liturgy celebrated by Father Uriel Molina at St. Mary's was the Campesino Mass, composed by the Nicaraguan composer Carlos Mejía Godoy in 1975. The following is part of the text of the mass:

You Are the God of the Poor

You go hand in hand with my people
In their struggle in the countryside and city.
You stand in line at the hacienda
To receive the day's wages.
I've seen you in the general store
or on the street.
I've seen you selling lottery tickets,
Without being embarrassed to do so.
I've seen you in the gas stations
Checking the tires of a truck.
And eating snow cones there in the park
With Eusebio, Pancho, and Juan Jose.

Chorus
You are the God of the poor.
The God that's human and simple,
The God that sweats in the streets,
The God with the weather-beaten face.

And so when I talk to you,
I speak as my people do.
Because you're the working-class God,
The Christ who's a laborer too.

The music to the mass was played at St. Mary's by a band of half a dozen young men, most of them (so we were told) veterans. One feature of the liturgy was the so-called Peace of God, when all present would circulate through the church, embracing or shaking hands with others. Many of the celebrants were elderly women, small in stature, who carried photographs of sons who had been killed in the war.

Staughton: At one Peace of God, a bearded, middle-aged man bounded across the church to embrace me. It was Abbie Hoffman, whom I had last seen in a Chicago jail in August 1968.

"We Shall Overcome" was sung in Spanish and in English as a regular part of the liturgy at St. Mary's. I felt that wild horses could not have kept me from taking communion at that Catholic church.

In 1987 our friend Joe Mulligan, a Jesuit priest from the States, arranged an interview with Father Uriel and translated. I explained my predicament to Father Uriel: "For the Christians in the United States I was too Marxist, and for the Marxists I was too Christian. I think Marxism is a very important tool of analysis, in fact, the best one I know; but when it comes to deciding what to do, how to live, Marxism is not sufficient. From the standpoint of the Christians, I was a poor Christian, and from the standpoint of the Marxists, a bad Marxist. Coming to Nicaragua, I have the feeling that there's a whole country that feels the way I do."

Father Uriel responded in part as had Miguel D'Escoto by pointing to the paradoxical nature of atheism. The Good Samaritan, D'Escoto had said in 1985, was an atheist, but "he did what our Lord said we all had to do if we wanted to be saved." Now Uriel remarked: "In the time of the New Testament, Christians were called atheists. They rejected the gods of the empire and the standard religious beliefs, so they were called atheists. Now there is a new need for a kind of atheist vision where the idols need to be knocked over and the true God is to be found, because the old conception of God doesn't speak to people today."

Father Uriel also commented that "we ourselves may not be the ones to discover our role but others may point us to it." He recalled that at one very grim moment in the struggle against the Somoza dictatorship, he had talked to "a young man who never came to church but was a very dedicated person. I said, things are looking very bad, maybe we better pull out because it is looking like it is all over and we are all going to be wiped out. And the young man, William, said: 'If you do, then the whole community will lose their hope, because your presence here is during the day like an open door and at night, a light'."

In El Bonete. On our last visit to Nicaragua, in 1990, we stayed for a week with two Catholic nuns in a village named El Bonete near the Honduran border. Our notes, written while there, say:

"Carmencita is from El Salvador, Nelly from Argentina. They belong to the Little Sisters of Jesus. A small *capilla* (chapel) is part of their house. It is about ten by twelve feet. The altar is a tree stump with a vase of flowers on the floor before it. Shoes are left at the door. Worshippers sit on planks resting on concrete blocks or on mats that cover most of the floor. On one wall hangs an orange fabric, with photographs of Archbishop Romero and of the six Jesuits killed in San Salvador in November 1989. On it Carmencita has embroidered Romero's famous

words about grains of corn that must die so that there may be new
growth, and two ears of corn, yellow and brown in their green sheaves."

The four of us sang a great deal. Some songs were primarily religious. Thus a song of this part of Nicaragua begins:

> When a group of brothers approaches the altar,
> God's smile is there.
> Lord, we are coming today
> To praise you
> And to thank you for so much goodness [*tanta bondad*].

In other songs the longing for a more just world is uppermost. El Salvador has its own campesino mass, the Salvadoran popular mass, written
in the base communities of San Salvador in 1978–1980. These are the
words to the dismissal (*despedida*) that closes the mass:

> When the poor come to believe in the poor
> Then indeed we will be able to sing of freedom.
> When the poor come to believe in the poor
> We will build fraternity.

> See you later, my brothers,
> The mass has ended
> And we've heard what God said to us.
> Now we are clear,
> We are able to sing,
> We need to begin our task.

> We have all committed ourselves
> At the table of the Lord
> To construct love in this world,
> To the brothers' struggle
> To become a community.

> When the poor seek out the poor
> And organization is born
> That's when our freedom begins.
> When the poor proclaim to the poor
> The hope that he gave us
> His Kingdom is born among us.

Return to Quakerism: Nonviolence

Our new friends in Nicaragua were not pacifists. D'Escoto considered revolutionary violence a "concession for a world in transition." Father Uriel spoke of the university students who had come to live with him in Barrio Riguero. "When many of these people went into the mountains to fight in the armed struggle, I stayed in this community . . . and felt that what we were forming here was the . . . spiritual rear guard for the people who were there fighting in the mountains." Sister Carmencita was the most direct. Several members of her family had been killed. In El Salvador, she told us, torture is the people's daily bread. She concluded: "I think there is a right to defend oneself."

The Gulf War. During the Gulf War in 1991, we picketed every day at noon in downtown Youngstown. We began by encircling a marble memorial on which were carved the names of local servicemen who lost their lives in Vietnam. Our presence there was particularly irritating to some Vietnam veterans. We talked with them. We agreed to move our picket line to a location that was just as visible but less offensive to them. It became a regular part of what we did to step out of the picket line and talk with any heckler or obvious opponent. We probably did not change any minds, but at least respectful relationships were established. Their presence rapidly diminished.

Alice: For me, the Gulf War brought a clear affirmation of Christianity. In my view, retaliation and retribution only lead to more suffering, more hatred, and intransigent obstacles remain to be overcome for generations. Unless we can learn to forgive, to forgive "seventy times seven" (Matthew 18:21–22), where is there hope for the future?

Nonviolence and forgiveness are not mere backing down. Nonviolence, as Barbara Deming describes it,[12] requires stepping forward, with one hand restraining while the other hand offers a better way, maintaining one's own presence and dignity while respecting the very different experience and outlook of one's adversary, appealing to basic values that all humans can understand. This is what I experienced on that picket line.

Staughton: I recall that when we decided to picket—and I was among those who suggested it—I felt, "Well, fifteen years of work in Youngstown may be going down the drain. But we have to do it anyway."

What actually happened surprised me. One very outspoken man looked me in the eye and said, "Lynd, you know I disagree with you about the war." Then every-

thing went on as before. Another man came up to me as I was walking with a group of retired steelworkers along a sidewalk in Cleveland. "You know I agree with you about the war," he said.

It seemed to me that for both men the critical thing was that they had known us personally for years. It was as if they figured, "This is what you'd expect Staughton to do." It made no difference whatsoever to our work or to the way in which the community viewed us.

Retirees. Much of our work in Youngstown has been with former steelworkers. Many of them proudly defended this country in World War II or the Korean War. Nonviolence is not part of their creed.

In 1986, when the second largest steel company declared bankruptcy and cut off medical benefits for retirees, an activist organization of retirees quickly formed. It was named "Solidarity USA" after Solidarność in Poland. The retirees collected petitions, went on bus trips to the court in New York City, and called on legislators in Washington, D.C. There were community rallies and pray-ins. One former local union president would often say, "It's time to get out the baseball bats!" But that never happened. Rather, a decision was made to go and confront whomever it was they thought had the capability of doing something that was needed.

Shortly before the Oklahoma City bombing in April 1995, a retired school teacher began to come to Solidarity USA meetings and to talk about the need for forming a posse to protect our rights. We, Staughton and Alice, were troubled. After the Oklahoma City bombing we raised the issue with Solidarity USA. The chairperson immediately spoke out: "Since 1986, we've had not one violent hand in this group! We've had our words. We've had our arguments. We've told them just what we felt. They don't like it. But that's the way to do it."

Return to Quakerism: A Believable Jesus

Is it necessary to believe in the virgin birth, Jesus Christ as the Son of God, and the resurrection of the flesh, in order to practice a preferential option for the poor? We don't think so.

John Dominic Crossan has described a believable Christianity in *The Historical Jesus*. Crossan is a Catholic scholar who has done a rigorous job of determining which passages of the New Testament most likely reflect what Jesus did and said. Jesus, as Crossan depicts him, was himself a poor man, who experienced the oppression of people living under the Roman Empire, who rejected guerrilla warfare, and who chose to be a healer, convincing others that "the kingdom of God is within you."[13] If Crossan is not mistaken, Jesus was a believer in the inner light and in equality, not church-building, and he lived among the poor, sharing whatever they set before him. He showed concern for the needs of their bodies as well as of their souls.

According to Crossan, the major thing on the minds of the Gospel writers was not fact but meaning. Crossan does not find a factual basis for the virgin birth or the details of Passion Week or the resurrection of the flesh. He thinks that in these passages, the canonical authors searched the Scriptures to determine what *must* have happened if the life and death of Jesus were to fulfill prophecies about the Messiah.

Crossan believes that myth is basic faith in story form. Whether or not the incident of the Good Samaritan occurred in fact, it is consistent with Jesus' message. After explaining that the Good Samaritan acted as a neighbor to the man who fell among thieves, Jesus concluded, according to Luke 10:37: "Go, and do thou likewise." This message is what is important, whether or not the incident actually took place.

Crossan suggests that whereas John the Baptist believed that God intended great, transformative changes in the near future, Jesus considered that the Kingdom of God was already here, already available to any seeker. In the apocryphal Gospel of Thomas (composed before the other Gospels in about A.D. 50–60), Jesus tells the disciples "that what they look for is already present, their error is in awaiting it rather than seeking to discover it."[14]

The way of life Jesus urged on his companions, according to Crossan, was sharing food for the body and healing for the soul: not "almsgiving but . . . a shared egalitarianism of spiritual and material resources."[15] In Crossan's view, Jesus' healing was empowerment, telling the poor not to take the ideology of the oppressor as their own, not to internalize the oppressor's image of themselves. (What Crossan articulates sounds like what we heard from "delegates of the Word" and members of base communities in Nicaragua.) Jesus looked at the world and said, this is not what God wants. Jesus' program was empowerment from the bottom up, to rebuild peasant dignity and hope without waiting for God to do it.[16]

We believe that there is Scriptural authority for an approach to Jesus' teaching based on what people *do*, not on what they *think*. Jesus says that people who feed the hungry, visit the imprisoned, and comfort the afflicted will experience salvation even if during their lives they are unaware of Jesus and give no thought to him (Matthew 25:31–46). Saying "Lord, Lord" is not the path to salvation, for the righteous will be known by their fruits not by their words (Matthew 7:20–21). The unbeliever who does good deeds—the Good Samaritan—will be preferred to the church member who passes by on the other side (Luke 10:30–37).

Conclusions

Like most other Friends, we ourselves are not poor. We have siblings, children, and grandchildren. We feel it would be irresponsible to desert those closest to us or to impose hardships on them for the sake of others. But our experience suggests to us that there is a middle path between, on the one hand, living in the inner city and giving all that one has to the poor, and, on the other hand, confining one's well-doing to financial contributions, demonstrations, and other occasional support for worthy causes.

The following are things we think we have learned. We offer them as challenges and concerns.

First, it seems to us that liberation theology teaches an important lesson for Friends concerned to practice reconciliation. Our goal must be a society of equals. Friends should be wary of mediation if it leaves in place the inequality between the rich and powerful, on the one hand, and the poor and oppressed, on the other. At a minimum one should seek what André Gorz calls "qualitative reforms," that is, reforms that give more voice in decision making to those with little power, and thus represent a step toward equality.

Second, if Friends are to address oppression and injustice, Friends need to encounter in a day-to-day manner the life situation of the poor and oppressed.[17] If we can rearrange where and how we live our lives, giving time and energy, that may be more important than giving money. (Of course, in the process of giving time one will also inevitably spend money.) The strategy we, Alice and Staughton, pursued in relation to the civil rights movement, the draft resistance movement, and the labor movement, was a strategy of acquiring a skill useful to the disadvantaged and then going to live where that skill could be made available. We propose this as a viable model.

Third, we believe that Friends must be willing to go to out-of-the-way places and stay there for long periods of time (as some already do). It is sobering that so many who called themselves "revolutionaries" in the 1960s burned out or dropped out when the movements of that decade failed to produce instantaneous, total transformation. (In any rational estimate, passing the Civil Rights and Voting Rights acts, ending the war in Vietnam, and starting the women's movement, were significant accomplishments for so short a time.) Friends must be prepared to be long-distance runners.[18]

Fourth, Friends need to be building community. Self-fulfillment is not a sufficient goal, for ourselves or for others. The labor movement has a slogan, "An injury to one is an injury to all." This means that people look out for each other. We want to encourage people to change the circumstances that bear down hard on them. This process requires not only individual growth but also the insights that come through shared experience and action with others. Travelers on this path also need periodically to meet with a community of seekers to re-center and re-energize themselves.[19]

Finally, we urge Friends to trust their weight to the idea that the Kingdom of God is available here and now. These words are written on a day when we made our monthly visit to a friend who is serving a long sentence at a local prison. The main subject of conversation with our friend in prison was his growing belief in nonviolence, which he is daily challenged to put into practice. For us, just to be in the visiting room of that penal institution, surrounded by children, parents, and siblings of the imprisoned men, all conversing with animation, laughing, expressing love, is to be convinced that the great majority of the prisoners would not be there if society gave them the chance to make a living. Going to that room is more like going to church for us than any other experience we have.

A young woman in one of Barbara Kingsolver's novels, a volunteer in revolutionary Nicaragua, describes what we think it might feel like to live as if the Kingdom of God were already here:

> [T]he very least you can do in your life is to figure out what you hope for. And the most you can do is live inside that hope. Not admire it from a distance but live right in it, under its roof. What I want is so simple I almost can't say it: elementary kindness. Enough to eat, enough to go around. The possibility that kids might one day grow up to be neither the destroyers nor the destroyed. That's about it. . . . [20]

PART **II**

Socialism with a Human Face

5 The First New Left ... and the Third

The first New Left was made up of radicals in the years 1930–1945 who broke not only from Stalinism but also from Leninism, and not only from Leninism, but also from Trotskyism, and not only from Trotskyism, but in part from Marxism itself.

In the United States many of those who should be considered members of the first New Left were associated with *Politics* magazine. Among this group were Dwight Macdonald, Conrad Lynn, William Worthy, Paul Goodman, and C. Wright Mills. It was also *Politics* that published Simone Weil for the first time in the United States. I shall return to *Politics* later.

First I want to make clear the reality of the first New Left as an international phenomenon. Then I will attempt to suggest the special contribution made to it by the lucid and thoroughgoing essays of Simone Weil. This will put us in a position to consider *Politics* in context and so

Originally published under the title "Marxism-Leninism and the Language of *Politics* Magazine: The First New Left ... and the Third," in *Simone Weil: Interpretations of a Life,* ed. George Abbott White (Amherst: University of Massachusetts Press, 1981).

come, finally, to the connection between this ancient history and where we find ourselves now.

I

The reality of the first New Left as an international phenomenon is sufficiently demonstrated by three lives: Ignazio Silone, A. J. Muste, and Simone Weil.

Ignazio Silone was a member of the Communist Party for ten years. Before leaving the party in 1931, he had risen to become a member of the Executive Committee of the Third International. In 1936 he published the magnificent novel *Bread and Wine*, written, so Silone states, "out of the fullness of my heart just after the Fascist occupation of Ethiopia and during the Purge Trials in Moscow, which had been set up by Stalin to destroy the last remnants of the opposition. It was hard to imagine a sorrier state of affairs. The inhuman behavior of General Graziani to Ethiopian combatants and civilians, the enthusiasm of many Italians for the conquest of the Empire, the passivity of most of the population, and the impotence of the anti-Fascists all filled the soul with a deep sense of shame. To this was added my horror and disgust at having served a revolutionary ideal in my youth that, in its Stalinist form, was turning out to be nothing but 'red Fascism,' as I defined it at the time."[1]

Bread and Wine concerns a Communist named Pietro Spina, who, having gone into exile after Mussolini seized power, secretly returns to Italy and falls desperately ill. A peasant shelters him. In his extremity, Spina adopts the vestments of a priest as a disguise. But as his clandestine existence takes him from person to person—old comrades, a Catholic monk who was his teacher in high school, a young woman preparing to enter a convent—the disguise becomes something more than that. Spina comes to feel that the Marxist abstractions he brought with him from exile do not describe the elemental realities of peasant life in southern Italy. He also comes to feel that Christianity, provided its tenets are fully acted out, can give him a new place to begin.

The dominant themes of *Bread and Wine* are characteristic of what I have called the first New Left as a whole. At one point in the novel, Spina, despairing of finding allies anywhere, takes charcoal and in the middle of the night writes on the whitewashed walls of the town buildings slogans such as "Down With the War." A girl who has befriended him is puzzled that so small an act could give the authorities so much

concern. Spina explains that in a dictatorship the act of one person's saying "no" calls into question the whole public order.[2] When, in 1946,
Dave Dellinger and others, who had served prison terms to protest
World War II, issued a call to a conference on nonviolent revolution,
they quoted this passage from *Bread and Wine*.

A second illustrative life is that of A. J. Muste, who from 1933 to 1936
belonged to a succession of Marxist parties and, in his own words,
"accepted fully the Marxist-Leninist position and metaphysics." For him
at the time, this commitment to Marxism-Leninism seemed the logical
culmination of his long experience with the labor movement, which he
began as an organizer of the Lawrence, Massachusetts, Textile Strike of
1919, and continued as director of the Brookwood Labor College. Nevertheless, Muste broke with Marxism in 1936. He explained his decision
in a letter to a friend:

> War is the central problem for us all today. . . . International war and coer-
> cion at home will continue to exist for just so long as people regard these
> things as suitable, as even conceivable instruments of policy. . . . The Chris-
> tian position does not mean to justify or condone the capitalist system. Quite
> the contrary. It provides the one measure by which the capitalist system
> stands thoroughly and effectively condemned. It stands condemned because
> it makes the Christian relation in its full sense, the relation of brotherhood
> between human beings, impossible. . . . So long, however, as the matter
> remains on the plane of economics and self-interest, no one is in a position
> to condemn another. When we feel indignation, as we do even in spite of
> ourselves, we then enter the realm of standards and values, the realm in
> which moral judgment is pronounced, the realm in which ethical and spiri-
> tual appeals are made . . . the realm of morality and religion.[3]

He elaborated these thoughts in an essay of December 1936 from which
I quote the following sentences, every one of which might have been
written by Simone Weil.

> The devoted members of any movement, among other reasons because they
> have experience of what is fine and true in the movement, are apt to ratio-
> nalize away its defeats as merely superficial and temporary. Personally, I have
> had to conclude that it is inexcusable, after all that has taken place in the
> labor movement since 1914, not to be willing to study the whole situation
> afresh, and as deeply and thoroughly as possible. . . .

If one looks squarely at [the facts] touching all organizations in the labor movement, then I think one is driven to the conclusion that the root of the difficulty is moral and spiritual, not primarily political or economic or organizational. Inextricably mingled with and in the end corrupting, thwarting, largely defeating all that is fine, idealistic, courageous, self-sacrificing in the proletarian movement is the philosophy of power, the will to power, the desire to humiliate and dominate over or destroy the opponent, the acceptance of the methods of violence and deceit, the theory that "the end justifies the means." There is a succumbing to the spirit which so largely dominates the existing social and political order and an acceptance of the methods of capitalism at its worst.[4]

If, with Muste and Silone in mind, one turns to a third life, that of Simone Weil, the impression is overwhelming, not only that these three are brothers and sisters of the spirit, but also that from her earliest essays Simone Weil anticipated every major theme of the second New Left of the 1950s and 1960s.

Consider her essay, "Are We Heading for the Proletarian Revolution?" published in the periodical *Proletarian Revolution* in 1933. In this essay Weil asserted among other things the following ten points:

1. In the Soviet Union, after fifteen years:

Instead of genuine freedom of the press, there is the impossibility of expressing a free opinion, whether in the form of a printed, type-written or handwritten document, or simply by word of mouth, without running the risk of being deported; instead of the free play between parties within the framework of the soviet system, there is the cry of "one party in power, and all the rest in prison"; instead of a communist party destined to rally together, for the purposes of free cooperation, men possessing the highest degree of devotion, conscientiousness, culture, and critical aptitude, there is a mere administrative machine, a passive instrument in the hands of the Secretariat, which, as Trotsky himself admits, is a party only in name; instead of soviets, unions and co-operatives functioning democratically and directing the economic and political life of the country, there are organizations bearing, it is true, the same names, but reduced to mere administrative mechanisms; instead of the people armed and organized as a militia to ensure by itself alone defense abroad and order at home, there is a standing army, and a police freed from control and a hundred times better armed than that of the

Tsar; lastly, and above all, instead of elected officials, permanently subject to control and dismissal, who were to ensure the functioning of government until such time as "every cook would learn how to rule the State," there is a professional bureaucracy, freed from responsibility, recruited by co-option and possessing, through the concentration in its hands of all economic and political power, a strength hitherto unknown in the annals of history.[5]

Thus Weil began where Camus, C. Wright Mills, Kolakowski, and E. P. Thompson would also begin a generation later: with the understanding that the Soviet Union has not fulfilled the great dream of a society where the free development of each is the condition of the free development of all.

2. Trotsky's view that the Soviet Union was a "workers' state," albeit with "bureaucratic deformations," obscured the reality that the oppression of the workers in the Soviet Union was not a step in the direction of socialism. One could conceptualize the Soviet Union as transitional only on the assumption that "there can at the present time be only two types of State, the capitalist State and the workers' State." The evidence, however, pointed to the conclusion that the Soviet Union was a third kind of state, unforeseen by Marx to be sure, but nevertheless there.[6]

3. Fascism, Weil continued, "fits no more easily into the categories of classical Marxism than does the Russian State." It was a mistake to believe that the Nazi regime was merely an instrument of German capitalism. The fact, she asserted, was that Stalinist socialism and National Socialism had much in common, and a military alliance between the two regimes was by no means excluded.[7]

4. However phenomena such as the Soviet Union, fascism, and the New Deal were categorized, the one movement lacking from the scene was "that very movement which, according to the forecasts, was to constitute its essential feature, namely, the struggle for economic and political emancipation of the workers." To be sure, scattered militants, little groups "divided by obscure quarrels," might be found. "But the ideal of a society governed in the economic and political sphere by co-operation between the workers now inspires scarcely a single mass movement, whether spontaneous or organized; and that at the very moment when, on every hand, there is nothing but talk of the bankruptcy of capitalism."[8]

5. The oppression of working people—and here Weil came to her affirmative analysis—was an oppression exercised neither in the name of

armed force nor in the name of wealth transformed into capital; rather it was oppression exercised in the name of management. That is to say—and here she strode beyond either Adolf Berle, who expressed a version of the same idea contemporaneously, or James Burnham, who echoed it superficially in his book *The Managerial Revolution*—the oppression of working people "has become, with the advent of mechanization, a mere aspect of the relationships involved in the very technique of production." Soviet experience demonstrated that if the ownership of production was changed but the technique of production was left unchanged, the oppression of working people continued. Weil then pointed, as have David Montgomery and other labor historians in the last few years, to the skilled machine workers who until early in the twentieth century "carried out their work while using machines with as much freedom, initiative and intelligence as the craftsman who wields his tool." It was these skilled machine workers who in every advanced capitalist economy had constituted the only hope of the revolutionary movement, for it was only they "who combined thought and action in industrial work, or who took an active and vital part in the carrying on of the undertaking; the only ones capable of feeling themselves ready to take over one day the responsibility for the whole of economic and political life." But it was precisely these skilled workers—who could in some sense be viewed as embodying the new society within the womb of the old—whom capitalism had largely eliminated with the introduction of the assembly line and the breaking-down of complex jobs into small, mindless, repetitive tasks. In place of the socialist machinists described by Montgomery (and, for that matter, in place of the metal workers of Petrograd and Moscow who formed the nucleus of the soviets), rationalization has "barely left more than specialized unskilled workmen, completely enslaved to the machine."[9]

6. "War, which perpetuates itself under the form of preparation for war, has once and for all given the State an important role in production."[10] As Walter Oakes would write a decade later in *Politics,* there had come into being a "permanent war economy."

7. Modern capitalism was governed by three bureaucracies: the industrial bureaucracy, the government bureaucracy, and the trade union bureaucracy.[11] C. Wright Mills would make the elaboration of this insight a life's work.

8. Left political parties cannot substitute themselves for the working class itself. In Weil's words: "Militants cannot take the place of the work-

ing class. The emancipation of the workers will be carried out by the workers themselves, or it will not take place at all." Any attempt to bring about revolution from above, by manipulation, ran the grave risk of creating, not revolution, but counter-revolution.[12]

9. Nevertheless, one should not despair. The fact that success is less likely than had been assumed is not a reason to cease struggling. "A man who is thrown overboard in the middle of the ocean ought not to let himself drown, even though there is very little chance of his reaching safety, but to go on swimming until exhausted. And we are not really without hope. The mere fact that we exist, that we conceive and want something different from what exists, constitutes a reason for hoping."[13]

10. Nor should the aforementioned analysis lead one to give up hope in the industrial working class. "The working class still contains, scattered here and there, to a large extent outside organized labor," working people prepared to devote themselves "with the resolution and conscientiousness that a good workman puts into his work" to the building of a rational society. The task of the revolutionary was to help these potential leaders in "think[ing] things out," in acquiring influence in trade unions, in banding together for such actions as were possible in the streets and factories.

An effort tending towards the grouping together of all that has remained healthy at the very heart of industrial undertakings, avoiding both the stirring up of primitive feelings of revolt and the crystallization of an administrative apparatus, may not be much, but there is nothing else. The only hope of socialism resides in those who have already brought about in themselves, as far as is possible in the society of today, that union between manual and intellectual labor which characterizes the society we are aiming at.[14]

II

Had Simone Weil died at twenty-four, the age at which she wrote the essay just summarized, instead of at thirty-four, her achievement would have been great. Forty-three years later [1976] I can find hardly a word I would wish to change. Further, her evocation of the nature of the task of the intellectual who seeks to work with industrial workers is more sensitive and more precise than any other I know.

In fact, between 1933 and her death in 1943 Weil conducted a richly complex and wide-ranging exploration of the themes set out in this initial essay. I lack the mastery of all her writings that could do justice to it, but it is possible to try to underline three themes that she comes back to again and again.

First, New Leftists are often accused of "mindless activism," but it is not a charge that will stick against Simone Weil. What the epithet accurately describes is the fact that in breaking with the mother church of Marxism and its well-elaborated creedal language, heretics of the New Left have often proceeded largely by intuition or, to say it better, have often lacked the new language to characterize the actions they felt drawn to undertake. Hence Simone Weil's intellectual clarity is a priceless gift to the New Left tradition. So persistent, so painstaking was her effort to think things back to their beginnings that, criticizing the critics, she found Marxism to be in many of its mansions a structure built on unexamined foundations and therefore, in the worst sense of the term, in many ways a "religion" rather than a "science." She was especially critical of the notion that the development of technology under capitalism was beneficent. As she interpreted Marx, the development of "productive forces" was simply *assumed* to be a positive historical force, of its own motion bursting through the restraints imposed by "productive relations" and automatically producing something better.

Simone Weil wrote in 1934 of this Marxist concept of productive forces that "to believe that our will coincides with a mysterious will which is at work in the universe and helps us to conquer is to think religiously, to believe in Providence."[15] The experienced reality is that assembly-line work and the specialization of tasks promoted by Taylorism destroy human dignity no matter who owns the productive forces. Instead of mass production, Weil wrote in fragments from the years 1933 to 1938, the need is for more flexible machines and a new science to invent them. Work, she wrote, should be coordinated by the best workers in rotation with no other reward for the responsibilities of coordination than the opportunity to comprehend the productive process as a whole. A liberated society would individualize the machine. Unless Western civilization could adapt itself to a decentralized world, with a material basis in cooperative production by small groups of workers using new kinds of flexible machines made possible by a science consciously directed to that end, Western civilization would collapse. Fortunately, in electricity there was available an appropriate form of power for a decentralized economy. It was then in no way irrational to assert that the main task of revolutionary thought was, not to promote leisure on the basis of a technology assumed to be unchanging, but to discover how it is possible for work to be free.[16]

Second, believing as she did that the problem of capitalist society is that human beings do not participate in the decisions that affect their work, Weil stood for the proposition that New Left values of activism and participatory decision making, far from being petty-bourgeois notions irrelevant to the world of work, are above all relevant to work and to the life of the industrial worker.

It occurs to me that a major cause of the disintegration of the movement of the 1960s was that when toward the end of the decade the movement recognized the importance of reaching out to industrial workers, it felt impotent to do so, and handed over that task to the sects. In this, our movement took its cue from Marx. Marx, as Simone Weil emphasized, described the alienation of work in a capitalist factory in words that it would be impossible to improve. We know, she wrote,

> Marx's terrible utterances on this subject: "In craftsmanship and fabrication by hand, the worker makes use of the tool; in the factory, he is at the service of the machine." "In the factory there exists a dead mechanism, independent of the workers, which incorporates them as living cogs." "It is only with mechanization that the inversion [of the relationship between the worker and the conditions of work] becomes a reality that can be grasped in the technique itself." "The separation of the spiritual forces of the process of production from manual work, and the transformation of the former into forces of oppression exercised by capital over labor, is fully accomplished ... in large-scale industry built up on the basis of mechanization. The detail of the individual destiny ... of the worker working at the machine disappears like some squalid trifle before the knowledge, the tremendous natural forces and the collective labor which are crystallized in the machine system and go to make up the owner's power."[17]

But Marx wrote these phrases *about* workers rather than *to* workers. In these phrases Marx memorably characterized the collective condition of those who worked in capitalist factories, but he did not suggest that revolutionaries agitate among workers around the concepts of fetishism and alienation. When it came to practical agitation, Marx assumed—in the *Communist Manifesto* for instance—that agitation among workers would be around matters such as the length of the work day and the level of wages, not around the undemocratic organization of the factory or the humiliating individual experience of work itself. Similarly, we in the movement of the 1960s, having said to ourselves that we should start to communicate with workers as well as students, simply assumed that this meant abandoning the rhetoric of the early Students for a Democratic Society's *Port Huron Statement* and adopting a new, grim language about material deprivation.

We were wrong. We were dead wrong, and the lack of life in the organizing that has gone on since proves this to be so. The best statement of this conclusion is Steve Packard's article "Steel Mill Blues" in *Liberation Magazine* (December 1975). Steve worked in a mill for six months. When he went to work there, he was a member of a Marxist-Leninist sect, but his experiences while at work convinced him to leave it. Summing up, Steve writes:

> I think the deepest needs of my friends here, the needs that require radical changes, are those unclear things that brought me into the Movement long ago. I felt then that history was ready for the development of a whole new kind of person. Somehow things like community, art, sex roles, justice, participatory democracy, creativity—somehow things like this were almost remolded into a new vision.
>
> Around 1970 I began to forget or abandon these politics. But that newer, free-er, wider, higher vision is what the average people need. It's the only thing that Billy and my other friends could really throw their lives into.

Simone Weil came to similar conclusions after nine months of factory work in 1934–35. The conclusions she reached then were confirmed by the French sit-down strikes of June 1936, when, in her words, "[a] tremendous, ungovernable outburst, springing from the very bowels of the masses, suddenly loosened the vice of social constraint, made the atmosphere at last breathable, changed opinions in all minds, and caused things that six months earlier had been looked upon as scandalous to be accepted as self-evident. . . . [M]illions of men made it clear—and in the first place to themselves—that they had a share in the sacred rights of humanity."[18] The earlier, personal experience of factory work was more important, however. Everyone knows that there are historical moments—as in the Paris Commune of 1871, the Russian Revolutions of 1905 and 1917, the general strikes in Minneapolis, San Francisco, and Toledo in 1934, or the General Motors sit-down strike of January 1937—when working people spontaneously demonstrate the most astounding capacity collectively to organize their affairs. Labor history can be written as a succession of such moments, like beads on a string. But that sort of history gives one no idea of what in the daily individual lives of working people acts as a source for the capacity for rebellion. In my opinion, Simone Weil's greatest single achievement as a social analyst was her insight into the oppressive character of capitalist factory work as an individual experience. It is easy to talk about socialism as the extension of democracy to the workplace. Historically and psychologically, however, the thirst for democracy requires a prior affirmation of personal, individual dignity. Only when peasants and artisans came to believe in the priesthood of all believers did they begin to think of themselves as collectively capable of governing. We must, absolutely must, find a language in which to talk with one another about the way in which we are robbed of our selfhood when we are denied the opportunity to participate as fully as we are capable of doing in decisions affecting our work. Simone Weil came closer to finding that language than anyone else to date.

She did so, for instance, in the essay "Factory Work" first published in *Politics* in December 1946.

Weil worked in a plant where she stamped out parts on a press. Some of the plant's production consisted of rush orders for armaments. There was a moving belt-line, as she called it, the speed of which, according to one of her fellow workers, had been doubled during the past four years.

The first point she makes about her experience of factory work is that one cannot discover workers' discontents simply by taking a poll. As André Gorz also has emphasized, those who have deep and painful feelings hide the feelings even from themselves. Weil writes: "The first effect of suffering is the attempt of thought to *escape*. It refuses to confront the adversity that wounds it. Thus, when workingmen speak of their lot, they repeat more often than not the catchwords coined by people who are not workingmen." Again she observes: "Humiliation always has for its effect the creation of forbidden zones where thought may not venture and which are shrouded by silence or illusion." The experience of shame at being treated as employees are treated, and underneath that, the belief that it is shameful not to have been able to escape the lot of an employee—these sentiments, so much the reverse of that brawny-armed confidence ascribed to proletarians by some Marxists, also separate workers from each other. "Each is isolated as though on an island," Weil relates. "Those who do escape from the island will not look back."

Why is work in a capitalist factory experienced as shameful? Because it is not free, answers Simone Weil. The workers are obliged to consider themselves as nothing. "What especially constrains them to this is the way in which they have to take orders." Since these orders are usually unexpected and unpredictable, the worker is unable mentally to anticipate the future, "to outline it beforehand, and in a sense, to possess it." Thought draws back from the future because the future, insofar as it is different from the present, will be so because of some arbitrary humiliating order. "This perpetual recoil upon the present produces a kind of brutish stupor."

Workers while at work are exiles, Weil comments in the language of her essay on "roots," uprooted, unable to feel at home. One cannot move freely, as is possible in a place that belongs to one. Nor can one pause and in small ways vary the rhythm of one's work.

> One can actually see women waiting ten minutes outside a plant under a driving rain, across from an open door through which their bosses are passing. They are working women and they will not enter until the whistle has blown. The door is more alien to them than that of any strange house, which they would enter quite naturally if seeking cover. No intimacy binds workingmen to the places and objects amidst which their lives are used up. Wages and other social demands had less to do with the sit-down strikes of '36 than the need to feel at home in the factories at least once in their lives. Society must be corrupted to its very core when workingmen can feel at home in a plant only during a strike, and utter aliens during working hours—when by every dictate of common sense the exact opposite ought to prevail.

Summarizing Simone Weil's experience of factory work, one might say that "work should involve incentives worthier than money or survival. It should be educative, not stultifying; creative, not mechanical; self-directed, not manipulated"; and one might say that, to bring about this change, society should consider "experiments in decentralization, based on the vision of man as master of his machines and his society," because "the personal capacity to cope with life has been reduced everywhere by the introduction of technology that only minorities of men (barely) understand." It is food for thought that the words I have just used to summarize, accurately I think, Weil's reflections on factory work, are words from the now-forgotten *Port Huron Statement*.

Simone Weil left the factory, but there was a sense in which for the remainder of her life she had won through to a sense of genuine identity with working people, exchanging it for her identification with the class into which she was born. I am not thinking of her later insistence on doing agricultural work, nor of her decision to eat no more as an exile in London than was permitted to civilians in occupied France. I am thinking of certain passages in a fragment she wrote entitled "On the Contradictions of Marxism":

> I do not think that the workers' movement in this country will become some-
> thing living again until it seeks, I will not say doctrines, but a source of inspi-
> ration, in what Marx and Marxists have fought against and very foolishly
> despised: in Proudhon, in the workers' groups of 1848, in the trade-union
> tradition, in the anarchist spirit.[19]

—that is to say, I think, in a tradition of common struggle and utopian hope created by workers *themselves*. Marx, she went on, was cruelly abstract in believing, on the one hand, that violent revolution is in real-ity the crowning point of a transformation that is already more than half accomplished, and brings to power a category of men who already more than half possessed that power, and, on the other hand, that the capi-talist proletariat, dehumanized by oppressive conditions of work, was prepared to assume command of the capitalist economy. Working peo-ple are not, Weil held, ready to run the workplace. The analogy to the medieval bourgeoisie, which in fact created a new society of cities within feudal society, is false. To propagate the hope of an imminent blessed catastrophe, which would miraculously make the last first, and the first last, is to stir working people into actions that would benefit, not them-selves, but their managers.

In what sense then can one rationally project a working-class revolu-tion? Perhaps, Weil wrote,

> being a revolutionary means calling forth by one's wishes and helping by
> one's acts everything which can, directly or indirectly, alleviate or lift the
> weight that presses upon the mass of men, break the chains that degrade
> labor, reject the lies by means of which it is sought to disguise or excuse the
> systematic humiliation of the majority.[20]

If this is revolution, she continued, it is a revolution as old as oppression, a spirit of revolt that quickened the Roman plebeians, and at the end of the Middle Ages, the wool workers of Florence, the English peasantry, and the artisans of Ghent; it is the struggle of those who obey against those who command, which will continue as long as there are societies in which some have more power than others.

In Weil's view Marxism had in some respects seriously debased this permanent spirit of revolution. Writing, as it were, from the standpoint of a worker misled by middle-class revolutionaries, she charged Marxism with "flashy pseudo-scientific trimmings, a messianic eloquence, an unfettering of appetites that have disfigured" the working-class tradition. "Nothing entitles one to assure the workers that science is on their side," she wrote. Further, nothing entitles one to assure the workers that it is up to them to save the world. This, she insisted, was the attitude of one who regards the working class as an instrumentality. Workers, she said, "are unhappy, unjustly so; it is well that they defend themselves; it would be better if they could liberate themselves; and that is all that can be said about it."[21]

From this perspective two corollaries followed. First, hostility to the Leninist project of substituting the party for the action of the working class itself. Weil, as already indicated, had set forth this position in her first writing on the subject. Later she added the perception that Marx, who was "struck by the fact that social groups manufacture moralities for their own use, thanks to which the specific activity of each one is placed outside the reach of evil," ironically "arrived at a morality which placed the social category to which he belonged—that of professional revolutionaries—above sin." Unlike Rosa Luxemburg, therefore, Simone Weil could not appeal from Leninist vanguardism to a Marxist model. In Weil's view, Marx himself had projected the concept of a party making use of the working class to achieve goals entertained not by workers but by the party in their name.

A second corollary, which for Simone Weil followed from the axiom of genuine identification with the working class, was that, if the workers seemed unrevolutionary, one did not casually abandon them in search of a functional equivalent, say in the Third World. Rather, if the workers seemed unrevolutionary, one took a second look at reform. Simone Weil came very close to the thesis of André Gorz in *Strategy for Labor,* that there are two kinds of reform: quantitative reforms, which lead to co-optation by the system as it is, and qualitative reforms, whereby the oppressed take partial control over decision making, which whets their appetite for more control and therefore leads to revolution. The antiwar movement of the 1960s developed a similar concept of "resistance," a form of struggle intermediate between reform and revolution. Simone Weil expressly conceptualized the possibility of nonviolent mass action.

> Antiquity has not only bequeathed us the story of the interminable and pointless massacres around Troy, but also the story of the energetic and pacific action by which the Roman plebeians, without spilling a drop of blood, emerged from a condition bordering on slavery and obtained, as the guarantee of their newly-won rights, the institution of the tribunate. It was in precisely the same way that the French workers, by their pacific occupation of the factories [in June 1936], imposed paid holidays, guaranteed wages and workers' delegates.[22]

I have emphasized two recurrent ideas in the social thinking of Simone Weil. In contrast to the common criticism of the New Left as mindless activism, this member of the first New Left rigorously explained her postulates and indeed turned the tables by accusing Marxism itself of logic repeatedly anchored in mere assumption. Thus Simone Weil exemplified the possibility of a rational New Left. Second, she demonstrated the fruitfulness of New Left categories such as participatory democracy in understanding the concrete individual experience of factory workers under capitalism. She showed that those seeking a more humane and democratic socialism need not draw back in fear, and abandon all that they have theretofore learned, in confronting the experience of industrial work. My own conversations with working people during the past six years [1970–76] are in accord. I think that all across the country there is a discussion not happening between former student radicals, who think that they must use the language of Marxism-Leninism in order to communicate with workers, and puzzled workers, who would like to talk about the lives they are leading and the decisions affecting those lives.

So third, I want to say that Weil offers one final theme or image which in a degree knits together her criticism of Marxism as unscientific and her concern with the actual experience of oppressed individuals. Marx, she said, thought he was using the method of Darwin but was actually using the method of Lamarck.[23] By this she meant that Marx, like Lamarck, assumed that the environment miraculously produced an adaptation of organisms to its requirements—as in the Lamarckian explanation that baby giraffes were born with longer necks because of their parents' attempts to reach bananas; so in Marxism, because capitalism was ripe for change, the proletariat was thought ready to change it. In either its Lamarckian or Marxist version, in this theory the environment was the protagonist of change.

A truly Darwinian social science would emphasize the ceaseless small initiatives whereby individuals seek to change the world around them. To be sure, such initiatives are selectively reinforced or destroyed by the social environment, just as are biological mutations by nature. The Marx who wrote that men make their own history, but that they make it under certain conditions, was absolutely right and consistent with Darwinian biology, so Weil believed. She often emphasized the many-sided, uneven, and ambiguous character of Marx's work; and if one prefers, one may see her, not as a critic of Marxism, but as a champion of the activist Marx against the Marx who, after the failure of the 1848 revolutions, and especially in old age, increasingly emphasized the impact of circumstances on man.

III

Having charted, to some degree, the first New Left and Simone Weil's place within it, I want to look more closely at the principal American embodiment of the first New Left, the magazine *Politics*.

Politics has a special place in the hearts and minds of its admirers. To read it, former SDS president Todd Gitlin wrote me, is like sipping rare old wine. To some of us it seems that there was more good sense and fresh thinking in this one magazine during the three or four years of its active existence than in all the pages of all the Left journals from that day to this. (Personally, one of the things I did when most disoriented by the events of the late 1960s was to read through *Politics* again from the first issue to the last.)

If there is such a thing as a review of a periodical, let me briefly try to write it. The first issue of *Politics* appeared in February 1944. The lead editorial by Dwight Macdonald stated:

> The next few decades require not an "oasis psychology" among left intellectuals, but rather a more conscious, active intervention in the historical process. It will be a period of tremendous suffering, tremendous revolutionary *possibilities*, in Europe and in the colonial countries. One's endeavor should be not to withdraw into illusory "oases" but rather to go out into the

desert, share the common experience, and try to find a road out of the wilderness.

Already in this first issue there was evidence of the effort to find a new language for the new realities of the mid-twentieth century. The system exemplified by both the Soviet Union and Nazi Germany, which Simone Weil had identified without naming, was termed "bureaucratic collectivism." Simone Weil's perception that henceforth capitalist economies would be symbiotically linked to war was developed, as I noted, by Walter Oakes, who, coining the term "permanent war economy," wrote: "The fact is that the capitalist system cannot stand the strain of another siege of unemployment comparable to 1930–1940. . . . The traditional methods . . . will not be followed." Paul Goodman contributed "The Attempt to Invent an American Style."

Politics followed with particular attention the growing movement for racial equality, exemplified by agitation in the army and by so-called riots in Harlem, which the magazine defended. Race, an editorial observed in August 1944, "is the one issue which really cuts to the bottom of things and so has an intrinsically revolutionary dynamic."

Also fully reported in *Politics* was the resistance movement in federal prisons by objectors to World War II. A single issue told of a work strike at Danbury against segregation, a hunger strike at Lewisburg over censorship of the mail, and the continuing noncooperation of Louis Taylor and Stanley Murphy, who, having fasted eighty-two days at Danbury, had been transferred to Springfield, Missouri, where they continued their protest.

Looking abroad, *Politics* saw most hope in the resistance movements of Europe on the verge of liberation. An article on "Dual Power in France" reported that the resistance committees saw themselves as continuing after the war and as constituting a new Estates General. Furiously *Politics* excoriated the *New Leader* magazine for withholding support from the Resistance because of Communist involvement in it. "This writer [Macdonald] is as much opposed to Stalinism as any of the *New Leader* experts, but he submits that 'to tell progress from reaction' is a somewhat more difficult job than just to look where the Communist Party has some influence and then throw one's weight into the other camp. . . . It is in the French popular liberation committees, in the FFI and in the workers' militia that democratic socialist elements are to be found, and not among the Paris ministerial bureaucracy or in the ranks

of over-aged former parliamentarians." Still listening for new language
and assisting in its invention, *Politics* declared in March 1945:

> Two new terms have emerged in this concluding phase of the war which are
> not [as yet] devaluated, which retain all their sharpness and moral purity:
> "collaboration" and "resistance." I think it deeply significant that these are
> becoming the great political watchwords in Europe today, since they indicate
> no specific, positive ideology, no aspiring faith, but simply the fact that peo-
> ple either "go along" or that they "resist." . . . To resist, to reject simply—
> this is the first condition for the human spirit's survival in the face of the
> increasingly tighter organization of state power everywhere. That this is not
> a sufficient condition is true—only a general, positive faith and system of
> ideas can save us in the long run. Such a faith and system are no longer held
> by significant numbers of people. But they will only develop, if they do, from
> the seeds of "resistance."

It was all the more disappointing to read this and in the spring of 1946
to read that *Politics* was obliged to present an analysis of "Why the Resistance Failed."

Politics was not without its humor. The high point, for this reader, was
a pyrotechnical exchange between Paul Goodman and C. Wright Mills
concerning modern psychology. According to Mills, Goodman preached
a "gonad theory of revolution." If anything, revolutionaries were sexual
ascetics, Mills went on. He concluded: "Leave Mr. Goodman with his revolution in the bedroom. We have still to search out the barricades of our
freedom." Goodman replied with dignity. When sexuality is free, he
wrote, "it is only one among several productive forces"; when repressed,
it is "the most important destructive influence that there is." The political energies of sexual ascetics "are precisely the energies that we see in
the sadism and masochism of monolithic parties and in transitional dic-
tatorships that become permanent." Marx, Goodman went on, appeals
to human nature against the alienation produced by "the collective conditions of work which exist under capitalism and which will continue to
exist in any modern industrial society."

These last words of Paul Goodman repeated the fundamental message of Simone Weil. She appeared as a contributor in *Politics* in February 1945, as a posthumous contributor to a symposium on "War as an
Institution." In her piece, entitled "Reflections on War," she stated:

"One point was common to all the Marxist trends: the explicit refusal to condemn war as such." Further, she asserted: "Armies wielded by the apparatus of the sovereign State cannot bring liberty to anybody."

With the advent of the atom bomb, war became *Politics'* preoccupation, and Simone Weil its patron saint. It was in this period that her essay on the *Iliad* was published, announced on the cover by the picture of a splendid Greek helmet with horsehair crest and nosepiece all but hiding the eyes. It was in this period also that Macdonald wrote the essays for which the magazine is best remembered: "The Responsibility of Peoples" and "The Root Is Man." I shall not attempt to summarize them. They are part of a living tradition, as suggested by Noam Chomsky's citation of them in his writings against the Vietnam War.

Rather, I want to call attention to the dramatic absence in *Politics* of that which was so crucial for Simone Weil: systematic attention to the particular experience of working people. To be sure, there were occasional articles on strikes. What there was not was that which illuminated *Politics'* reporting of the black, pacifist, and European resistance movements: letters from participant observers, individual accounts of little-known skirmishes, in short, the reporting in depth that can happen only when people who are publishing a magazine are personally in touch with people taking part in a certain form of struggle. *Politics* was not in touch. Its failure to include in its developing articulation of New Left ideology the experiences and insights of contemporary working-class struggle, a failure inherited by our movement of the 1960s, was a principal cause of its demise and ours. And this is why, the richness and vitality of *Politics* notwithstanding, today as we make a new beginning we appropriately look back over its head to Simone Weil, who in her incipient New Leftism found the working class to be absolutely central.

There was much in American working-class life that *Politics* might have reported.

During World War II itself there took place a rash of wildcat strikes in defiance of the no-strike policy of the union leadership. In 1944, the year in which *Politics* began publication, more workers went on strike than in 1937, the year of the General Motors and Little Steel strikes. In 1944, also, the United Automobile Workers (UAW) national convention very nearly repudiated the no-strike policy in the midst of war. As a statistical phenomenon, the World War II strike wave is well known. Its causes are much less clear, though worth serious attention. The financial status of the average worker was better than before the war. Women, blacks, and Southern whites moved into industry in large numbers during the war, and the role of each of these groups in the strike movement is uncertain. Nor is it clear to what extent the rank-and-file workers who went on strike despite the no-strike policy would have responded to the idea of a *labor* party, endorsed by the Michigan state CIO Convention in 1943. On the whole, the wildcat strikes appear usually to have been catalyzed by just that sort of arbitrary discipline that was so offensive to Simone Weil. In March 1944, for example, two war veterans working at the massive Ford River Rouge plant were caught smoking and fired. Two hundred and fifty of their fellow workers hurried to the labor relations office to protest. When a plant protection guard attempted to intervene, they physically attacked him and, breaking into the labor relations office, spent two hours knocking over desks, destroying documents, emptying files, and breaking windows. The two discharged workers were quoted as saying that they "would just as soon be in a prison camp as work under the conditions imposed by the labor relations division at the Ford plant."

Politics might also have reported local experiments such as the formation of the United Labor Party in Akron and nearby cities in 1946. I have told this story in *Liberation* (December 1973). What especially leaves one with a sense of lost possibilities is that the rank-and-file workers, former Trotskyists and former Wobblies who tried to create a labor party in northeastern Ohio, had much the same sense of making a New Left beginning as that expressed by Dwight Macdonald and *Politics*. The United Labor Party deliberately broke with both the Social Democratic and Bolshevik models of a radical party. They opposed the use of party pseudonyms as a conspiratorial practice inappropriate in America. They prided themselves on their comradely and libertarian practices; a member recalls that the United Labor Party said it was the only Left party that treated members as well as nonmembers, and that it was the only group to which he ever belonged in which everyone seemed to trust one another. There was a strong Wobbly-like emphasis on *doing* rather than *talking*. Indeed, in the spring of 1947 United Labor Party members joined Dwight Macdonald, A. J. Muste, and Dave Dellinger in a national "Break with Conscription" action by publicly mailing their draft cards to President Truman.

One would have liked to see in the pages of *Politics*, rather than in a less accessible publication, the following description of the United Labor Party by two of its members:

[W]hat marks the ULP most of all, is the basic work it has done *in mobilizing and articulating a folk culture in politics*. It does not possess, nor does it hanker after, a unique, gobbledegook "party environment" separate from all else. It wants to encompass everything that is common to plebeian culture, excluding what is not. This may seem like gibberish to those who have been weaned on manifestoes and programmatic differentiation. But for those who have waited and wondered what an American party might look like, it is something to ponder.

To do this, it has first of all renounced the precious cannibalism of the orthodox Left. . . . It does not regard itself, and does not operate, *as a competitor to other minority parties*. . . . It aims at the untouched workingclass for its recruits (welcoming all others, of course). It reserves its offensive artillery for the major parties, who deserve the maximum fire-power. It refuses to hang about its neck the stinking albatross of being "The Chosen Party."[24]

Such a description of a political style on the Left was presumably as refreshing a quarter of a century ago as it would still be, alas, today.

The point, in sum, is that the New Left as it first manifested itself in the United States was brilliant, but one-sided. Many of the persons associated with *Politics* were to play central roles in the creation of a second New Left in this country. The failure of our first New Left to incorporate within itself a language descriptive of the day-to-day experiences of working people has accordingly continued to cripple the effort to move beyond orthodox Marxism without losing what remains valuable and essential in its teaching.

It may be objected that neither Marxism nor Simone Weil provides proof as to why any special importance should be attached to the experience of work, and to working people. This is a legitimate objection to which there may be more than one solution. Marxism, I take it, holds that in the last analysis working people are important because they and they alone have in their hands the power to overthrow capitalism and so usher humankind from the realm of necessity to the realm of freedom. If I read Simone Weil correctly, her feeling was that working people are important because they are oppressed and need help, and because, also, work provides human beings a unique opportunity to come into contact with the order of the world outside themselves. Affirming all these sentiments, I would emphasize another: that the dependence and relative helplessness of employees oblige them to turn to one another for mutual aid, in strikes and trade unions. No matter how bureaucratized trade unions may become, it remains true for working people as for no other group in capitalist society that "an injury to one is an injury to all." In this sense, perhaps, industrial life does create a new society or at least a seed of it within the shell of the old.

IV

Although the connection between this ancient history and where we find ourselves now may be clearer, perhaps I should underscore what I perceive as most important.

One comes away from encounter with Simone Weil refreshed in the belief that a small piece of *good work*, for instance, a single life well lived, makes a difference. It is so in the life of the spirit; and it is also so in science, where progress may wait on a particular experiment, an individual discovery. Perhaps in the small-scale organizing that many of us have been doing since the disintegration of SDS we have been thus experimenting. Perhaps, if none of our experiments has yet been successful, one day soon it will be otherwise. At that point a new movement—a third New Left—will regroup around that solitary advance.

In the life of the spirit, too, small things may count for much. In her later writings Simone Weil spoke of seeds, of catalysts, of points of gravity: physical small things to show how it is that the spirit may part waves and move mountains.

Simone Weil teaches that the first step in advancing toward our end is to desire it greatly. "The first condition for moving in this direction is to let one's thoughts dwell on it. It is not one of those things that can be obtained by accident. Maybe one can receive it after desiring it long and persistently."

6 Communal Rights

How, if at all, should a radical movement for a more just and communal society make use of the language of rights embodied in documents like the Declaration of Independence, the First and Fourteenth Amendments of the United States Constitution, Title 42 United States Code section 1983, or section 7 of the National Labor Relations Act? Legal workers in the movement for a new society answer this question very differently. Arthur Kinoy summed up his odyssey as a people's lawyer in the phrase "rights on trial."[1] The National Lawyers Guild devoted its 1983 convention to the theme of economic rights.[2] The American Civil Liberties Union has announced a nationwide litigation strategy that seeks to formulate and protect economic rights.[3] On the other hand, many participants in the Conference on Critical Legal Studies appear to believe that a rights-oriented legal practice necessarily conflicts with the attempt to create a more cooperative society.[4]

"Communal Rights," by Staughton Lynd, was published originally in 62 *Texas Law Review* 1417 (1984). Copyright 1984 by the Texas Law Review Association. Reprinted by permission. I thank Jules Lobel, Glorianne Leck, David Rabban, Lee Lynd, and especially Karl Klare, for helping me think through the ideas in this essay.

Here I attempt to resolve these differences. I argue that the traditional rights rhetoric is properly criticized to the extent that it conceptualizes rights as a kind of individual property. I argue further, however, that instead of scrapping the language of rights, it would be better to explore the possibility that rights can be restated in a manner congruent with a community founded on love and mutual respect. Finally, I identify particular "communal rights" consistent with and perhaps indispensable to such a society.

The Critique of the Traditional Rights Rhetoric

What is it that the Left has found lacking in the United States Constitution and other declarations of rights? First, these documents often include questionable metaphysical assertions about the origin and nature of rights. The Declaration of Independence, for example, states that men are endowed with rights by a Creator.[5] Even if the term "Creator" could be explained to everyone's satisfaction, the word "endowed" creates other problems. The concept of natural or God-given rights is, to say the least, arguably inconsistent with the modern understanding that the particular society into which a person is born shapes that person's ideas about the world. The Declaration of Independence also asserts that governments are freely created "to secure these rights."[6] In truth, governments perhaps have originated more often in conquest, or in the imposition of the will of one class on the will of another, than by consent. To that extent the premises of the Declaration of Independence are no longer "self-evident" for all contemporary readers.

Second, scholars associated with the Critical Legal Studies movement argue that the traditional rights rhetoric is necessarily incoherent because it is highly abstract. Because the language of rights is formalistic and indeterminate, rather than concrete and specific, the application of a "right" in a particular setting will depend on factors external to the legal concepts involved. This causes rights rhetoric to become incoherent, because decision makers arbitrarily select varied and often contradictory rationales to justify outcomes that are not logically compelled by the premises chosen.[7] This aspect of the critique of rights does not claim that rights rhetoric is more incoherent than other varieties of formal legal reasoning, but that, with rights as well as with other conventional legal rules, no particular outcome can be predicted when the rules are applied to a given set of facts.

Finally, the language of rights is permeated by the possessive indi-
vidualism of capitalist society. Rights, in the conventional view, are
assumed to be *individual* rights. Thus the author of a book called *Taking
Rights Seriously* states, "Rights-based . . . theories . . . place the individual at the center."[8] Moreover, in the conventional view individuals are
imagined to *possess* rights in the same way that they possess more tangible kinds of property.[9] A court that wants to ensure that individuals will
not be deprived of rights is likely to call them "vested," using a term bor-
rowed from property law. Consistent with this analysis of rights as property, the conventional view implicitly assumes that the supply of rights is
finite, and thus that "right" is a scarce commodity. In this view the assertion of one person's right is likely to impinge on and diminish the rights
of others. Thus, as Karl Klare has suggested to me, conventional rights
rhetoric assumes a "zero-sum" game. If we desire a society in which we
share life as a common creation and genuinely care for each other's
needs, then this rhetoric, which pictures us as separated owners of our
respective bundles of rights, stands as an obstacle.

Notwithstanding these criticisms of traditional rights rhetoric, I
believe that wholly to discard the language of rights would present serious dangers and forego obvious opportunities. First, demolishing the
conceptual underpinning of the Bill of Rights, without putting something in its place, would deprive dissenters of such protection as they
now have under our Constitution. I simply do not believe that we are less
free because there is such a thing as the First Amendment: that has not
been my experience as demonstrator, traveler to hostile nations in
wartime, or discharged teacher. And while persons associated with the
Critical Legal Studies movement often close their essays with vague,
affirmative descriptions of what a better society might be like, these
utopian declarations lack the legal enforceability the Bill of Rights
presently provides. Nor is the situation much improved by the suggestion that instead of talking about rights we should talk about "empowerment."[10] To invite ourselves to think of power rather than of rights
necessarily extends the same invitation to others, hostile to our utopias,
who have much more power than we do.

There is also a positive reason for reworking rather than discarding
rights rhetoric. A theory that is merely critical erodes the legitimacy of
what is but does not project an alternative. I think of the effort to restate
rights theory as an affirmation that a new society is possible, so that,
rather than merely deploring the present state of affairs, we can begin

to glimpse how law and justice might be understood in a better society. Rights need not be conceptualized as property. Bourgeois rights theory, which does conceptualize rights as property, is quite different from feudal rights theory, which visualized rights as arising from hierarchical relationships between persons of different status. Why should not socialism, in its turn, have its own rights theory? I believe a future society without *any* theory of rights would be a society without law, in which conflicts would be decided on the basis of the distribution of power. E. P. Thompson is surely right when he says: "Everything we have witnessed in this century suggests that no serious socialist thinker can suppose that a rule of some kind of law—albeit, socialist law and not capitalist law—is not a profound human good."[11]

Further, if legal workers who use the language of rights in the courtroom wholly discredit that language in their discourse with fellow radicals, they will create a contradiction of theory and practice that has disturbing parallels in American history and that will impair the credibility of their politics. Spokespersons for the Critical Legal Studies movement recognize this problem but have not resolved it. One of them states: "[T]he critique of rights as liberal philosophy does not imply that the left should abandon rights rhetoric as a tool of political organizing or legal argument."[12] Two others write: "That one must use the language of rights in court does not necessarily mean that one must use it with one's clients and in everyday political activity."[13] I am concerned that these attitudes, systematically pursued, might reproduce the political schizophrenia of the 1930s, when radicals talked about democracy in public and about socialism in private; the American people concluded that radicals could not be trusted to mean what they said. For these reasons, I agree with Duncan Kennedy that "[w]e need to work at the slow transformation of rights rhetoric, at dereifying it, rather than simply junking it."[14]

In this effort, we can be sensitive to the legitimate warnings contained in the critique of the traditional rights rhetoric. One important way to dereify rights rhetoric is to avoid discussion of rights in general, and to talk instead about particular rights. To pose the problem of rights in general, as if all rights were essentially similar, rather than to grapple with the differences among, for example, the right to own a factory, the right to confront one's accusers, and the right to engage in concerted activity for mutual aid or protection, creates a version of what Hegel called "the night in which . . . all cows are black."[15] It does what any kind of formalism does: it uses a general concept to describe particular realities that are significantly different from one another. As a result, one discusses not the underlying realities, but mere words. To direct attention to rights in general rather than to particular rights is to succumb to the fallacy of reification, mistaking abstract words for concrete things.

Rights rhetoric is no more prone to incoherence and indeterminacy than any other form of legal reasoning. We can all agree that words in themselves offer no protection to anyone, that words can be made to mean almost anything, and that decisions about what words mean are often based on political and economic considerations extrinsic to legal arguments. Nor will use of the term "communal rights" magically resolve difficult conflicts between different values and different rights. Rather, my object is the more modest one of designating rights that, standing alone, do not require a choice between our own well-being and the well-being of others. Similarly, I would protest any asserted correlation between use of rights language and belief in the efficacy of the legal system. I, for example, am comfortable using the language of rights, but I also believe that "whenever a problem can be solved without the help of a lawyer, do it"[16] and that "[l]egal activity can be very useful when it is one part of a larger struggle, but should not be relied on alone."[17]

By far the most important element in the critique of rights rhetoric is the insight that rights in capitalist society invariably are treated as a kind of individual property. If this aspect of existing rights rhetoric can be overcome and if rights can be given a "positive-sum" character so that one person's exercise of a right enhances rather than diminishes another's, the Left appropriately can use the language of rights. The burden would then shift to anyone still arguing for the abandonment of rights. At the same time, the property-like character of many rights in our society should make us particularly watchful lest communal rights come to be seen merely as a new form of property, belonging to groups rather than to individuals,[18] "public" rather than "private."[19] The persistence of a property-oriented approach might lead to the separation of new "communal rights" from traditional "individual rights." An individual who sought to exercise a right that had been categorized as communal might then be told that the right was not his or hers to exercise, for it was vested only in some group or collective representative, or in society at large. Because this problem has arisen in labor law in the name of so-called "collective rights,"[20] I prefer the term "communal rights" to "collective rights."

In opposition to this property-oriented rights thinking, the Left should stress two things. The first is that rights do not come neatly divided into inherently individual and inherently communal rights. Most rights are sufficiently ambiguous that they can be pushed in different directions by political and intellectual struggles. Thus, the point may be less to identify and champion peculiarly communal rights than to fight for communal content in as many rights as possible. Even more important, "communal rights" are not the opposite of "individual rights." Communal rights, whether exercised by groups or individuals, are rights characteristic of a society in which the free development of each has become the condition of the free development of all. The opposite of a communal right is any right which presupposes that what is accessible to one person is therefore unavailable to another.

Examples of Communal Rights

If a new society is struggling to be born from the womb of capitalist society, one would expect to find a rudimentary world view and a corresponding new conception of right. The new kind of right would not be conceptualized as individual property, nor would it presuppose that one person's gain was inevitably another's loss. It would articulate, in however preliminary a form, the values of community, compassion, and solidarity.

The Right to Engage in Concerted Activity. I suggest that the right of workers to engage in "concerted activities for . . . mutual aid or protection"[21] now guaranteed by federal labor law is an example of a communal right. More than any other institution in capitalist society, the labor movement is based on communal values. Its central historical experience is solidarity, the banding together of individual workers who are alone too weak to protect themselves.[22] Thus, there has arisen the value expressed by the phrase, "an injury to one is an injury to all." To be sure, at times particular labor organizations, and to some extent trade unionism in general, fall short of this communal aspiration. Yet it is significant that trade union members still address one another as "Brother" and "Sister" and sign their correspondence "Fraternally yours." These conventions evidence an underlying attitude and practice fundamentally different from that in business and even in academia, where one person's job security subtracts from, or at most is separate from, another's.

Whatever rights the critique of the traditional rights rhetoric properly calls into question, it misses the mark when it applies its critical analysis to the right to engage in concerted labor activities. There is nothing metaphysical or indeterminate about this right. It articulates the historical experience of rank-and-file workers. It is, if anything, more specific in content than most legal rules. No one has ever doubted that "concerted activity" meant strikes, picketing, the formation of labor organizations, and related activities. And it is clearly not a right akin to an individual's ownership of property. On the contrary, it is a right to act together, to engage in activity commonly and most effectively undertaken by groups.

This in no way endorses the National Labor Relations Act, in which the right is presently embodied. On the one hand, the protection of concerted activity in section 7 of the NLRA makes it "perhaps the most radical piece of legislation ever enacted by the United States Congress."[23] On the other hand, the American Civil Liberties Union predicted at the time the act was passed that it would "impair labor's rights in the long run, however much its authors may intend precisely the contrary."[24] I have felt for some years that this assessment by the ACLU was correct:

> [I]t took a lot of backtracking by the Supreme Court to get there, but maybe that was part of the prediction, at least in its more sophisticated form: no matter how the law was written, once you had the government that far into controlling the labor movement, given the nature of power in American society, it was going to wind up controlling the labor movement for the sake of business.[25]

But from my point of view, the historical miscarriage of the NLRA makes it more and not less important to "celebrate and seek to restore to its intended vigor the right to engage in concerted activity for mutual aid or protection."[26]

It may not be immediately clear why this right is so different from other rights.[27] The best approach to understanding the special features of this right is to examine the underlying forms of struggle from which the right is derived. Consider the following example.

After Anna Walentynowicz was discharged from her job as a crane operator in the Lenin shipyard in Gdansk in August 1980, her workmates struck demanding her reinstatement.[28] Other shipyards struck in sympathy. In two days the workers at the Lenin yard had won their demands. Walentynowicz and Lech Wałęsa were reinstated and the Polish government promised to build a monument honoring workers killed in the strike of 1970. The strike would have ended in failure, however, had it not been for the intervention of two individuals, Walentynowicz and her friend Alina Pienkowska. As Walentynowicz tells the story:

> Alina Pienkowska and I went running back to the hall to declare a solidarity strike, but the microphones were off. The shipyard loudspeakers were announcing that the strike was over and that everyone had to leave by six P.M. The gates were open, and people were leaving.
>
> So Alina and I went running to the main gate. And I began appealing to them to declare a solidarity strike, because the only reason that the manager had met our demands was that the other factories were still on strike. I said that if the workers at these other factories were defeated, we wouldn't be safe either. But somebody challenged me. "On whose authority are you declaring this a strike? I'm tired and I want to go home." I too was tired, and I started to cry. . . .
>
> Now, Alina is very small, a tiny person, but full of initiative. She stood up on a barrel and began to appeal to those who were leaving. "We have to help the others with their strikes, because they have helped us. We have to defend them." Somebody from the crowd said, "She's right!" The gate was closed.[29]

The strike that gave birth to Polish Solidarity followed.

I believe that this piece of history embodies a good deal of what legal workers for a new society care about. In Gdansk, one worker was fired and a whole shipyard walked off the job in protest. Although one recounts this as if it were an everyday occurrence, I have never known a university faculty to do this for a colleague who had been fired or denied tenure. It does, however, occur regularly in the labor movement. Ed Mann tells of an incident in Youngstown in the late 1960s:

> We had a man killed in the open hearth. . . . He had seven days to go to retirement. Two or three months before that I'd filed a grievance, requesting that certain safety features be adopted. The grievance was rejected out of hand. He was killed by a truck backing up. One of the items on the grievance was that trucks backing up have a warning system.
>
> The guy gets killed. Everybody liked him. He'd worked there . . . how many years? . . . you know. All right, I led a strike. I had to scream and holler, drag people out by the heels, but I got them out, shut the place down.[30]

In Gdansk, after the first yard struck in protest, workers at other shipyards also left their jobs. As is often the case in wildcat strikes, the workers developed their own demands,[31] in addition to demanding Walentynowicz's reinstatement. When the question was posed whether the
Lenin yard strikers should stay out on behalf of the demands of other
shipyards, Anna Walentynowicz took the position that only if the Lenin
workers continued their strike on behalf of the workers at the other
shipyards would they be "safe." Clearly she was saying that workers, to
secure their rights, need above all else to preserve their solidarity.

This distinctive experience of solidarity, underlying the right to
engage in concerted activity, has three unusual attributes. First, the well-
being of the individual and the well-being of the group are not experienced as antagonistic. Justice Sandra Day O'Connor has written that
"the concepts of individual action for personal gain and 'concerted
activity' are intuitively incompatible."[32] This is the view from the outside,
the view of someone who has not experienced the wage worker's elemental need for the support of other workers. Learned Hand came
much closer to the reality in a passage written soon after the enactment
of section 7:

> When all other workmen in a shop make common cause with a fellow work-
> man over his separate grievance, and go out on strike in his support, they
> engage in a "concerted activity" for "mutual aid or protection," although the
> aggrieved workman is the only one of them who has any immediate stake in
> the outcome. The rest know that by their action each one of them assures
> himself, in case his turn ever comes, of the support of the one whom they
> are all then helping; and the solidarity so established is "mutual aid" in the
> most literal sense, as nobody doubts. So too of those engaging in a "sympa-
> thetic strike," or secondary boycott; the immediate quarrel does not itself
> concern them, but by extending the number of those who will make the
> enemy of one the enemy of all, the power of each is vastly increased.[33]

I have heard a rank-and-file steelworker use almost identical language in
trying to persuade fellow workers to support each other's grievances.
What is counterintuitive to Justice O'Connor is the common sense of
those engaged in the struggle.

Second, the group of those who work together—the informal work
group, the department, the local union, the class—is often experienced
as a reality in itself. Thus, Hand's rationale misses something crucial to

the right to engage in concerted activity. I do not scratch your back only because one day I may need you to scratch mine. Labor solidarity is more than an updated version of the social contract through which each individual undertakes to assist others for the advancement of his or her own interest.

In a family, when I as son, husband, or father, express love toward you, I do not do so in order to assure myself of love in return. I do not help my son in order to be able to claim assistance from him when I am old; I do it because he and I are in the world together; we are one flesh. Similarly in a workplace, persons who work together form families-at-work.[34] When you and I are working together, and the foreman suddenly discharges you, and I find myself putting down my tools or stopping my machine before I have had time to think—why do I do this? Is it not because, as I actually experience the event, your discharge does not happen only to you but also happens to *us*?

Justice William Brennan's majority opinion in *NLRB v. City Disposal Systems Inc.*[35] portrays this experienced reality of the working group. The case dealt with a truck driver who refused to drive an unsafe truck. Nobody was with Brown, the driver, when he told two supervisors that the truck in question, No. 244, "has got problems and I don't want to drive it."[36] One of the supervisors went on to tell Brown that "[w]e've got all this garbage out here to haul and you tell me about you don't want to drive."[37] Brown responded, "Bob, what are you going to do, put the garbage ahead of the safety of the men?"[38] Thus Brown, although he was quite alone, put his case as a matter of "the safety of the *men*," because this is how he experienced it. And in fact, Brown initially had become aware of the problems with the truck when, two days earlier, he had been driving a different truck and, because of its brake problems "truck No. 244 nearly collided with Brown's truck";[39] when that happened, Brown and the driver of No. 244 together brought No. 244 to the employer's repair facility. Accordingly, Justice Brennan is profoundly right to say in *City Disposal* that when Brown invoked the clause in the collective bargaining agreement permitting a driver to refuse to drive an unsafe truck, he did "not stand alone" but brought "to bear on his employer the power and resolve of all his fellow employees."[40] When James Brown refused to drive a truck he believed to be unsafe,

he was in effect reminding his employer that he and his fellow employees . . . had extracted a promise from City Disposal that they would not be asked to drive unsafe trucks. He was also reminding his employer that if it persisted in ordering him to drive an unsafe truck, he could reharness the power of that group to ensure the enforcement of that promise. *It was just as though James Brown was reassembling his fellow union members to reenact their decision not to drive unsafe trucks.*[41]

Finally—and again in dialectical tension with the attribute just emphasized—the solidarity of workers articulated in the right to engage in concerted activity can and must be individually exercised. The Walentynowicz story contains this theme, too. When Walentynowicz was asked, "On whose authority are you declaring this a strike?," she began to cry. But her friend, now acting completely alone, stood up on the barrel and finished the job.

Any conception of the right to concerted activity that might make the rights to strike and to picket less capable of exercise by individuals flies in the face of legislative history.[42] In the late nineteenth and early twentieth centuries, workers were understood to be free to quit work or to picket individually (however ineffectual that might be), but were found liable under conspiracy or common law tort theories if they performed the same acts jointly. The intent of the Clayton and Norris-LaGuardia Acts was to protect activities by groups that were assumed to be protected when practiced by individuals. Both laws expressly protected striking, and Norris-LaGuardia protected picketing as well, whether undertaken "singly or in concert."[43]

Section 7 of the Wagner Act,[44] enacted only three years after the passage of the Norris-LaGuardia Act, protected "concerted activity" against the private employer but failed to add that individual exercise of the same rights was also protected. There is not the slightest evidence to suggest that this omission indicated any change in the conception of the rights as expressed in the Norris-LaGuardia Act. Nonetheless, for many years the National Labor Relations Board and the United States Supreme Court took advantage of the omission, finding "statutory protection for an activity engaged in by two employees while the very same activity engaged in by one remains unprotected"[45] and creating the concept of the right to engage in concerted activity for mutual aid or protection as a "collective right" that can be exercised by individual workers only with the approval of their union representatives.[46] These doctrines are contrary to the legislative history and policy of the statute. Professors Gorman and Finkin conclude an authoritative survey as follows:

[T]here are not two abstract and distinguishable categories of action—individual action for self-interest and collective action for mutual interest—one which Congress chose not to protect and the other which Congress chose to protect, but rather a continuum of individual activity—of individuals choosing to speak and act on their own behalf, singly and in small and large groups. Thus, the narrow reading of the Act proceeds upon a false dichotomy, for at the core of the freedom of the individual to protest in a group necessarily lies the freedom of the individual to protest at all.[47]

In *City Disposal,* the Supreme Court acknowledged the Gorman-Finkin critique and accepted it in situations where a union has been recognized and a collective bargaining agreement has been negotiated. The majority opinion points out that the language of section 7 protects the rights "to join, or assist labor organizations . . . and to engage in other concerted activities," although both joining and assisting are "activities in which a single individual can engage."[48] Brown's individual refusal to drive an unsafe truck was, according to the Court, "integrally" related to the group activity that had created the union and brought into being a contract protecting the right to refuse to drive an unsafe truck:

> When an employee joins or assists a labor organization, his actions may be divorced in time, and in location as well, from the actions of fellow employees. Because of the integral relationship among the employees' actions, however, Congress viewed each employee as engaged in concerted activity. The lone employee could not join or assist a labor organization were it not for the related organizing activities of his fellow employees. Conversely, there would be limited utility in forming a labor organization if other employees could not join or assist the organization once it is formed. Thus, the formation of a labor organization is integrally related to the activity of joining or assisting such an organization in the same sense that the negotiation of a collective-bargaining agreement is integrally related to the invocation of a right provided for in the agreement. *In each case, neither the individual activity nor the group activity would be complete without the other.*[49]

This extraordinary opinion comes close to suggesting that even without a collective bargaining provision articulating the right to refuse unsafe work, such refusal might be an "efficient substitute" for filing a "formal" grievance.[50] Under this suggestion, the right to refuse unsafe work could be exercised by an individual, as well as by the union as representative of the individuals.

The right to engage in concerted activity for mutual aid or protection is the paradigm communal right. Neither a narrowly individual nor a merely collective right, it is a right derived from the actual character of working-class solidarity and accordingly a right that foreshadows a society in which group life and individual self-realization mutually reinforce each other.

The First Amendment. As I initially formulated this idea a few years ago, I may have seemed to say that the right to engage in concerted activity is the *only* communal right and that all other rights, including the rights associated with the First Amendment, are individualistic property rights.[51]

The late Edward Sparer read my words this way and understandably protested. "It would be unfortunate," he wrote,

> if Lynd is too readily accepting a narrow conception of such rights as speech and dissent. Such rights do not necessarily subtract from or function separately from "the right to engage in concerted activity for mutual aid." Indeed, the former rights are indispensable to the maintenance of the latter right. Where would the right of working people to unionize and strike be without the right to free speech?[52]

Sparer made the same point in this way:

> While it is easy to understand how one person's right to separately possess property limits another person's separate possession of property, I fail to see how one person's exercise of, for example, free speech and dissent *necessarily* limits another person's. Quite the contrary; the exercise of these latter rights can increase the next person's ability to exercise them.[53]

Pondering Sparer's words, it gradually became clear that the rights represented by the First Amendment might themselves be seen as what I have called "communal rights," more like the right to engage in concerted activity than individualistic property rights.

For one thing, I knew that when Congress enacted section 7 of the Wagner Act the sponsors of the legislation analogized section 7 rights to

First Amendment rights. Picketing in particular was regarded as protected *speech*. Moreover, during the early years of the Wagner Act's administration, the Board and the Supreme Court articulated a single developing body of doctrine for both section 7 and First Amendment cases, applying essentially the same test whether speech was regulated by a private employer or by the state.[54]

Then I came across a remarkable passage from one of Thomas Jefferson's letters in which he memorably portrayed the self-contradictory character of intellectual property.

> If nature has made any one thing less susceptible than all others of exclusive property, it is the action of the thinking power called an idea, which an individual may exclusively possess as long as he keeps it to himself; but the moment it is divulged, it forces itself into the possession of every one, and the receiver cannot dispossess himself of it. Its peculiar character, too, is that no one possesses the less, because every other possesses the whole of it. He who receives an idea from me, receives instruction himself without lessening mine: as he who lights his taper at mine, receives light without darkening me.[55]

These words suggested that the communal search for truth is no more compatible with the right to private property than is the concerted activity of workers for mutual aid or protection.

Finally, I looked again at the text of the First Amendment itself:

> Congress shall make no law respecting an establishment of religion, or prohibiting the free exercise thereof; or abridging the freedom of speech, or of the press; or the right of the people peaceably to assemble, and to petition the Government for a redress of grievances.[56]

Insofar as the First Amendment specifies to whom the rights it enumerates belong, the rights belong not to individuals, but to "the people." The two clauses concerning religion describe arguably communal rights: the right not to be forced to support a particular denomination, and the right to be free to meet in religious assemblies of any persuasion without state interference. The free speech clause is linked with freedom of the press, which even in the eighteenth century required a group of persons for its exercise. Finally, it is difficult even to imagine an individual exercising alone the rights to assemble and petition.[57]

All of this suggests that the critique of rights, valid as it may be when applied to property rights, does not adequately confront the communal character of the First Amendment any more than it adequately characterizes the right to engage in concerted labor activity. If the rights associated with the First Amendment can be viewed as communal rights, it might be possible to celebrate and defend them along with the communal rights of workers, without weakening the critique of rights associated with private property. First Amendment rights would then be seen not as "bourgeois rights" to be cast aside along with private property, but as communal rights prefiguring the qualities of a future, better society.

The modern history of the law concerning allegedly seditious political speech—the only branch of First Amendment doctrine considered here—provides important evidence in the search for the communal content of the First Amendment. As with the right to engage in concerted activity, we find the conception—alien to the general thrust of existing law and difficult even to express—that certain rights represent *both* affirmations of public values *and* protection for individual self-realization. This part of First Amendment doctrine also suggests that an individual's exercise of certain freedoms can best be safeguarded not by likening them to property, but simply by emphasizing the importance to the community that the rights should flourish.

The modern history of seditious speech law begins with a cluster of Supreme Court opinions written just after World War I. In March 1919 Justices Oliver Wendell Holmes and Louis Brandeis, writing for a unanimous Court, upheld the convictions of socialists (including Eugene Debs) who had spoken out against the war.[58] In November 1919, in a case presenting essentially similar activity, Justice Brandeis joined the first of Justice Holmes's famous First Amendment dissents.[59]

Interestingly, the "speech test" employed by the Justices did *not* change. Justice Holmes used the same "clear and present danger" speech test to send Debs to jail that he used less than a year later to argue against sustaining the conviction of Abrams. What changed was the weight Holmes gave to uninhibited political speech as a public value.[60] When Holmes first suggested the phrase "clear and present danger" he saw it as a distillation of the law of criminal attempt; he used it to assess purported speech crimes as he would have used it in any other criminal case. During the summer of 1919, however, Holmes appears to have been persuaded by Zechariah Chafee, among others, that free speech was a preeminent community value and that the First Amendment was "a declaration of national policy in favor of the public discussion of all public questions."[61] As a result, in his dissent in *Abrams v.*

United States, Holmes implicitly distinguished between the ordinary criminal prosecution of an individual and a prosecution for speech "where private rights are not concerned."[62]

The subsequent opinions of Justice Brandeis, culminating in his concurrence in *Whitney v. California*[63] in 1927, expressly set forth the dual character of First Amendment rights. Political speech is a public value because it is necessary to democratic self-government: "The fundamental right of free men to strive for better conditions through new legislation and new institutions will not be preserved, if efforts to secure it by argument to fellow citizens may be construed as criminal incitement to disobey the existing law."[64] But free speech and assembly are also "fundamental personal rights."[65] Accordingly, an adequate description of the First Amendment must incorporate both its public and private aspects. Except for the recurrence of the male pronoun, Brandeis's characterization seems difficult to improve upon:

> The right of a citizen of the United States to take part, for his own or the country's benefit, in the making of federal laws and in the conduct of the Government, necessarily includes the right to speak or write about them; to endeavor to make his own opinion concerning laws existing or contemplated prevail; and, to this end, to teach the truth as he sees it.[66]

One striking theme of Brandeis's pronouncements is his insistence that the rights at issue are just as real and important as property rights. "I cannot believe," he wrote, "that the liberty guaranteed by the Fourteenth Amendment includes only liberty to acquire and to enjoy property."[67] The power of the courts to strike down an offending law, he stated, "is no less when the interests involved are not property rights, but the fundamental personal rights of free speech and assembly."[68]

The critique of traditional rights rhetoric and the character of what I term "communal rights" converge at this point. It does not make a right more real, or more protected, to analogize the right to property and say that it is "vested." The rights to speak, associate, assemble, and petition will be protected only so long as they are valued by society; the best of speech tests will be readily circumvented if that valuation fades. This does not mean that we should cease to struggle for the speech tests that are most protective of political speech and speech in the workplace.[69] Still less does it mean that because these rights depend on social consensus for their enforcement, the First Amendment is superfluous as a legal right. The First Amendment as social and moral value and the First Amendment as legal right stand in symbiotic relation to one another. The value requires the right to be legally enforceable, and the right requires continuing nurture of the value so that the political will that the right be enforced will not cease to exist.

The Communal "Rights of the Citizen" according to Karl Marx

Karl Marx is unquestionably the single most important source of the critique of liberal rights rhetoric. His most explicit discussion of rights rhetoric, in the 1843 essay *On the Jewish Question*, frequently is cited as a demonstration of the inadequacies of liberal rights theory.[70] Thus it seems useful to show that Marx articulated in that very essay the distinction urged here between two different kinds of rights.

In *On the Jewish Question* Marx differentiated between *droits de l'homme*, "the rights of man," and *droits de citoyen*, "the rights of the citizen." *Droits de l'homme* are the rights of the human being as a bourgeois, or member of civil society. Above all these are rights to property itself, but they also include liberty in the sense of "the right to do everything which does not harm others" and equality understood as "the equal right to liberty as defined above."[71]

Droits de citoyen, on the other hand, are characterized as "*political* rights, which can only be exercised if one is a member of a community. Their content is *participation* in the *community* life, in the *political* life of the community, the life of the state. They fall in the category of *political liberty*, of *civil rights*."[72] Far from criticizing these rights "which can only be exercised if one is a member of a community," Marx celebrated them. He contrasted the egoistic *droits de l'homme* with the communal *droits de citoyen*. The tragedy for Marx was that the communal rights of the citizen are made to serve the egoistic rights of man, which are grounded in the last analysis on the right to private property. He criticized the fact that the French and American Revolutions reduce

> citizenship, the *political community*, to a mere *means* for preserving these so-called rights of man; and consequently, that the citizen is declared to be the servant of egoistic "man," that the sphere in which man functions as a species-being [*Gemeinwesen*] is degraded to a level below the sphere where he functions as a partial being, and finally that it is man as a bourgeois and not man as a citizen who is considered the *true* and *authentic* man.[73]

On the Jewish Question does not tell us exactly what rights Marx considered to be the communal rights of citizens. In the 1840s, however, Marx and Engels drafted or helped draft three programs containing political demands: the *Manifesto of the Communist Party*, which includes a ten-point program;[74] the *Demands of the Communist Party in Germany*,[75] adopted a few weeks after the publication of the *Manifesto*, and according to historian David Ryazanov a more accurate reflection of the thinking of Marx and Engels; and an exposition by Engels entitled *Principles of Communism*.[76]

Among the rights demanded in one or more of these three programs are: the right of persons having attained the age of twenty-one to vote and to be elected to office;[77] the right of representatives to receive salaries, so that manual workers may become representatives;[78] universal arming of the people;[79] free legal services;[80] equalization of salaries for civil servants, except that those with families to support should receive more;[81] complete separation of church and state;[82] a steeply graduated income tax and abolition of taxes on consumption;[83] free public education and the abolition of factory work for children in its then present form;[84] abolition of the right to inheritance.[85]

Marx and Engels later took pains to indicate that the particular demands contained in *The Communist Manifesto* ought not be canonized. They stressed particularly that the experience of the Paris Commune of 1871 had led them to conclude that workers could not simply take over the existing state machinery.[86] With variations in detail and emphasis, however, Marx throughout his life expressed strong interest in the rights he characterized in 1843 as the communal "rights of the citizen." He came of age politically at a time when workers all over Europe were demanding the opportunity to participate as equals in political decision making. Marx's *Critique of Hegel's Philosophy of Right*, written the same year as *On the Jewish Question*, eulogized democracy as a political form transcending alienation. In a democracy, he wrote, "[m]an does not exist because of the law but rather the law exists for the good of man"; in a democracy, "the law . . . is itself only a self-determination of the people."[87] Throughout the 1840s Marx and Engels were deeply involved in the British Chartist movement, a working-class movement with exclusively political demands for universal adult male suffrage protected by the ballot, the abolition of property qualifications for members of parliament, payment of members of parliament, equal electoral districts, and annual parliaments.[88] In their response to a draft program of the

German socialist parties in 1875, Marx and Engels vigorously criticized the program's political demands. But they did not attack the demand for abolition of laws restricting "the press, associations and assembly," and they chided the drafters for failing to mention the self-organization of the working class in trade unions.[89] Thus, even toward the end of their lives, Marx and Engels were sympathetic to the communal political and economic rights discussed earlier in this article.

Communal Economic Rights

There is a growing awareness that, as Marx argued, political rights without an economic foundation inevitably will lack substance. The American Civil Liberties Union has made the most elaborate attempt to date to provide a rationale for economic rights. Part of an ACLU policy statement is pertinent:

> The government now substantially controls the economy, and therefore the distribution of economic benefits. . . .
>
> Such "state action" largely determines . . . macroeconomic factors [which] in turn result in adequate subsistence or security for most Americans while leaving others without the necessities of life. . . .
>
> Life, liberty and property include the fundamentals of a life and, under these circumstances, we believe the government is constitutionally required to provide the necessities of life to all persons.[90]

The ACLU, like some abolitionists before and during the Civil War, is arguing for the incorporation into the United States Constitution of rights proclaimed by the Declaration of Independence. Having done so, it will argue that because government is created to secure those rights, there is a constitutional claim to those necessities of life included in the phrase "life, liberty, and the pursuit of happiness," particularly because, according to the policy statement, "[t]he government now substantially controls the economy."

But the Declaration of Independence is not part of the Constitution, and the government does not substantially control the economy. The ACLU's actual litigation strategy for economic rights proceeds on the quite different argument that *if* the government willingly undertakes to provide a benefit, then it must do so consistently with constitutional requirements of due process and equal protection.[91]

There is, however, an alternative approach to economic rights, which begins, not with the individual rights of the Declaration of Independence, but with the idea of communal rights. In most countries, the foundation for the tradition of communal values and rights is common ownership and use of the land. Ideologically, this social practice is reflected in the belief that the good things of the world are intended for the common use of humankind as one family. The idea has repeatedly forced itself to the surface of British history, as in the movement against enclosure of village common lands and the Digger movement of the 1640s.

In American history, the concept of the earth and its bounty as a common inheritance is much more attenuated but not entirely absent. The Quaker John Woolman voiced the ancient conception that "[t]he Creator of the earth is the owner of it."[92] Thomas Paine wrote in his *Preface to Agrarian Justice:* "It is wrong to say God made *rich* and *poor;* He made only *male* and *female;* and He gave them the earth for their inheritance."[93] Thomas Jefferson held that the earth belongs to the living generation, and wrote, even more radically, in 1785:

> Whenever there is in any country, uncultivated lands and unemployed poor, it is clear that the laws of property have been so far extended as to violate natural right. The earth is given as a common stock for man to labour and live on. If, for the encouragement of industry we allow it to be appropriated, we must take care that other employment be furnished to those excluded from the appropriation. If we do not the fundamental right to labour the earth returns to the unemployed.[94]

This idea reappeared almost a century later when Radical Republicans sought to make the public lands of the West available to homesteaders and to give the freed slaves access to the plantation land of the South.[95]

In the modern industrial economy, the concept of common ownership survives in the law of eminent domain. Labor law, as the Supreme Court has recently reemphasized, attributes to management an absolute "prerogative" to make unilateral investment decisions without considering the welfare of employees or communities.[96] But the law of eminent domain gives communities a residual authority to do what is necessary to preserve themselves. Private property may be taken by public bodies, so long as the property is taken for a public purpose and the owner is compensated at fair market value.

In colonial America, the power of eminent domain was often used (as it still is today) to take private property for public roads.

> Anyone, such as a town, that wanted a new road applied to the county court, which appointed a commission to report on the need. Upon the commissioners' report, if the court found the road needed, a local "jury" was appointed to lay out the route. Compensation was provided for [if the land taken was improved; wild land was not paid for, on the theory that the road created more benefit to the owner of the land than it destroyed].... An owner aggrieved by the "jury's" estimate could appeal to the county court. Once a road was built, it was maintained by the citizens of the town through which it ran, who, under the direction of town "surveyors," had to donate labor and materials.[97]

Corporations used the power of eminent domain in the nineteenth century to assemble land for mill sites and railroad rights of way. The public can use it today to acquire factories that corporations have shut down. Recent decisions by the supreme courts of Michigan,[98] California,[99] and the United States,[100] suggest that legal (as distinct from political) obstacles to the taking of industrial property by eminent domain can be overcome. A Pittsburgh-based group, TriState Conference on Steel, has proposed that one or more local public bodies, acting under the Pennsylvania Municipal Authorities Act of 1945, might create a regional development authority that would use the eminent domain power to acquire abandoned industrial facilities and ensure their continued operation, either by operating them itself (in the manner of the Tennessee Valley Authority) or by transferring them for operation to groups of employees.[101]

I believe that strategies to implement the communal right to economic survival increasingly will commend themselves to thoughtful persons in the labor movement. When management can relocate product lines or declare bankruptcy for the express purpose of avoiding a labor contract, labor is no longer able to pursue its short-run objectives without facing the long-run question of control of investment decisions.

In the final analysis, a communal approach to economic rights seems inseparable from the vision that the earth belongs to all humankind and should be accessible to those who need it most. I favor building on this ancient wisdom, rather than on the concept of an individual right to livelihood, because I believe it is more consistent with the kind of society we desire.

REINTERPRETING RIGHTS such as the right to engage in concerted activity, the rights guaranteed by the First Amendment, and the rights associated with the power of eminent domain, as communal rights, would give new meaning to the concept of "inalienable" rights. One respect in which the Declaration of Independence no longer seems self-evident is in its characterization of life and liberty as "inalienable" *individual* rights. Life and liberty are rights possessed by individuals, yet surely an individual can give up his or her life and individuals effectively can permit themselves to be made slaves.[102]

But no *individual* can give up a right which belongs to the whole community, and no current majority can give up rights belonging to future generations. One is reminded of the United States soldiers seeking an Indian spokesperson who could be induced to give up the land belonging to the tribe. The Indians typically replied: "It is not ours to give." Similarly, trade unionists from whom contract concessions have been demanded have sometimes responded "that this generation of members does not have the right to willingly give up the contractual gains made by our fathers and their fathers before them."[103]

The attribute of inalienability underscores the fundamental character of communal rights. Communal rights can help define the long-term objectives of a society or a movement for change and give them stability from one generation to the next. The language of communal rights seems appropriate for a movement of long-distance runners, of advocates who will not be denied.

7

In Memoriam:
E. P. Thompson

And did those feet in ancient time,
Walk upon England's mountains green;
And was the holy Lamb of God,
On England's pleasant pastures seen!

And did the Countenance Divine,
Shine forth upon our clouded hills?
And was Jerusalem builded here,
Among these dark Satanic Mills?

Bring me my Bow of burning gold:
Bring me my Arrows of desire:
Bring me my Spear: O clouds unfold!
Bring me my Chariot of fire!

I will not cease from Mental Fight,
Nor shall my Sword sleep in my hand:
Till we have built Jerusalem,
In Englands green & pleasant Land.

—William Blake, Preface to *Milton* (1804)

I had only one conversation with Edward Thompson. It was in the spring of 1966, at the apartment of Eugene Genovese in Manhattan. A few hours before I had been in London speaking at a rally against the war in Vietnam. I believe I introduced myself to Edward Thompson by offering greetings from the pigeons in Trafalgar Square.

Four things from that conversation remain in my mind. Thompson spoke with disdain of historians who, in his phrase, "never untied a bundle" of manuscripts. I formed a mental picture of bundle upon bundle of manuscripts at the British Home Office, each tied with string. Be that as it may, the message was clear. Radical historians may make political demands of themselves over and above the requirements of good historical scholarship, but the requirements of historical scholarship are the same for everybody. We have to be good craftspersons, whatever else we may be.

Second, I said something to the effect that it might be the Third World, rather than the working class of advanced industrial societies,

Originally published in 82 *Georgetown Law Journal* (July 1994).

that took the lead in the transition from capitalism to socialism. Had it been a year or two later I might have cited Frantz Fanon or Regis Debray. In 1966, I believe I referred to Sartre.

Thompson reacted sharply. He did not believe for a moment that the industrial working class was finished as an historical agent. Why, there was this strike and that struggle that had just happened in Britain, and he felt sure that there was more to come.

I recall being very surprised. The message to be drawn from this exchange, I think, was not that anyone could say with confidence what the respective roles of First and Third World proletariats would be in the long run; it was simply that one ought not to give up on the workers of one's own country. I apparently was influenced. I have spent the past twenty-five years as a historian and a lawyer trying to do what Thompson suggested. My clients have typically been discharged or displaced industrial workers.

A third point Thompson made in our 1966 conversation had to do with what he called "doing history" and "doing politics." He did not see how one could do both at the same time. He suggested then, and his later life seems to exemplify, that one must do history and politics in alternation, for separate periods of time.

I find this idea inadequate. Surely it falls short of what Marx called a unity of theory and practice. I wonder if the difficulty Thompson found in connecting theory and practice was related to something else: that the focus of his scholarly inquiry shifted further and further back in time, from William Morris (late nineteenth century), to the formation of the English working class (early nineteenth century), to studies in seventeenth- and eighteenth-century popular culture.

Finally, there was the question of Edward's acerbic dialogue with Perry Anderson and other British Marxists (about which I say more below). I cannot remember what point this exchange had reached at the time I spoke with Thompson in 1966. Nor can I recall any particular words that Thompson used. What came through and what stays in mind is the passion with which he spoke. Thompson's biographer Bryan Palmer describes his attitude as follows:

> Though retaining from Marxism a set of central questions and analytical methods, Thompson conceived of himself less and less in terms of traditional Marxism and more and more in terms of a moral agenda that turned on opposition to power and its abuses. "We need, in some new form," he

would write in *The Nation* in 1983, "a 'Wobbly' vocabulary of mutual aid and of plain duty to each other in the face of power."[1]

The "Double Service" of the Law

In the conclusion to his book *Whigs and Hunters*, Thompson expresses a view of the law with which every legal worker on the Left should grapple. His imagined interlocutors were the British Marxists grouped around Perry Anderson and the French structural Marxists influenced by Louis Althusser. But what Thompson had to say is equally subversive to the views of Critical Legal Studies scholars in the United States.

Thompson did battle with the notion that because law is nothing more than an instrument of the ruling class, legal rhetoric is a sham. He conceded, indeed insisted, that law *is* an instrument of the ruling class, and nowhere more so than in eighteenth-century England. But this is not all that law was, or is.

> [The] oligarchy employed the law, both instrumentally and ideologically, very much as a modern structural Marxist should expect it to do. But this is not the same thing as to say that the rulers had need of law, in order to oppress the ruled, while those who were ruled had need of none. What was often at issue was not property, supported by law, against no-property: it was alternative definitions of property-rights.[2]

It is not possible to conceive of productive forces as a substructure of society distinct from the law, Thompson argued. "How can we distinguish between the activity of farming or of quarrying and the rights to this strip of land or to that quarry? The farmer or forester in his daily occupation was moving within visible or invisible structures of law."[3]

In Thompson's view, the law does not belong wholly to the powerful. It is contested terrain. "There were alternative norms; that is a matter of course; this was a place, not of consensus, but of conflict."[4] On behalf of its own self-interest, the ruling class must let the law have some autonomy.

> If the law is evidently partial and unjust, then it will mask nothing, legitimize nothing, contribute nothing to any class's hegemony. The essential precondition for the effectiveness of law, in its function as ideology, is that it shall display an independence from gross manipulation and shall seem to be just.

It cannot seem to be so without upholding its own logic and criteria of equity; indeed, on occasion, by actually *being* just.[5]

Like religion, then, law in the Thompsonian view performs a "double service."[6] Law simultaneously advances the agenda of the ruling class and inhibits it. For the oppressed, also, law is more than empty rhetoric, more than a mask. "[S]o far from the ruled shrugging off this rhetoric as a hypocrisy, some part of it at least was taken over as part of the rhetoric of the plebeian crowd, of the 'free-born Englishman' with his inviolable privacy, his *habeas corpus,* his equality before the law. If this rhetoric was a mask, it was a mask which John Wilkes was to borrow, at the head of ten thousand masked supporters."[7] (Likewise, a few pages later, "it was a mask which Gandhi and Nehru were to borrow, at the head of a million masked supporters.")[8]

Law was for Thompson a "cultural achievement . . . towards a universal value," "an unqualified good."[9] To those who believed that new and superior socialist arrangements were just over the historical horizon, he observed dryly: "[W]atch this new power for a century or two before you cut your hedges down."[10]

The difference between Thompson and Critical Legal Studies is not that one adheres to moral values and the other does not. Critical Legal Studies writers, I believe, tend to project moral vision in the form of personal utopias, unconnected to any hard-won institutional precedent. I think Thompson would have considered this attitude cavalier. Thompson viewed "norms" and the law that articulates these norms as products of centuries-long human agency, precious collective capital that should not lightly be discarded. I think he would have tried to talk to the Critical Legal Studies folk about what he called "political culture."[11] The entire history of such a nation as England might be understood as a struggle to create, maintain, and expand a political culture.

The law-and-order brigade would like us to think that the constitution is a generous provision, made at some time by Them to Us. But they know in their hearts that the opposite is true. They know that one way of reading our history is as an immensely protracted contest to subject the nation's rulers to the rule of law.

This contest has swayed backwards and forwards, through a thousand episodes, and with each generation it has been renewed. We have subjected

feudal barons, overmighty subjects, corrupt Lord Chancellors, kings and
their courtiers, overmighty generals, the vast apparatus of Old Corruption,
inhumane employers, overmighty commissioners of police, imperial adven-
turers and successive nests of ruling-class conspirators to the rule of law.
Every now we have notched up a victory, and every then the ratchet has
slipped back.[12]

In my opinion we will best serve the memory of Edward Thompson
not by refighting in the abstract the issue of the nature of law, but by
attending to the preservation of those aspects of "bourgeois law" that
will have continuing validity in a socialist society, or in any democratic
society. Civilian control of the police and military was one such permanently good arrangement, Thompson believed. He was even more
strongly committed to trial by jury. The place of the jury in English constitutional history, he wrote,

> does not rest on a naive belief that every jury verdict must be true, rational
> and humane.

> It rests upon a total view of the relation between the legislature, judiciary
> and the people; upon a notion of justice in which the law must be made to
> seem rational and even humane to lay jurors (hence inhibiting a thousand
> oppressive processes before they are even commenced, through the knowl-
> edge that no jury would convict); and upon a particular national history of
> contests between "the people" and the Crown or state, in which the jury has
> won and reserved for itself, in its verdict, a final power.[13]

An English citizen charged with a serious crime has the option to be
tried by jury: to "put himself upon his country." Were it otherwise,
Thompson thought, "I would no longer know who the British people
are."[14]

Academic Blindness

Edward Thompson, the most influential historian writing in the English language during the second half of this century, never received a
Ph.D. He wrote his masterpiece, *The Making of the English Working Class*,
while serving as a sort of adjunct professor at a provincial university; the
book was originally to be an introductory essay for a text to be used in

his workers' education classes. In 1965, Thompson was appointed to a regular academic position at Warwick University, and for years I have wondered if I erred in turning down an invitation to join him there on a one-year basis. Now I learn from Edward's obituaries that in 1970 he became involved with students who had invaded the university offices and held a sit-in, and in 1971 he resigned, after writing stingingly about the ethos and administrative arrangements of this new "business university."[15] Thereafter, until his death, Thompson lived as an independent writer and peace agitator, supported in part by the academic income of his wife, Dorothy Thompson.

Thompson's life accordingly should challenge us to consider the relationship between academic livelihood and intellectual life on the Left. Perhaps more particularly, we may wonder if some of Thompson's originality and incisiveness arose precisely because he was not, during most of his life, a university professor.

For Thompson, academic custom often ran counter to the values that meant most to him. He believed in human agency, as opposed to any form of determinism; in the rationality and dignity of working people; and in the necessity of moral values and moral choices. By contrast, academic life tended to segregate teachers from practice; to persuade them that they were better than ordinary people; and to lead to amoral and sterile theorizing.

An early and much-quoted passage from "Outside the Whale" (1960) sounded Thompson's theme of human agency. During the confining years of the Cold War, Thompson wrote:

[M]en had abandoned human agency. They could not hold back change; but change went with the shuffling gait of circumstance. It did not stem from the operation of human consciousness and will upon circumstances. Events seemed to will men, not men events. For meaning can be given to history only in the quarrel between "ought" and "is"—we must thrust the "ought" of choice into the "is" of circumstance which in its turn defines the human nature with which we choose.[16]

Likewise, in *The Making of the English Working Class*, Thompson said it was a study "in an active process, which owes as much to agency as to conditioning," and criticized prevailing orthodoxies that "tend to obscure the agency of working people."[17] He insisted that the poor be remembered as protagonists, as thinking men and women guided by norms of their own. In rioting for food in the eighteenth century, or in smashing machines in the early nineteenth century, those who took direct action had in mind a "legitimizing notion." They were the champions of a "moral economy" derived in part from late medieval English laws that sought to ensure access to good wheat bread at reasonable prices or to maintain the quality of English textiles. As these laws were evaded and ignored, the poor turned first to others to enforce them, but if the Justice and the Parliament refused to act, they took matters into their own hands. Against academics of Right *and* Left who wished to reduce culturally mediated behavior to economics, Thompson counterposed an anthropological view, claiming that these common folk displayed "a pattern of behavior of which a Trobriand islander need not have been ashamed."[18]

The themes of agency, working-class rationality and dignity, and the need for moral values are summoned as prosecutors of the academic way of life in "The Poverty of Theory." The essay confronts academic intellectuals who (according to Thompson) are the product of a rupture "between intellectuality and practical experience." It attacks the "characteristic delusion of intellectuals, who suppose that ordinary mortals are stupid."[19] Further,

> I must remind a Marxist philosopher that knowledges have been and still are formed outside the academic procedures. Nor have these been, in the test of practice, negligible. They have assisted men and women to till the fields, to construct houses, to support elaborate social organisations, and even, on occasion, to challenge effectively the conclusions of academic thought.[20]

Thompson reached out to popular culture, even to religion, as an antidote to two-dimensional academicism. It is "profoundly important that our protestant prejudice should be renewed, that we should *think* ourselves to be 'free.'"[21] The Marxism of "closure," which he deplores, has arisen and been replicated "not in the Soviet Union, but within an advanced intellectual culture in the West. Its characteristic location has been in universities."[22] A merely theoretical Marxism "allows the aspirant academic to engage in harmless revolutionary psycho-drama, while at the same time pursuing a reputable and conventional intellectual career."[23] Rather than be that kind of Marxist, Thompson exclaims, "I would rather be a Christian (or hope to have the courage of a certain kind of Christian radical). At least I would then be given back a vocabulary within which value choices are allowed."[24]

Morris, Blake, and Love

In a 1976 postscript to a new edition of his biography of William Morris (first published in 1955), Thompson went further than before in delimiting the proper scope of Marxist theory. It should now be clear, runs the crucial paragraph,

> that there is a sense in which Morris, as a Utopian and moralist, can never be assimilated to Marxism, not because of any contradiction of purposes but because one may not assimilate desire to knowledge, and because the attempt to do so is to confuse two different operative principles of culture. . . . Marxism requires . . . a sense of humility before those parts of culture which it can never order. The motions of desire may be legible in the text of necessity, and may then become subject to rational explanation and criticism. But such criticism can scarcely touch these motions at their source. "Marxism," on its own, we now know, has never made anyone "good" or "bad." . . . So that what Marxism might do, for a change, is sit on its own head a little in the interest of socialism's heart. It might close down one counter in its universal pharmacy, and cease dispensing potions of analysis to cure the maladies of desire. This might do good politically as well, since it would allow a little space . . . for the unprescribed initiatives of everyday men and women.[25]

William Blake was the one radical intellectual about whom Thompson had no such mixed feelings. To begin with, unlike John Thelwall and Brontierre O'Brien, both sons of merchants,[26] or William Morris, whose father made his fortune in mining stocks, Blake's father and brother were hosiers, as was the first husband of his mother, Catherine Hermitage. Thus Blake "straddled two social worlds: that of intellectuals and artists, and that of tradesmen and artisans."[27]

Moreover, Thompson saw Blake as the last English intellectual at home both in working-class resistance to industrial capitalism and the Romantic critique of Utilitarianism.[28] Thompson's admiration for Blake, now poignantly available in the posthumously published *Witness against the Beast: William Blake and the Moral Law,* is very closely tied to his view of academic culture and his convictions about the limitations of theory.

> Despite every precaution, we have a continuing difficulty in our approach to Blake, which derives from our tendency to make overly academic assumptions as to his learning and mode of thought. It takes a large effort to rid our-

selves of these assumptions, because they lie at an inaccessible level within
our own intellectual culture—indeed, they belong to the very institutions
and disciplines with which we construct that culture. That is, we tend to find
that a man is either "educated" or "uneducated," or is educated to certain
levels (within a relatively homogeneous hierarchy of attainments); and this
education involves submission to certain institutionally defined disciplines,
with their own hierarchies of accomplishment and authority.

Blake's mind was formed within a very different intellectual tradition. In the
nineteenth century we sometimes call this, a little patronisingly, the tradition
of the autodidact. This calls to mind the radical or Chartist journalist, lec-
turer or poet, attaining by his own efforts a knowledge of "the classics." This
is not right for Blake. For a great deal of the most notable intellectual energies of the eighteenth century lay outside of formal academic channelling.[29]

The particular non-academic intellectual tradition in which Thompson seeks to place Blake is a small but persistent Protestant sect, the
Muggletonians. Like the Quakers, the Muggletonians were antinomians:
that is, they believed in an "inner light" that enabled ordinary men and
women to find ultimate spiritual truth, without the mediation of any
externally defined moral law. Unlike the Quakers, Muggletonians
refused "submission to the rationalism and civilizing modes of the time,
with an accompanying upwards drift in the social status of their following,"[30] and maintained their plebeian character into the second half of
the eighteenth century.

Blake's supposed link with the Muggletonians derives from the fact
that a man with the same last name as Blake's mother (Hermitage), who
lived in the same London parish where the Blakes lived, wrote Muggletonian songs of praise. On this foundation Thompson erects the following hypothesis:

We could suppose that William Blake in his childhood was made familiar
with the structure of antinomian thought and the central images of *Genesis*
and *Revelation* in a Muggletonian notation; that he turned sharply away from
this in his teens, rejecting the know-all dogmatism of the sect, and its philis-
tinism towards all the arts (except divine songs); read widely and entered the
artistic world without restraint; took stock of works of the Enlightenment;
was led back toward his origins by reading Boehme and Swedenborg; and
then, in his early thirties (the years of the *Songs* and the *Marriage of Heaven*

and Hell) composed a symbolic world for himself in which the robust tradition of artisan and tradesman antinomianism reasserted itself, not as literal doctrines, but as a fund of imaginative possibilities and as intellectual footholds for an anti-Enlightenment stance.[31]

The critical affirmation in Blake's intelligent anti-intellectualism, Thompson says, was love. His antinomian heritage

enabled Blake to question and resist the simplicities of mechanical materialism and Lockean epistemology, in which the revolutionary impulse was to founder. For in shedding the prohibitives of the Moral Law, Blake held fast to the affirmative: Thou Shalt Love.[32]

And:

Hence Blake, however close he is to the Painites, will not dispense with "The Divine Image" and the "Everlasting Gospel." Just as with deism or atheism, he can agree with the analysis but still require, at the end of it, a utopian leap. . . . To create the New Jerusalem something must be brought in from outside the rationalist system, and that something could only be found in the non-rational image of Jesus, in the affirmatives of Mercy, Pity, Peace and Love.[33]

And last:

The busy perfectionists and benevolent rationalists of 1791–6 nearly all ended up, by the later 1800s, as disenchanted men. Human nature, they decided, had let them down and proved stubborn in resistance to enlightenment. But William Blake, by denying even in the *Songs of Experience* a supreme societal value to rationality, did not suffer from the same kind of disenchantment. His vision had been not into the rational government *of* man but into the liberation of an unrealized potential, an alternative nature, within man.[34]

The practice of love and solidarity by working people emerges as E. P. Thompson's great theme. The early nineteenth century experienced "the loss of any felt cohesion in the community, save that which the working people, in antagonism to their labour and their masters, built for themselves."[35] At the end of the nineteenth century, the "social sense" had been "brought near to extinction everywhere except in the centres of working-class life."[36] Thompson valued the working class no less than did Karl Marx. But in the end the working class mattered, not because it was destined to overthrow capitalism, but because it kept alive among Satanic Mills an ethic of mutuality that prefigured a better society.

Thompson perceived the *problem* as capitalism and imperialism, but the *answer* as mutual aid, plain duty to each other, building community, and creating a culture of solidarity within the shell of the old society. The special responsibility of anyone who wishes to carry on the work of Edward Thompson, it seems to me, is to seek in our own time, in whatever places we live and labor, to nurture the spirit of working-class solidarity.

8

Toward a Program for Publicly Financed Jobs

As a candidate, Bill Clinton ran on a program of "jobs." But the fundamental goal of President Clinton's administration is not to create jobs. It is to help firms based in the United States compete and make profits in the international market: as the President put it in his 1994 State of the Union address, "to take full advantage of the opportunities before us in the global economy."[1]

In their concern to become lean, mean, and internationally competitive, United States corporations are systematically cutting jobs, not creating them. Companies that since January 1, 1993, have announced the elimination of five thousand or more jobs include:

General Motors	69,650
Sears, Roebuck	50,000
I.B.M.	38,500
A.T. & T.	33,525
Boeing	31,000

Unpublished paper prepared for a Legal Services task force. Published in condensed form in *Social Policy* (Fall 1994). Used by permission.

GTE	27,975
Nynex	22,000
Phillip Morris	14,000
Procter & Gamble	13,000
Woolworth	13,000
Martin Marietta	12,060
Eastman Kodak	12,000
Xerox	11,200
McDonnell Douglas	10,966
Raytheon	10,624
Pacific Telesis	10,000
General Electric	9,825
Westinghouse	9,345
U S West	9,000
Pratt & Whitney	8,514
Scott Paper	8,300
Bristol-Myers Squibb	7,600
American Airlines	8,769
Hughes Missile Systems	6,000
RJR Nabisco	6,000
Phar-Mor	5,962
Du Pont	5,700
Texas Instruments	5,675
Lockheed	5,600[2]

An American Management Association survey concluded in September 1993, "There's no end in sight to the downsizing that is sweeping through corporate America."[3] As of mid-1994, this forecast appeared correct. The *AFL-CIO News* reported early in 1994 that "according to analysts at a Chicago job placement firm, 645 companies have announced layoffs of more than 600,000 workers for 1994; that amounts to more layoffs than for all the 1991 recession year."[4] In January 1994 announced staff cutbacks totaled 108,946, a record for a single month, and the total of 143,564 for the first two months of 1994 exceeded the record January–February totals the previous year.[5]

Downsizing is one of several cost-cutting alternatives to productive capital investment. The rate of profit on capital investments decreased from 10 to 15 percent in the early 1970s to 6.8 percent in 1993.[6] Profit-maximizing managers accordingly have turned to squeezing from factory labor an average of 3.8 percent more output per hour from 1990 to 1993;[7] investing (when they do invest) not in new plants in the United States but in replacement technology,[8] or overseas[9] or in high-tech industries that employ relatively few workers;[10] and . . . relentlessly and implacably consolidating and eliminating jobs.

Corporate downsizing is not a temporary fad, but a structural, long-term trend. "In each year of the 1980s, roughly 2 million full-time workers reported losing jobs because their employers either went out of business or laid them off for other reasons and had not recalled them over a year later." Thus, during the 1980s "roughly 20 million workers . . . were displaced" (i.e., "permanently terminated from one's job").[11]

The number of unemployed persons—a yardstick that should always be preferred to percentages[12]—is increasing. "In November 1991, when President Bush signed a bill extending jobless benefits, there were 1.3 million Americans officially designated as long-term unemployed, meaning they had been out of work for six months or longer. . . . [In January 1994] the number of long-term unemployed was 1.7 million."[13] Unofficial estimates of the total number of persons unemployed are staggering. Former Senator William Proxmire writes: "Current 6.8 percent unemployment idles nearly 10 million American workers. It discourages 1 million more from trying to find a job. It forces 3 million who want and need full-time employment to work part time (usually 15 to 20 hours a week)."[14]

And the number of those unemployed and underemployed still does not adequately measure the number of persons who are in poverty because of lack of good jobs. More than 9.4 million *working* Americans have incomes under the federal poverty guidelines, with the result that more than 30 million persons live in homes "where paychecks and poverty go hand in hand."[15] One in six workers earned poverty-level wages in 1992, up from one in eight in 1979; whereas in 1977 only 7.7 percent of working families with children had household incomes below the poverty level, in 1991 11.2 percent of these families were poor.[16]

The Problem: Jobless Recovery, Jobless Job Training, Jobless Welfare Reform . . . Jobless Everything

Clinton administration spokespersons candidly recognize the fact that economic recovery may reduce, not increase, the number of jobs.

"We used to think that jobs and the economy were the same thing," the United States Secretary of Labor, Robert B. Reich, said. "But we have learned in recent years that the paper economy and the people's economy are not always the same thing."

"There is now a much greater sensitivity," Mr. Reich said, "that the challenge of creating good jobs must be dealt with on its own terms" and not by relying on economic growth alone.[17]

The President himself has stated, "There is a great insecurity that productivity, for the first time, may be a job threat, not a job creator."[18]

But rather than condemn corporate downsizing with its deliberate job destruction, President Clinton and Secretary of Labor Reich offer job training as the answer to structural unemployment. This perspective is a snare and delusion.

In the first place, the training promoted by the Clinton administration encourages workers to disregard traditional job classifications. The result will be fewer jobs, because workers will be more able to do one another's work. The effect of this kind of training is to facilitate corporate downsizing, rather than to resist it.

In the second place, retraining for dislocated workers is self-evidently effective only when there are jobs at the end of the training. All too often there are not. For example, the *New York Times* reports that in Springfield, Missouri, the jobs that "hundreds of former Zenith workers have been training for [after the plant moved to Mexico] often pay much less than their former jobs, or simply do not exist."[19]

Secretary Reich assumes that there is "a surplus of high-skill jobs awaiting workers who undergo training."[20] But there isn't. One in five college graduates in the 1980s (as compared to one in ten in the 1970s) ended up working at a job that did not require a college degree. Employment projections for the 1990–2005 period indicate that "average annual openings in jobs requiring a degree will be fewer than the jobs available in the 1984–90 period."[21]

Reich the high-tech trainer is also Reich, advocate of labor-management cooperation. Companies that sponsor the joint labor-management formats favored by Secretary Reich are often the same companies who practice downsizing, and who do so the more savagely because the union has thrown away its weapons in advance.[22]

Clinton's Welfare Reform Will Increase the Number of Persons Seeking Jobs. As a candidate, President Clinton proposed to end "welfare as we know it" and specifically suggested that after two years of training, persons presently on welfare would be forced off welfare and into jobs. Public service jobs would be created for persons unable to find jobs in the private sector.

In office, however, the Clinton administration [even before approving federal "welfare reform" legislation in August 1996] approved a Wisconsin plan whereby in two experimental counties persons would be forced off welfare after two years, and denied public cash assistance for the next three years, whether or not there were jobs available. Mark Greenberg, author of an incisive critique of the Wisconsin "waiver" program, commented, "It is extraordinary to think that the federal government wants to run an experiment to test what will happen when poor families with children have nothing to live on," and the *New York Times* asked editorially: "What happens to parents who, through no fault of their own, can't find work. Where will they get cash to buy their children soap, clothes, bus fare—let alone an occasional book or movie ticket."[23]

The draft welfare reform bill of the Clinton administration likewise did not answer "the question of what comes next for families that, at the end of the program, could still not find work."[24] In March 1994 the drafters were still debating "the question of what happens to a welfare recipient who joins a yearlong work program but is still unable to find private employment when the program expires. Should that person be allowed to return to the welfare rolls, or should the family's benefits be reduced or even eliminated?"[25] The number of families now on welfare who will need jobs when federal "welfare reform" is implemented has been estimated at five million.[26]

Other Clinton Administration Programs Will Not Help and May Make the Problem Worse. Other Clinton initiatives will also reduce jobs rather than create them. Defense cuts are expected to eliminate 1.8 to 2 million jobs. Vice President Gore's plan to streamline the federal bureaucracy proposes to cut 252,000 federal jobs.[27] President Clinton's economic advisers forecast that his health plan, had it been adopted, would have cost about 600,000 jobs.[28] However desirable each of these initiatives may be for other reasons, all will aggravate, not reduce, the problem of unemployment.

But Aren't There More Jobs Now? The Contingent Reserve Army

Clinton administration officials appear to refute the foregoing analysis when they state, for example, that 1.6 million new private sector jobs were created in 1993, that 245,000 net new jobs a month were added to the economy in January through May 1994, or that 3.8 million new jobs had been created under the Clinton Presidency as of July 1994.[29]

How can one explain the simultaneous occurrence of job loss caused by corporate downsizing and apparent job growth? The answer is like the answer to other Zen koans: the "jobs" that are being lost are not the same as the "jobs" that are increasing in number. An estimated 21 million workers in the United States now have part-time jobs; they "are usually paid about 60 per cent of the hourly scale of full-timers and often don't get any fringe benefits."[30] If leased, contracted, and temporary employees are added, this "contingent" work force totals about 34 million, or one in every four workers.[31] The number of such contingent workers in the United States is expected to double by the year 2000, and the percentage of contingent workers in the total labor force is growing about twice as fast as is the labor force as a whole.[32] Similarly, the Canadian Labour Congress reports that 42 percent of that country's workers are now part-time, seasonal, or temporary.[33]

A summary of the Clinton welfare reform proposal presented to television viewers in my Legal Services office by a public service think tank indicates that the "jobs" former welfare recipients will be required to accept can be from 15 to 35 hours a week, as each of the fifty states may determine. Correspondingly one wonders about the "jobs" that administration officials tell us have increased. Could it be, for example, that a federally subsidized task in the private economy, filled by a series of casual workers, is reported to the government as two or three new jobs?

Institutionally, the new contingent work force is channeled to employment by a plethora of new temporary employment agencies. One Youngstown-area job seeker reports:

> Every summer for the past five years I have come home to the Mahoning Valley to find work. My first and last stop was always the classified section. I've had bad jobs and I've had good, but each summer I found something through the paper, on my own. My experience this summer [of 1994], however, was different. The paper carried the usual restaurant help and lawn care ads, but virtually everything else—most factory, warehouse, and office

jobs that looked like they might hold the potential for more than minimum wage—were advertised through a temporary service. For the first time I could not find a decent job on my own. I was forced to go through an agency.[34]

Ninety percent of all United States companies now use temporary agencies.[35] As of only a few years ago, the typical temp was a young female, and her typical place of employment was an office. Temporary help was just that, an efficient way to cover for an ill or vacationing employee on a short-term basis. But due to downsizing, and the subsequent need for a readily available and disposable work force, companies are finding that temporary agencies offer a convenient way to do much if not all of their hiring. And temp help is no longer necessarily short-term. More and more positions previously held by a permanent employee are now given to a series of temps on a permanent basis. In the words of a manager's guide to temp services, "The cost of temporary help is *always* lower than the transaction costs or hidden costs associated with putting a permanent employee on the payroll."[36]

In the Mahoning Valley, all six temporary employment agencies report that business is booming. The placement officer of a local business college says, "I encourage each and every one of our graduates to go to a temp agency."[37] Each agency named manufacturing firms as the source for most of its recent business. A representative of Cancor Services, in the area for thirty-three years, estimates that 75 percent of recent placements have been in manufacturing settings and only a quarter in office positions. In the mid-1980s the numbers were reversed.[38]

Steve Burnett points out the result of this new practice for what is left of union labor in a place like Youngstown. Area employers such as Easco Aluminum, a medium-size aluminum processor, respect the rights of their older unionized workers but hire all new employees through an agency.[39] In Burnett's words:

> Thus, especially during peak months, groups of permanent unionized employees work alongside groups of temporary workers. These people earn as little as half the wage of the unionized employee, enjoy no benefits, and have no job security past the next day. The unionized employee sees the constant influx of temporary workers and is thus constantly reminded of the tenuousness of his/her own position. The temp sees the union members with their solid wages and job security and is inspired to keep in mind the "possibility of full time employment" always vaguely promised by the company.

The temp's only hope of becoming a union member is to impress the foreman, Burnett argues.

In this way, unions become less a right than a benefit. It is up to the employer who is allowed to stay and who is not. The union is thus associated with the company rather than with the work force. On the shop floor, the dichotomy is between new temporary worker and older unionized worker, not between worker and foreman. The union is a reward bestowed upon the hard-working, loyal employee by the employer. It is a symbol of employer's power instead of a source of worker empowerment.[40]

The Youngstown Area as a Microcosm

A salutary aspect of Legal Services work is that most of us operate out of local offices. Necessarily we must deal with unemployment, not just as a national problem, but as a local catastrophe with names and faces. In this spirit I offer a few words about the unemployment problem in the microcosm of the Mahoning Valley (Mahoning and Trumbull Counties, Ohio).

According to the labor force estimates of the Ohio Bureau of Employment Services for May 1994, unemployment in Mahoning and Trumbull Counties was:

	Labor Force	Employment	Unemployment
Mahoning County	123,100	113,500	9,700
Youngstown	37,100	32,100	5,100
Trumbull County	113,700	105,900	7,800
Warren	23,100	20,700	2,400

Thus about 17,500 persons are unemployed in Mahoning and Trumbull Counties.

The private sector does not have plans to employ any significant part of the unemployed. A survey of employment prospects at Mahoning Valley firms showed that 10 percent planned to add workers in the first quarter of 1994 and 10 percent planned to reduce staff.[41] The vice president of economic development for the Youngstown Warren Regional Chamber of Commerce forecasts that in 1994 the expansion of existing firms and arrival of new firms will create the same number of jobs (1,900) that were lost through major closings and cutbacks in 1993.[42] A joint plan of the Niles, Warren, and Youngstown Chambers of Commerce projects 2,500 new and retained jobs over the next four years.[43] Even if we assume that all 2,500 jobs are created rather than retained, and that the plan will be completely successful, it would solve less than 15 percent of the Valley's unemployment problem.[44]

Accordingly, the jobs problem in the Mahoning Valley is that 15,000 persons (17,500 – 2,500) have no jobs and no prospect of obtaining jobs from the private sector. This is the local figure corresponding to the approximately 10 million persons unemployed nationally.

Summary So Far. So far, we have defined the problem: 10 million unemployed persons nationally, and 15,000 unemployed persons locally, whom the private sector has no plans to employ. Additionally, we have determined that the Clinton administration is likely to be of little help.

Therefore, we shall have to do the job ourselves, as grassroots activists. This does *not* mean that all the money for what we do must come from poor and working people. On the contrary, while self-help initiatives are important, in themselves they cannot possibly provide enough capital to wipe out unemployment. We shall need federal money, but *we* must design the strategies for getting the money, and *we* must decide how to use it once it is in our hands.

In the remainder of this essay I discuss strategies for beginning to build the kind of movement and program required to solve the problem of jobs. They are: cutting defense spending and using the money to create jobs; Felix Rohatyn's notion of raising money *without* cutting defense spending, and using it for the same purpose; and drawing on our own Legal Services program as a model that can powerfully counteract the ideological obstacles to a publicly financed jobs program.

The Clinton Administration Does Not Intend Further Cuts in Defense Spending

Since the beginning of World War II—a period of more than a half century—the United States has been a permanent war economy. The private economy experienced cyclical peaks and valleys, but prosperity was always underwritten by huge public spending on so-called defense.

With the end of the Cold War in the late 1980s, many voices called for dramatic reduction in military spending while rolling over the same amount of public money into domestic projects, such as rebuilding roads, bridges, and homes. This was the project of a "peace dividend."

The peace dividend was and is the obvious and best answer to the problem of unemployment. Jesse Jackson observes:

> For the country, the first priority should be to expand investments vital to our future.
>
> Children must be given a healthy start. We must provide them with the best primary and secondary education possible. We need to make college affordable for all who qualify. We should join every other industrial nation in providing apprenticeship training for those who don't go to college.
>
> Our cities are a disgrace that can no longer be ignored. Investments in fast trains and other mass transit are central to a prosperous economy. By fulfilling the president's campaign promise to rebuild America's infrastructure, we can help areas hurt by defense cuts and put people back to work.[45]

Where would the money come from to rebuild America? the Reverend Jackson asks, and answers:

> It would make sense to start with where the money is. The Pentagon still consumes more than half of all discretionary spending. This year we will spend about $274 billion on defense, more than the average Cold War budget. The Russians—with the next biggest military budget in the world—will spend less than $40 billion.[46]

The Youngstown National Priorities Program has spelled out what deeper cuts in military spending could mean in our community. Youngstown businesses and residents paid $59 million for the military in 1992 and will pay an estimated $260.2 million during the next five years. Meantime, Youngstown receives $28 million less today than it did in 1980 for revenue sharing, community development block grants, job training, and anti-poverty.

	Federal aid in 1980	Federal aid in 1993
Revenue Sharing	$4 million	$0
Community Development Block Grants	$11 million	$5.5 million
Job Training	$21 million	$1.5 million
Anti-Poverty	$259,650	$145,687[47]

The Congressional Research Service has estimated what it would mean for Youngstown and other local communities if $3 billion in military spending was shifted to such activities as State and local education, highway and street construction, and construction of sewer facilities. After deducting for the *loss* of jobs that would be caused by cutting $3 billion from defense-related activity, the CRS estimates the *net* addition to employment in the private and public sector as a result of the shift of $3 billion from defense to State and local government-related activities to be 18,762 jobs.[48]

But the Clinton administration is not pursuing the peace dividend. In his first year in office, President Clinton *reduced* federal public investment in such programs as education and training, rebuilding infrastructure, and children's welfare, below its level under President George Bush.[49] The Clinton proposal to provide national service jobs for 250,000 young people was scaled back to a program of only 25,000 jobs; Clinton's modest proposal for retraining and apprenticeship programs was slashed by 70 percent; his original proposal of $80 billion over four years for an array of infrastructure projects was reduced to $20 billion, mostly for traditional outlays such as road repair; and of the $16.3 billion "stimulus package" designed to respond to the crisis in Los Angeles and other inner cities, only 3 percent remained when the deficit bill was enacted.[50]

The President put what might be described as the last nail in the coffin of the peace dividend in his State of the Union speech on January 25, 1994. Although the words were little noted in media commentary, the President said—with emphasis, and to applause from both sides of the aisle—that there would be no further cuts in "defense" spending.

> This year, many people urged us to cut our defense spending further to pay for other government programs. I said no. The budget I sent to Congress draws the line against further defense cuts.[51]

Even the *New York Times* editorialized that "the Administration refused to reduce Pentagon programs enough, despite the end of the cold war. . . . Unless Mr. Clinton finds the courage to trim defense, he will be forced to shortchange domestic investment for years to come."[52] The Clinton administration is spending $2.8 billion more on the military in 1994 than was spent in 1993, more than Richard Nixon spent two decades ago, and more than the rest of the world combined.[53]

I believe that we should never omit from our presentations about jobs the simple theme that a solution to jobless recovery is available: cut defense spending, and spend the same money on public works and public service jobs. At the same time, however, prudence suggests that we should also explore other strategies.

Toward a Program for Publicly Financed Jobs

How to Pay for It. Investment banker Felix Rohatyn believes that our economy "has forgotten how to create jobs." In a luncheon conversation with columnist Hobart Rowen, Rohatyn recognized that business corporations are cutting their payrolls mercilessly. According to Rowen, Rohatyn "has come to the conclusion that it is government's responsibility to step into the jobs breach because private institutions alone can't handle the problem. But he would shun, or at least downplay, the role of retraining and education, the standard nostrum dragged out by bureaucrats at the first sign of growing unemployment. Retraining for what? he asks."[54]

Specifically, Rohatyn proposes a ten-year, $250 billion public works program, financed outside of the regular budget, which could create one million jobs a year. He described it as follows in a speech at the Kennedy School of Government at Harvard:

[A] large-scale public works program should be undertaken, federally financed and supplementing state and local programs. A $250 billion ten-year program would be a fraction of what is needed to bring this country's infrastructure to satisfactory condition and should be considered as a minimum first step; it could create about 1 million jobs annually and could serve as one component of a defense conversion effort. High speed rail; mass transit; airport construction and many others would be a more effective use of defense contractors capabilities than building redundant Seawolf submarines. The use of some military bases, which are presently scheduled to be closed, for CCC-type programs to train inner-city youngsters, would be another benefit. The financing for such a program could be separated from the federal budget, with special issues of infrastructure bonds, secured by modest increases in gasoline taxes or other recurrent revenues. These would pay off the bonds in 30–40 years and could make them eligible for investment by private and public pension funds, which now amount to about $3 trillion and will probably double in size over the next ten years.[55]

This proposal, coming from the man who rescued the finances of New York City, takes the financing issue out of discussions of the jobs problem. If the peace dividend cannot be financed by diverting general tax revenues presently spent on defense to the creation of public works and public service jobs, it can be financed a different way.[56]

What Should Be Done with the Money. One respect in which Rohatyn's proposal is, as he says, only "a minimum first step," is that it seems to be limited to construction and related physical work. He appears to have in mind the seven thousand public works projects proposed by the nation's mayors after the Los Angeles riots, which, according to Holly Sklar, would create a million jobs a year.

> [A]fter the Los Angeles riots the U.S. Conference of Mayors identified in their report, *Ready to Go,* over 7,000 public works projects on hold for lack of funds. As reported by the Milton S. Eisenhower Foundation (created in part by members and staff of Johnson's Advisory Commission on Civil Disorders, known as the Kerner Commission) in *Investing in Children and Youth, Reconstructing Our Cities,* these projects would generate over 400,000 construction jobs and, calculating the multiplier effect of such investment, over one million jobs within a year.[57]

The number of jobs that Rohatyn's program could generate would increase if service as well as construction jobs were included. A Congressional survey of federal counter-cyclical spending programs since 1962 found that "public service" jobs are in some respects preferable to "public works" jobs.

> Public service programs are thought to have certain advantages over public works programs. In addition to the quicker startup typical of public service jobs programs, relatively more of their expenditures go toward wages, which means that more jobs can be created per dollar of spending (i.e., "more bang for the buck"). Public service employment programs also tend to reach a broader spectrum of workers by employing relatively more low-skilled and unemployed workers than do public works programs.[58]

A campaign to create more publicly funded *service* jobs might grow naturally from efforts, such as that in Pittsburgh, to save existing social service safety nets.[59] It could provide a context for programs to fund tutoring for inner-city youth, like that proposed by Dawud Abdullah of the Youngstown Area Urban League. The AmeriCorps program of the Corporation for National and Community Service is a tiny ($153 million) step in this direction.

By creating one million jobs a year over a ten-year period, Rohatyn's program could put to work *all* ten million of those currently unemployed nationwide. It would do the same for the Mahoning Valley. The Youngstown-Warren Metropolitan Statistical Area contains about 0.2 percent of the population of the United States (500,000 of 250,000,000). 0.2 percent of the 10,000,000 jobs that would result from Rohatyn's program comes to 20,000 jobs, a figure slightly higher than existing unemployment in the Valley.

Mahoning Valley legislators have compiled an inventory of construction projects they desire to have funded by the state.[60] While a congress of citizens might well propose a quite different list, still these items are of interest:

YOUNGSTOWN JUSTICE CENTER. $2.5 million.

KENT TRUMBULL SCIENCE CENTER. $6.95 million.

CANFIELD FAIRGROUNDS GRANDSTAND. $1 million for renovation.

MAHONING COUNTY EXPERIMENTAL FARM. $2.2 million to keep the educational facility open. Ohio State University funding expected to dry up this year.

YOUNGSTOWN LIBRARY. $212,000 to build a connector atrium between the library and a proposed $2.8 million annex behind the Wick Avenue building.

AUSTINTOWN POLICE DEPARTMENT. $250,000 for communications center to accommodate emergency 911 service and to expand the Juvenile Services Bureau.

ART CENTER. $2.75 million for a Youngstown State University–sponsored National Center for the Study of American Art; $1 million in private funding has already been secured.

EDWARD W. POWERS AUDITORIUM. $169,000 to begin reconstructing emergency exit stairs and help replace aging air-conditioning system. Building dates back to 1931.

WEATHERSFIELD. $750,000 to construct a water tower to relieve a lack of water pressure that lawmakers say poses a fire hazard.

NILES. $20,000 and $34,000, respectively, for the city to purchase a van to transport handicapped senior citizens, and to renovate tennis courts and restrooms at Waddell Park.

GIRARD. $890,000 for city hall renovations for handicapped access and $50,000 for renovations at Liberty Park.

STRUTHERS. $200,000 to stabilize Mahoning River bank to alleviate flooding problems dating back to 1985.

CAMPBELL. $47,000 to repair leaky city hall roof, which has begun to cause structural damage.

A special irony should be noted. The "Youngstown Justice Center" listed is one of at least four prisons under construction or on the drawing boards in our Valley. Building prisons is the only public works program that here, as elsewhere in the United States, is being vigorously pursued. In 1993 the Senate, after appropriating just $100 million for a school-to-work program, authorized the expenditure of $3 billion to finance the construction of ten new regional prisons, and another $3 billion for boot camps and other programs for young offenders.[61] The Eisenhower Foundation comments:

> One exception to the federal government's domestic disinvestment was prison building . . . costing $37 billion at the federal and state level over the decade [of the 1980s]. Because the inmates were disproportionately young, in many ways prison building became the American youth policy of choice over the mid 1980s and early 1990s. . . . Given that the population in American prisons more than doubled over the decade, while funding for housing for the poor was cut, incredibly, by more than 80 percent from 1978 to 1991 [after accounting for inflation], and given that the cost of a new prison cell in New York State was about the average cost of a new home purchased in the U.S. nationally, in some ways prison building became the American low-income housing policy of the 1980s.[62]

A less ambiguous strategy was proposed in Illinois. There, in spring 1993, the Illinois General Assembly considered a measure that would have reserved 5 percent of the jobs that flow from State of Illinois public works contracts and subcontracts for welfare recipients and those financially eligible for aid. With fifty thousand new jobs being created under the governor's public works budget, enactment of the bill would have resulted in twenty-five hundred well-paying jobs in trades that have been "historically inaccessible to the poor, to women, and to racial minorities." The State would have realized a saving of over $10 million in cash assistance payments alone. But the measure was scuttled due to opposition from both contractors and construction unions.[63]

Conclusion

An adequate response to long-term, structural unemployment seems to require a synthesis of *analytic and strategic radicalism* with *tactical flexibility and creativity*. The particular points suggested thus far include:

1. The private sector will not employ most of the unemployed.
2. Clinton administration programs will not help significantly and may make the problem worse.
3. In particular, the Clinton administration's welfare reform will increase the number of persons seeking work.
4. The Clinton administration does not intend further cuts in defense spending.
5. Felix Rohatyn has proposed a plan to create ten million jobs (and thus wipe out unemployment in the United States) without cutting defense spending or raising income taxes, but at this point the only public enterprise that has broad public support—apart from military spending—is building prisons.

A fundamental obstacle in moving toward a program of government-guaranteed investment in jobs is ideological. It is the conviction, or alleged conviction, of many Americans that anything funded by the government must be centralized, bureaucratic, and wasteful. Thus in the health care debate of 1993–94, one oft-expressed opinion was that a single-payer plan is obviously best, but unacceptable to the American people because of its "socialist" appearance.

Legal Services workers are in an opportune position to rebut this nonsense. We know, from experience, that money can be appropriated by Congress, allocated to offices in the field on the basis of objective criteria, administered in communities by more-or-less democratic boards of directors, monitored to assure compliance with national statutes and regulations, and spent to provide a needed service free of charge. If legal services can be provided in this way, so might health services. So, indeed, might be provided a variety of goods and services now offered to the community by hierarchically organized, publicly unaccountable, profit-maximizing corporations.

Helen Merrell and Robert Lynd in the early 1920s.

Alice Niles and Staughton Lynd in the summer of 1950, about a month after they first met.

The log cabin in which the Lynds lived at the Macedonia Cooperative Community in Georgia.

Staughton's student Alice Walker on the porch of her home in Eatonton, Georgia, with Barbara and Lee Lynd.

Staughton Lynd at the Freedom School convention, Meridian, Mississippi, summer 1964.

David Dellinger, Staughton Lynd, and Robert Moses march to the steps of the Capitol to declare peace with the people of Vietnam, August 1965.

Staughton Lynd in North Vietnam, December 1965–January 1966. Herbert Aptheker of the American Communist Party, who invited Staughton, in background.

Staughton Lynd speaking to National Guardsmen at rally shortly after the assassination of Dr. Martin Luther King, Chicago, April 1968.

Writers' Workshop in Gary, Indiana, where Staughton and Alice Lynd recorded many of the interviews later published in their book *Rank and File.*

The Rank and File Team (RAFT). John Barbero is sixth from the left. Ed Mann is at right. Staughton, Alice, and Martha Lynd are at left.

The interviews with three women in *Rank and File* were made into the movie *Union Maids*. Shown at the movie's premiere in Dayton, Ohio, Spring 1976, are Alice Lynd, union maids Vicki Starr ("Stella Nowicki" in the book) and Sylvia Woods, and filmmakers Jim Klein and Julia Reichert.

Attorney Staughton Lynd at Northeast Ohio Legal Services, Youngstown.

Lee, Martha, and Staughton Lynd.

Demonstration in the lobby of U.S. Steel's Pittsburgh headquarters, November 30, 1979

Photo by Rob Engelhart.

Staughton Lynd with Rosa Solis and members of her family, Barrio Riguero, Managua, Nicaragua, 1985.

1988 Reunion of Students for a Democratic Society (SDS). Alice and Staughton Lynd are standing in the middle of the back row. Carl Oglesby is to the left of A

Staughton Lynd, Father Uriel Molina, and Alice Lynd, in Managua, Nicaragua, 1990.

Staughton Lynd speaking at Labor Day rally of Workers' Solidarity Club, Youngstown.

PART **III**

Solidarity Unionism

9 The Possibility of Radicalism in the Early 1930s: The Case of Steel

Historians associated with the Left have found industrial union organizing in the 1930s puzzling. We have declined to join in the liberal celebration of its results, pointing to "the partial integration of company and union bureaucracies" in administering CIO contracts (C. Wright Mills)[1] and the CIO's "definition of union organizing that made it impossible . . . to concentrate on political organization that challenged capitalist institutions" (Mark Naison).[2] We have dwelt on happenings which for liberal historians are merely preliminary or transitory, such as the mass strikes in Toledo, Minneapolis, and San Francisco in 1934,[3] the improvisation from below of local industrial unions and rank-and-file action committees,[4] or the many indications of interest in a Labor Party or Farmer-Labor Party.[5]

This essay brings together material some of which was initially presented in "Guerrilla History in Gary," *Liberation* (October 1969); "What Happened to the Militancy of the CIO? Some Rank-and-File Views," a paper read at the American Historical Association meeting (December 1970); and "Personal Histories of the Early CIO," *Radical America* (May–June 1971). The essay appeared in *Radical America* (November–December 1972). Reprinted by permission.

But this is not enough. In the 1890s, the drive for industrial unionism under Eugene Debs led to a confrontation with a Democratic President, recognition of the need for independent labor politics, and the
formation of the Socialist Party. There was a step-by-step transition, first
to economic organization on a broader scale, then to political organization, very much in the manner outlined in *The Communist Manifesto*. This
did not happen in the 1930s (or at first glance appears not to have happened), and we must ask why. I believe that there is a connection
between the difficulty experienced by New Left historians in answering
this question, and the difficulty experienced by New Left working-class
organizers. If we had a better idea how radicals should have acted while
unions were being organized, we might better understand how they
should act today.

This essay considers the case of steel.

When the National Recovery Administration (NRA) came into existence in June 1933, the feeble AFL union in the steel industry—the
Amalgamated Association of Iron, Steel, and Tin Workers—reported
fewer than five thousand members. By the time of the Amalgamated's
annual convention in April 1934 its membership had increased to a
number variously estimated at fifty thousand to two hundred thousand.[6]
Harvey O'Connor, then a labor reporter living in Pittsburgh, remembers
it this way:

> Along came the New Deal, and then came the NRA, and the effect was elec-
> tric all up and down those valleys. The mills began reopening somewhat, and
> the steelworkers read in the newspapers about this NRA Section 7A that
> guaranteed you the right to organize. All over the steel country union locals
> sprang up spontaneously. Not by virtue of the Amalgamated Association;
> they couldn't have cared less. But these locals sprang up at Duquesne,
> Homestead, and Braddock. You name the mill town and there was a local
> there, carrying a name like the "Blue Eagle" or the "New Deal" local. These
> people had never had any experience in unionism. All they knew was that,
> by golly, the time had come when they could organize and the Government
> guaranteed them the right to organize![7]

This remarkable organizing drive was carried out by rank-and-file steelworkers with little help from full-time organizers of the Amalgamated.
At the U.S. Steel Edgar Thomson Works in Braddock, for example, an

Amalgamated organizer provided membership cards, and volunteer organizers from the mill returned in a week with five hundred of them signed.[8] Walter Galenson wrongly terms the Amalgamated organizing campaign of 1933 "unsuccessful."[9] As a matter of fact, the Amalgamated drive between June 1933 and April 1934 signed up about the same number of steelworkers that the Steel Workers Organizing Committee (SWOC), using two hundred full-time organizers, signed up in a comparable period of time, from June 1936 to March 1937.

The self-organization of the rank and file was at least as effective as the top-down professionalism of the CIO, which had far greater resources at its disposal. Galenson himself quotes Lee Pressman as saying that as of the spring of 1937 SWOC could not have won a National Labor Relations Board (NLRB) election "on the basis of our own membership or the results of the organizing campaign to date" in either Big or Little Steel.[10] The best testimony to this effect comes from the man who collected SWOC dues, David J. McDonald, later president of the United Steelworkers of America. "Contrary to union propaganda—some of which I helped to write—the steelworkers did not fall all over themselves to sign a pledge card with the SWOC," McDonald states in his autobiography.

> What we hoped would be a torrent turned out, instead, to be a trickle. Under our arrangement with the Amalgamated, it would charter a local union as soon as we had enough men signed up in a plant to form the nucleus of an effective organization. Oftentimes the locals consisted of the half-dozen men daring enough to sign the charter application. When these skeleton requests straggled in, we assigned impressively high lodge numbers in the hope that outsiders would think we had that many locals. Only Murray and I knew how thin the tally was, although Lewis would insist on the truth whenever I visited Washington, then would shake his head in wonderment at the lack of progress.[11]

According to McDonald, SWOC membership was a "shaky 82,000" at the end of 1936, and when U.S. Steel signed a contract in March 1937 SWOC had signed up only 7 percent of its employees.

McDonald offers a hatful of explanations for steelworkers' absence of response to SWOC: a 50-year tradition of non-unionism, the fear of losing jobs, and the fact that some workers "were as apprehensive about dictatorship from an international union as they were of arm-twisting from their employer." Only the last of these makes any sense when one recalls that just three years earlier the same steelworkers had enthusiastically organized local unions. The question presents itself: Why did the organizing drive of 1933–34, strongly supported by the rank and file, fail to achieve the union recognition accomplished by the SWOC drive of 1936–37 with weaker rank-and-file backing?

The rank and file sought to achieve union recognition through the Amalgamated in 1933, 1934, and 1935. The 1933 effort was the by-product of a spontaneous strike by coal miners in the "captive mines" of western Pennsylvania owned by the steel companies.[12] These miners joined the United Mine Workers (UMW) after the passage of the National Industrial Recovery Act (NIRA) just as steelworkers were joining the Amalgamated. Late in July, miners at the H. C. Frick mines owned by U.S. Steel struck for recognition of their new UMW locals and the right to elect checkweighmen. UMW president John L. Lewis agreed with President Roosevelt that the men would go back to work and that their grievances would be referred to a special government board. The men refused, their representatives voting 123 to 4 against returning to work for the present. A 44-year-old Irish immigrant named Martin Ryan emerged as their spokesman. By the end of September 1933 seventy thousand miners were on strike.

Then the strike spread to steelworkers. On September 26 miners marched into Clairton, Pennsylvania, where the largest coke plant in the United States made fuel for U.S. Steel mills throughout the Monongahela Valley. Hundreds of coal miners and an estimated half of the workforce at Clairton "circled the gates of the Clairton steel and by-products works in an endless march, day and night." Meanwhile at Weirton, West Virginia, fifty miles away, twelve thousand more steelworkers went out demanding recognition of their new lodges of the Amalgamated. The national president of the Amalgamated, Michael Tighe, declared both the Clairton and the Weirton strikes "outlaw."

John L. Lewis and Philip Murray, leaders of the UMW and future leaders of the SWOC and CIO, persisted in attempting to get the miners back to work. O'Connor describes the part played by Murray:

> Vice President Murray of the United Mine Workers summoned the rank-and-file leaders to Pittsburgh. "Today," he warned them, "you are fighting the coal companies; but tonight, if you remain on strike, you will be fighting the Government of the United States. Today you are conducting a strike;

tonight you will be conducting a rebellion. Today we may say we are going to defy the greatest friend we've ever had in the history of this nation (President Roosevelt). But I tell you, friends, he can turn against you as strong as he's been for you. He can call out the Army and Navy."

Martin Ryan, leader of the striking miners, answered Murray: "Why do you ask 75,000 men to go back to work instead of telling one man (President Moses of the Frick Company) to sign the contract?" The rank-and-file delegates returned to Fayette County and called twenty thousand miners together to consider Murray's back-to-work order. The miners voted to continue their strike until the Frick Company signed a contract.

Finally, on October 30, 1933, Lewis and Murray signed a contract on behalf of Frick's miners with none other than Myron Taylor, the same man who would sign a contract with them in March 1937 concerning steelworkers employed by U.S. Steel. Historians differ as to how much this contract achieved for the miners, but whatever it achieved was thanks to the pressure from below of men who struck without authorization and who refused Lewis's and Murray's orders to go back to work. The striking steelworkers achieved nothing. At Weirton, the strikers returned to work with a promise that an election for union representation would be held on December 15. The election turned out to be an election for company-union representatives. In the words of O'Connor: "The grand tactical plan for the united front of steel's mine and mill workers, conceived on the spur of the moment by local rank-and-file leaders in both industries, had been scuttled by a stronger united front, that of Washington, the union leaders, and the steel companies."

The leaders of the Weirton strike, Billy Long and Mel Moore, now joined with other presidents of new Amalgamated lodges to launch a second effort to unionize steel. On March 25, 1934, 257 delegates from fifty of the newly formed lodges met in Pittsburgh to plan strategy for the Amalgamated convention the following month.[13] First among equals was Clarence Irwin, president of the Amalgamated lodge at the Brier Hill works of Youngstown Sheet and Tube, Youngstown, Ohio, and of the Sixth District of the Amalgamated, which included Youngstown, Canton-Masillon-Mansfield, and Cleveland.

Irwin is dead now, but Robert R. R. Brooks of Yale University interviewed him in the late 1930s, and further information can be gleaned from a scrapbook in the possession of his wife. Irwin was the antithesis of the demagogue usually placed at the head of crowds by historians.

Forty-two years old in 1934, he had worked at steel mills in the Mahoning Valley since 1906 and had belonged to the Amalgamated since 1910.
He was chairman of the strike committee in his mill during the 1919
steel strike. He was married and had three children. He was a skilled
roller and had voted Democratic all his life, except in 1932, when he
voted for Norman Thomas.

Irwin describes the other rank-and-file leaders as very much like
himself:

> Almost all of us were middle-aged family men, well paid, and of Anglo-Saxon
> origin. Most of us were far better off than the average steelworker and did-
> n't have much to gain from taking part in the movement except a certain
> amount of personal prestige. Almost all of us could have done better for our-
> selves if we had stuck with the companies and not bothered about the rest of
> the men. But for various reasons we didn't.

We were sure, he goes on,

> that the mass of steelworkers wanted industrial unionism, and so did we. But
> it wasn't clear to us until we set out to get it that we would have to fight not
> only the companies but our own international officers and even the Gov-
> ernment. The process of learning was slow and painful, and a lot of us
> dropped by the way.[14]

Contrary to John L. Lewis's subsequent allegations, "All these fellows
had a union inheritance of one kind or another." Long's father had
been a militant in the Amalgamated Association of Iron, Steel, and Tin
Workers, and Earl Forbeck's father had been a Knight of Labor.[15] Moreover, the rank-and-file presidents of the new lodges developed the practice of calling together lodge representatives in district conferences.
These district meetings had no constitutional standing. They had been
used years before for the purpose of informal discussion of common
organizational problems, and in the course of time had died out. Now
they were revived, at first with the sanction of the national officers, who
attended and spoke at many of the conferences. In time more or less
permanent officers were chosen for each district.[16]

The March 25 gathering brought together delegates from lodges all
over the country. A general strike was in progress in Toledo; the very day

the steelworkers met a national strike in auto had been averted; general strikes in Minneapolis and San Francisco were little more than a month in the future. Steelworkers, too, turned to the strike weapon. Delegates decided to take back to their lodges, for proposed presentation to the Amalgamated convention on April 17, the following strategy: All lodges should request recognition from management at the same time; if recognition is denied, a strike date should be set; the Auto Workers, the Mine Workers, and the Railroad Workers should be approached with the idea that these three groups, together with steelworkers, should act together if necessary to gain collective bargaining for any one group. What was envisioned was a national strike—and if need be, a national general strike—for union recognition.

The Amalgamated convention adopted this strategy. The convention also adopted resolutions to the effect that the Committee of Ten rank-and-file leaders which had drawn up the strike program should be included in all negotiations arising from it, that no lodge should sign an agreement until all could sign at once, that full-time Amalgamated organizers should be elected rather than appointed, and that the national union should no longer have the power to declare locally initiated strikes unauthorized.[17] The new members of the union appeared to have taken it over from the incumbent leadership.

The rank-and-file leaders understandably found this historic opportunity frightening. "Most of us were capable local or district leaders," Irwin recalls, "but we had very little idea what the national picture was like. . . . We were completely unprepared for a strike. We had no funds, no central leadership, no national organization except the Amalgamated's officers, and they were opposed to strike action." Irwin and his co-workers began to look for help.

They turned first to a group of four intellectuals: Heber Blankenhorn, Harold Ruttenberg, Harvey O'Connor, and Stephen Raushenbush. Blankenhorn had edited the Interchurch World Commission report on the 1919 steel strike. He was close to John L. Lewis and Senator Robert Wagner, and later helped to create the LaFollette Civil Liberties Committee. Ruttenberg was a student at the University of Pittsburgh doing research on the steel industry, O'Connor a labor journalist who during this period published *Mellon's Millions,* and Raushenbush an investigator for the Nye Committee.

Appearing at the 1934 Amalgamated convention with a typewriter, Ruttenberg and O'Connor assisted the rank-and-file delegates in "putting together the resolutions they wanted the way they wanted them and getting things going."[18] Thereafter they functioned as a behind-the-scenes leadership group cryptically known (because Blankenhorn in particular was concerned lest his association with the rank and file become public) as "The Big Four." "Although they had no money and had to work on the q.t.," remembers Irwin, they "gave us something like national leadership. In a way, they were a forerunner of the Steel Workers Organizing Committee."

I believe it is fair to characterize the Big Four (with the partial exception of O'Connor) as Social Democratic intellectuals, in the sense that they had a tendency to rely on publicity and government intervention rather than on the collective power of the workers, and to avoid cooperation with the Communist Party.

But four men with typewriters and connections could not really be the functional equivalent of a SWOC. According to the decisions of the Amalgamated convention, all lodges were to ask for recognition on May 21, and if recognition was refused a strike date was to be set for the middle of June. On May 7 Irwin wrote to Ruttenberg asking if Ruttenberg could get him the addresses of the men who had led the 1933 strike in the captive mines, and of the leaders of the Steel and Metal Workers Industrial Union (SMWIU).

The SMWIU was one of the dual unions sponsored by the Communist Party during the so-called Third Period of international Communist strategy.[19] It was founded in August 1932 and claimed a membership of ten thousand to fifteen thousand. The SMWIU justly denounced the NRA. It called on working people to rely on their own power rather than on Presidential promises, government boards, and so-called labor leaders. By May 1934 it had led local strikes, for instance in Warren, Ohio; East Chicago, Indiana; and Ambridge, Pennsylvania. These had often ended in violent defeat.

After the Warren strike, which resulted in the discharge of many strikers and the departure from the city of an entire community of Finnish steelworkers, the local Communist Party "was convinced of the impossibility to organize independent labor unions in opposition to the old AFL"[20] and sought to persuade William Z. Foster and other national Party leaders to abandon dual unionism in steel. The rank-and-file movement in the Amalgamated offered the SMWIU an opportunity to overcome its isolation from the mass of steelworkers. And the SMWIU offered the rank-and-file movement, which had lost its own local strikes at Clairton and Weirton, the national structure and resources so badly needed if a national steel strike were to become a reality.

The difficulty was that in May 1934 the SMWIU had not abandoned the dual unionist line. SMWIU literature urged its members and sympathizers simultaneously to "take the lead in the organization of united committees" to implement the decisions of the convention and to prepare for a strike—and "to build the SMWIU into a powerful organization in their mill."[21] This was a tactic that looked two ways at once. It never has worked; it never will work; and it did not work in the spring of 1934.

Irwin and Ruttenberg arranged a meeting with the SMWIU leadership for May 20. They urged all members of the Committee of Ten and of the Big Four to be there so as "to determine [in Irwin's words] a central plan of attack, set up a central office with a secretary, determine a uniform method of demanding recognition, find out what help the SMWIU could give us, and discover what the national officers were going to do to bust up our plans." Three days before the meeting, Irwin wrote to Ruttenberg that the only alliance which should be sought with the SMWIU was cooperation on the conduct of the strike. That cooperation should be basically through local joint committees that would work in unison even against the orders of the Amalgamated national office, Irwin believed.[22]

Tragically, Irwin was unable to attend the meeting because his wife was seriously ill. He was represented by Ruttenberg, subsequently research director for SWOC, co-author with Clinton Golden of *The Dynamics of Industrial Democracy,* and steel-company executive. Blankenhorn was apparently not at the meeting, but his taped reminiscences make it clear that he was part of the discussion.

> There were telegrams to me, and as a matter of fact I was in Pittsburgh when that meeting was held, and talked with Pat Cush [one of the SMWIU leaders] and the SMWIU boys, and tried to get the brass tacks on it, and in front of them I advised the rank-and-filers: "If these boys won't walk out of here and keep their mouths shut instead of making public pronouncements, you have no choice but simply to say that they came and saw you but you had nothing to do with them. If they have any paid members to deliver, let them deliver them quietly."

Blankenhorn and Ruttenberg persuaded the rank-and-file leaders not to work with the SMWIU.[23]

Yet responsibility for the failure of the May 20 meeting falls equally on the SMWIU. In contrast to Irwin's proposals for cooperation visible at a local level but behind-the-scenes nationally, "They [the SMWIU] wanted the rank-and-file group and the SMWIU to issue a joint statement from this meeting, a joint call for a joint convention to focus public attention on the issues, and local organizations to issue joint statements and call joint mass meetings. It was perfectly clear that they wanted to formalize the whole affair, and to be sure that the SMWIU was in the limelight as an organization. As soon as they had withdrawn (from the meeting), the rank-and-file group voted thumbs down on the whole proposition. We'd have been smeared immediately as Communists if we had accepted."

These words from Irwin's interview with Brooks are perhaps more those of Ruttenberg than those of Irwin, who was not at the meeting.[24] But the fact remains that the SMWIU approach counterposed a Left dual union not only to the national structure of the Amalgamated but also to the independent local lodges that the steelworkers had built for themselves. Then and later the rank and filers showed themselves quite able to stand up to Red-baiting, and had the SMWIU not placed so much emphasis on its own organization, I believe united action might have been possible. The fact that (to look ahead) the rank-and-file leaders and the former SMWIU leaders easily established a working relationship the next November, after the SMWIU finally abandoned dual unionism, is strong evidence to this effect.

In May and June, after the failure of the May 20 meeting, things went from bad to worse. On May 22 five of the rank-and-file leaders went to the national office of the Amalgamated and demanded $100,000 from the union to help run the strike, the use of the union's printing press, and rooms in the union's building for strike headquarters. They were contemptuously refused. Irwin then proposed to the rest of the Committee of Ten "that we would take over the running of the strike altogether, call upon the lodges for money (my lodge had already put up a hundred dollars), and select a secretary from our own group." Only two other members of the Committee supported this leap into the unknown. "I was never so disgusted in my life," Irwin remembers.

At this point the four intellectuals stepped back onto center stage, urging the rank and filers to take their campaign to Washington, where they could attract national press attention and hopefully embarrass the President into intervening on their behalf. Desperate, the rank-and-file leaders agreed. They got the publicity, but killed the possibility of a successful strike. As one of them commented after it was all over, "They spent most of their time in Washington in a futile attempt to 'see Roosevelt.' This running around after Roosevelt created the impression among the steelworkers that a strike was unnecessary, that Roosevelt would step in at the last minute and help them."[25] The precious weeks that might have been used for local strike preparation were squandered, as the national secretary of the SMWIU rightly observed.[26] In the First District of the Amalgamated near Pittsburgh, where more than a thousand steelworkers gathered to support the strike movement on May 27, a meeting a month later, after the strike had collapsed, attracted only fifty-three.[27]

It now appears that in directing the rank-and-file leaders to Washington, Ruttenberg, Blankenhorn, and Raushenbush acted as agents for John L. Lewis. In interviews conducted by the Pennsylvania State Oral History Project in 1968 and 1969, Ruttenberg stated that a steel strike "did not come off because of the intervention of John Lewis and Philip Murray, who counseled against it for fear that an abortive strike would thwart their contemplated plans to move in and really organize the steel industry." The UMW had no contact with rank-and-file steelworkers until spring of 1934, Ruttenberg went on. "At that point they began to exercise influence through myself, and they assigned John Brophy from the UMW to be the liaison man. . . . Blankenhorn was the one who kept telling John Lewis and Philip Murray that they should get control of the rank-and-file committee and use them as a basis for their unionizing work. . . . And so the counsel that I got from Blankenhorn, which I in turn passed on to the steelworkers, was not to strike now because John Lewis was going to come here and have a big organizing campaign that would stand a chance of being successful." Raushenbush, for his part, "said that we have to show strength among the rank-and-file steelworkers in order to encourage John Lewis to take the risk. . . . And so you had the whole threatened strike and activity to influence John Lewis to come in as well as to influence Congress to pass a National Labor Relations Act."

Through Ruttenberg, Blankenhorn, and Raushenbush the rank-and-file leaders were brought before Senator Wagner, the sponsor of that act, who "gave them a lecture about not engaging in a premature strike and gave them a lecture that John Lewis was 'going to come in here and do this job right and don't you fellows mess it up.'"[28] Putting this evidence together with Lewis's role during the coal and steel strikes of 1933, the hypothesis suggests itself that if Lewis succeeded in 1937 where the rank and file failed in 1934, it was partly because Lewis did his best to make sure that industrial unionism would come to steel only if he controlled it.

Meantime the steel companies had disdainfully refused to recognize the Amalgamated lodges, and the strike date approached. The companies placed large orders for the purchase of arms and, at least in Gary, arranged to house strikebreakers in the mills should a strike occur.[29] As tension mounted, the Amalgamated leadership called a special convention in Pittsburgh for mid-June, the time at which, according to the mandate of the convention, a strike date was to be set if recognition had been refused. Reporters, government mediators, delegates, and a confused group of rank-and-file leaders assembled for the convention.

The strategy of President Roosevelt, of the Amalgamated leadership, and apparently of Ruttenberg and associates and of John L. Lewis, was to have William Green, AFL president, come to the convention and propose yet another government labor board as an alternative to a walkout. Ruttenberg reports on the mood of labor officials and government representatives at the convention: "Social revolution was on hand. Bill Green was their only hope." Clinton Golden was one of three people who met Green at the train and "coached him as to what to say. He said it."[30] The strike was called off. As the news came over the radio in the bars in Braddock, steelworkers tore up their union cards.[31] Ruttenberg also tells us that Irwin got dead drunk and lost the confidence of many delegates, a situation for which Ruttenberg appears to feel he had no responsibility.

There was to be one more effort at unionization by the rank and file, in 1935. During the summer of 1934, Irwin "tried to keep the rank-and-file movement together by supporting the rank-and-file slate of officers that was running in the Amalgamated's fall referendum." In the October 1934 convention of the AFL a resolution was passed urging the AFL executive council to take action in organizing steel. Meanwhile the government board created in June to head off the threatened walkout had done nothing. "Production was picking up," Irwin remembers, "and the steelworkers were stirring again."

More important than any of these events was the fact that—six months too late—the Communist Party abandoned dual unionism. SMWIU chapters dissolved so that their members could join the Amalgamated. According to Irwin, in November 1934 rank and filers and

SMWIU finally got together. Money became available for steelworkers to travel to conferences,[32] and a series of meetings began to heat up the idea of a national strike again. But whereas in the spring of 1934 the Communist Party wanted a steel strike only if the SMWIU could publicly help lead it, in the spring of 1935 the Communist Party wanted a strike only if expulsion from the Amalgamated could be avoided. Remaining part of the organization they had previously scorned became the primary goal of Party members in steel.

These forces came to a head at a meeting of four hundred rank-and-file steelworkers and one hundred rank-and-file miners in Pittsburgh February 3, 1935. Our four intellectual friends played their by-now-familiar role. Ruttenberg wrote to Irwin before the conference warning him of Communist influence, and O'Connor wrote to Irwin after the conference, acting as an intermediary for an unnamed third party in Washington, to urge the rank and file not to act by itself but to consider cooperation with a committee of the AFL executive council to organize steel.[33]

Lewis, too, played a predictable part. Just as Michael Tighe, president of the Amalgamated, threatened to expel from the Amalgamated any steelworkers who attended the February 3 meeting, so Pat Fagan, district director of the UMW, issued similar warnings to dissident miners. After the meeting both men carried out their threats, Fagan stating: "You can't be a member of the UMW and be affiliated with a Red group. That meeting was absolutely Red. Those fellows don't believe in authority or law and order or anything else. They're an asinine crowd of parlor bolshevists!"[34] This is the same Pat Fagan who in April 1936 led a delegation of the Pennsylvania AFL state convention to the national Amalgamated convention nearby, and proposed that the Amalgamated accept $500,000 from John L. Lewis and work with him to organize steel.

Ruttenberg, Tighe, and Fagan notwithstanding, the gathering of rank-and-file steelworkers and miners took place as scheduled. It was an extraordinary occasion. Mr. and Mrs. Irwin, Bill Spang, Mel Moore, Roy Hallas, Cecil Allen, and Lew Morris represented the rank-and-file leadership in the Amalgamated. Present on behalf of the rank-and-file miners was Martin Ryan, leader of the 1933 strike in the captive mines. The lesson of 1933–34 had been learned. A resolution was adopted that "the steelworkers know from their own experience that they can secure no help in their struggles from the labor boards or other Federal agencies, but that their only defense . . . is the power of their own organization, exercised by the calling of strikes if and when necessary."

This time, organization was not left to afterthought. A committee was named to open headquarters in Pittsburgh. Local finance committees were to be pressed into service at once. Most remarkable, in view of subsequent history, were speeches by Martin Ryan and (according to the press) numerous other speakers equally denouncing Michael Tighe and John L. Lewis. The one had betrayed the steelworkers and the other had betrayed the miners, according to the prevailing sentiment at this meeting. "Lewis and Tighe have crucified you for years," declared Ryan, "and will continue to do so until you demand and get their resignation and removal."[35]

Why did these rank-and-file steelworkers and miners fail to press on toward a national organizing campaign? This time around, the Amalgamated leadership were not going to permit their national convention to be captured and used to legitimize a rebel movement. Within days of the February 3 meeting Tighe expelled the lodges represented there. What was critical was the rank and file's response to the expulsions. Here the Communist Party, with its newfound concern for labor unity, and John L. Lewis, jockeying in Washington for passage of the Wagner Act and Guffey Act, again had determining influence.

The expelled lodges represented the overwhelming majority of the Amalgamated membership.[36] They might simply have declared that they were the Amalgamated, or reorganized as federal unions directly affiliated with the AFL, and in either case proceeded to organize steel. It appears that many members of the rank-and-file movement—the rank and file of the rank and file, so to speak—wanted to do this. O'Connor reports that at the February 3 meeting "some difficulty was experienced in stemming the apparently powerful sentiment of many delegates . . . that an independent union should be started now."[37]

An independent union was exactly what the Communist Party had been trying to build the year before, but now no longer desired. The resources which might have financed an organizing drive were used instead to campaign for reinstatement in the Amalgamated. The National Organizing Committee set up by the February 3 meeting distributed fifty thousand leaflets in April calling for "Unity For All Steel Workers." "Our program," the leaflet stated, "is the restoration of unity in the union and the organization of the unorganized steel workers."[38] Lawsuits followed to compel Tighe to reinstate the expelled lodges. These were successful, and on August 1, 1935, it was announced that unity had been restored. In the meantime, however, another strike threat had swelled up and been dissipated, with the result that the Amalgamated, to which the expellees won reinstatement in mid-summer 1935, had by then been reduced to the empty shell it was two years before.

In dissipating the strike threat of 1935, Lewis's misleadership augmented the misleadership of the Communist Party. Early in March a meeting to implement the February 3 decisions was held in Weirton, attended by steelworkers from Illinois, Indiana, Ohio, Pennsylvania, and West Virginia. Conference speeches, the Federated Press reported, showed great sentiment for a strike in steel. Clarence Irwin declared that "the kind of union we are going to have will not depend on courts, but on organization and the picket line."

Later that month William Spang, president of District 1 of the Amalgamated, tied a steel strike to a strike of four hundred thousand soft-coal miners threatened for April 1. "Rank-and-file committees of steel workers and coal miners have been meeting to set up plans to strike April 1. If the United Mine Workers of America does not get a new contract, both unions will join in united strike action," Spang said. He added: "We have decided to disregard all arbitration boards. . . . There is only one way we can win our demands—by an industry-wide strike. That's just what we're building up for now."[39]

But there was no coal strike April 1. On the eve of the miners' walkout, John L. Lewis postponed action till June 16 "out of consideration of the President of the United States and the National Industrial Recovery Board."[40] On Memorial Day 1935, just two years before the Memorial Day strike sacred in CIO annals, the steel strike almost happened from below.

What at first seemed to the Federated Press "the long-expected clash in the steel industry" began in Canton, Ohio. "Rank-and-file leaders led it; not one union-paid official had a directing hand in it," Ruttenberg wrote. The strike began at the Berger Manufacturing Company, a wholly owned subsidiary of Republic Steel employing four hundred fifty persons. An AFL federal union at the plant struck to enforce a government finding that the company was refusing to bargain collectively. Two hundred fifty thugs attacked the strikers with tear gas and lead pipes. One striker, Charles Minor, had the side of his face torn off, and fourteen persons in all were hospitalized. As so often in those years, this picket-line brutality triggered a general strike. Within twenty-four hours four thousand Republic Steel employees in the Canton area had walked out in protest, led by Lewis Morris, one of the Committee of Ten of 1934.

Two other members of the Committee from nearby communities, Mel Moore from Weirton and Clarence Irwin from Youngstown, apparently tried to call a national strike. On May 29 they asked "all Republic mills to send delegates to Canton to formulate plans for spreading the strike nationally." On May 31 "The Central Strike Committee [in Canton] issued a call for support from all lodges of the Amalgamated." The only response, or parallel action, which has come to light was by Bill Spang's Fort Dukane Lodge in Duquesne, Pennsylvania. There a strike at the U.S. Steel mill was called for 3 P.M., May 31, but short-circuited when Spang and other officers of the lodge were arrested for parading without a permit. Meanwhile in Canton an attempt to spread the strike to neighboring Masillon collapsed when non-union employees flooded the Amalgamated lodge meeting and voted not to go out. County and city police broke up the Canton picket lines, and the men started back to the mills.[41]

Once more the rank and file looked to the UMW. "Following Spang's release, the Fort Dukane Lodge decided at a mass meeting to issue a call to other lodges to 'strike all Carnegie Steel Company [U.S. Steel] mills June 16,' the date set by the United Mine Workers of America for its strike in the bituminous fields." But Lewis postponed this strike too. On June 14 he promised President Roosevelt not to strike till June 30 so that Congress could act on the Guffey bill. On July 1 the coal strike was postponed for a third time, and on July 29 for a fourth. Meanwhile on July 5 the Wagner Act became law, and late in August the Guffey Act, setting up NRA-like machinery for the coal industry, finally made it through both houses of Congress.[42]

Two philosophies of industrial union organization expressed themselves in these events. Lewis's approach stressed governmental intervention so as to make possible a "responsible" unionism which would avoid strikes. As Len DeCaux summarized it at the time, Lewis and a number of other union officials told the Senate Education and Labor Committee considering the Wagner Act: "Allow the workers to organize, establish strong governmental machinery for dealing with labor questions, and industrial peace will result." DeCaux noted that some employers favored this approach, and that the expectation in Washington of international war made its adoption more likely.[43]

The second approach relied on strike action, and insisted on writing the right to strike into any labor-management contract that resulted. No one can prove that a national steel strike in 1934 or 1935 would have been any more successful than the defeated national steel strike of 1919. Yet it was Blankenhorn's retrospective judgment that "without even the pretense of Amalgamated leadership" the rank-and-file movement would have involved seventy-five thousand to one hundred fifty thousand steelworkers in a national strike; and O'Connor argued at the time that any strike in steel was likely to reach a climax within a few weeks, because the government could not allow it to continue "in view of the restiveness of workers in the auto industry and other industries."[44]

Seeking proof in the experience of SWOC, one can argue that the Little Steel strike of 1937 shows what would have happened had steelworkers struck in 1934 or 1935. One can also argue that SWOC would never have gotten its contract with U.S. Steel in March 1937 had auto workers for General Motors not been willing to strike and occupy their plants just previously.

The trade-union line of the Communist Party after mid-1934 dovetailed neatly with the approach of John L. Lewis. The Party maneuvered brilliantly within the skeleton Amalgamated to have Lewis offer $500,000 to the Amalgamated for a steel drive, with the understanding that the money would be administered by Lewis, and to have the Amalgamated accept that offer.[45] When SWOC was formed, the Party made available sixty organizers.[46] The rank-and-file dream passed into the hands of Lewis in the bastardized form of an organizing committee none of whose national or regional officers were steelworkers, an organizing committee so centralized that it paid even local phone bills from a national office, an organizing committee, in DeCaux's words, "as totalitarian as any big business."[47]

It could have been otherwise. The critical weakness of the rank and file was its inability to organize on a national scale. Had the Communist Party thrown its organizers, its connections, and its access to media, lawyers, and money in a different direction, there might have come about an industrial unionism not only more militant and more internally democratic, but also more independent politically.

Coming about as it did, industrial unionism in steel lacked any thrust toward independent political action. By 1935 the rank-and-file leaders had lost confidence in the "National Run Around" and, to a considerable degree, in President Roosevelt. Experience daily brought more and more workers to the position that "we are through forever with Washington" (Mel Moore); "we're through with weak-kneed appeals to government boards" (Clarence Irwin).[48] They were prepared to defy the national government through strike action and to seek parallel strike action from workers in other industries. In effect they wanted to duplicate Toledo, Minneapolis, and San Francisco on a national scale. And despite Roosevelt's genius in letting local Democrats take the onus of state action against striking workers, a national steel strike might have brought steelworkers into collision with Roosevelt just as a national rail strike had brought Debs into collision with Cleveland in 1894.

Even as it was, there were indications of support among steelworkers for independent political action. In 1935, along with many other unions in that extraordinary year, the Fort Dukane and South Chicago lodges of the Amalgamated passed resolutions for (in the South Chicago wording) an "anti-capitalist Labor Party."[49] In 1936, Clarence Irwin stated that "I am in favor of a real Labor Party with no connection with any of the existing parties." The last clipping in his scrapbook describes a 1939 regional SWOC meeting which passed a motion stating: "Whereas labor's experience in the political field has been anything but satisfactory, therefore be it resolved that our ultimate goal be the fostering of a third party called the Labor Party."[50] Given the existence of this sentiment, at the very least it should have been possible to organize local labor parties which, after the death of Roosevelt in 1945, could have joined to form a deeply rooted national third party.

But industrial unionism came to steel and to the CIO generally under the auspices of a longtime Republican who at no point favored a third party, and of a national radical party which, by mid-1936, was uncritically supporting the incumbent Democratic President. The new industrial unions lost little time espousing the political company unionism of the two-party system.

10 The Genesis of the Idea of a Community Right to Industrial Property in Youngstown and Pittsburgh, 1977–1987

The right to private ownership and management of property is a basic value—some would say, *the* basic value—of American society. So pervasive, so deeply rooted, and so systematically internalized is this value that it has often been considered a "consensus" norm.

The right to private ownership and management of property draws support from the United States Constitution. Nowhere expressly set forth in the Constitution, the right to private property is reinforced by several passages and especially by the Fifth Amendment. A view of the Constitution that shields private property from community intervention has been more or less blatantly enforced by the courts for the past two hundred years.[1]

Between 1977 and 1987, in the industrial heartland communities of Youngstown, Ohio, and Pittsburgh, Pennsylvania, consensus support for the right to private ownership and management of property eroded. The traumatic collapse of the steel industries in those communities, with the social distress that followed, led to the appearance of new ideas.[2]

Originally published in 74 *Journal of American History* (3) (December 1987), pp. 926–58. Reprinted by permission.

Local residents began to articulate and explore the ideas that private decisions with catastrophic social consequences are really public decisions, that some kind of community property right arises from the long-standing relation between a company and a community, and that the power of eminent domain (the power of government to take private property for a public purpose without the owner's consent) should be used to acquire industrial facilities when corporations no longer wish to operate them. As a result, media stereotypes about the inherently conservative views of blue-collar workers, as well as historiographical chestnuts about the inevitable absence of socialism in the United States, seem a good deal less compelling.

The entire experience suggests some thoughts about how community ideas of constitutional rights may change. First, economic hardship makes people open to new ideas. It does not guarantee the emergence of any particular new ideas, and I do not deny that the presence of John Barbero, Ed Mann, Charley McCollester, Mike Stout, and for that matter, Staughton Lynd, helped shape the ideas that were brought forward. But we would not have gotten anywhere had the mills not first been shut down.

Second, ideas are likely to be judged on the basis of results. Corporate ideology has been significantly discredited in the Mahoning and Monongahela valleys. But radical alternatives have yet to take firm hold because we have yet to produce a successful worker- or community-owned steel mill.

Third, building a mass movement against plant shutdowns is a little like pouring water through a sieve. Plants are closed one by one. At each facility, there is a typical life cycle of protest: first, overflow public meetings and a brief season of unfocused militancy; later, an ebbing of group support as each displaced worker concludes that the plant will probably not reopen and begins to devise a private strategy for survival. When the next plant closes, the movement arising from the first shutdown is gone, and everyone starts all over again. The dissipation of protest energy was if anything more significant in Pittsburgh than in Youngstown, for in Pittsburgh the shutdown process stretched over a longer period of time, and in Pittsburgh the steel companies—learning from Youngstown—tended to close their mills department by department, to avoid displacing thousands of workers at once.

Fourth, obstacles that hinder the formation of any radical mass movement in the Western world also affected the movements in

Youngstown and Pittsburgh. The transition from capitalism to socialism presents problems that did not exist in the transition from feudalism to capitalism. In late medieval Europe, a discontented serf, a Protestant artisan, an experimental scientist, or an enterprising moneylender could do small-scale, piecemeal things to begin to build a new society within the old. He could run away to a free city, print the Bible in the vernacular, drop stones from a leaning tower, or organize a corporation—all actions requiring few persons and modest amounts of capital, actions possible within the interstices of a decentralized feudal society. The twentieth-century variant of the process, in Third World countries, also permits revolutionary protagonists in guerrilla enclaves, like Yenan in China or the Sierra Maestra in Cuba, to build small-scale alternative societies, initiating land reform, health clinics, and literacy. But how can people take such meaningful small steps, begin such revolutionary reforms, in an interdependent society like that of the United States? A localized strategy runs into what might be called the problems of "socialism in one steel mill": the effort to do something qualitatively new, requiring tens of millions of dollars, in a hostile environment. However, when the commanding heights of the economy are still in the hands of profit-making corporations, attempts to use the national state are likely to encounter the frustrations we in Youngstown experienced in seeking grants and loan guarantees from the Carter administration. It is true today, as it was when Werner Sombart wrote his famous essay, that *es gibt kein Sozialismus* (there is no socialism) in the United States. But if *Sozialismus* means not just the existence of a political party that calls itself socialist, but the existence of a socialist society, then *es gibt auch kein Sozialismus* (there is also no socialism) in England, France, Germany, Italy, or Japan.[3]

The breakthrough achieved in Youngstown and Pittsburgh is partial but significant. The idea of unrestricted corporate ownership of industrial property is not dead in these communities, nor has a new consensus in support of worker or community ownership formed. Thus in 1985, toward the end of the decade considered, the Youngstown-Warren area participated in "Saturn mania," the effort to attract General Motors' new Saturn plant. The community offered GM a sizable development package, organized a one-hundred-car caravan to GM headquarters to deliver two hundred thousand letters from residents and school children, and bought billboard and television space in Detroit. Yet at roughly the same time Patrick Ungaro, the mayor of Youngstown, asked United States Steel to donate its former mill site to the city and, when U.S. Steel refused, threatened to use eminent domain to take it anyway.

> "We've done a lot for them," [the mayor] said of U.S. Steel's long presence in Youngstown and the Mahoning Valley. "A lot of people worked for them and now they're gone. Morally and philosophically I believe they should do something for the community."

A previously unthinkable community right to industrial property has been legitimized and can now be asserted; although by no means uncontested, it is no longer taboo.[4]

One might compare what has occurred to a successful laboratory experiment, the results of which have yet to be applied industrially, or on a large scale. What has been shown in the Youngstown and Pittsburgh laboratory is that ordinary middle Americans may endorse public acquisition of corporate property by legal compulsion.

One cannot dismiss the Youngstown-Pittsburgh experience on the ground that the communities are atypical. Youngstown and Pittsburgh are not noted for political radicalism. They are blue-collar towns historically dominated by the steel companies headquartered there: United States Steel Corporation and Jones & Laughlin Steel Corporation in Pittsburgh, Youngstown Sheet & Tube Company in Youngstown. Both are heavily populated by immigrants from eastern Europe. Those defining characteristics have opened as well as closed doors: in each community strains of working-class radicalism played a critical part, and in each the centrality of Catholicism made public opinion susceptible to new currents in the worldwide Roman Catholic Church. But on balance, it seems safe to say that any ideological novelty that emerged in Youngstown and Pittsburgh could readily take root anywhere in the United States.

The emergence and evolution of new ideas in Youngstown and Pittsburgh between 1977 and 1987 suggests a final point about how community ideas of constitutional rights undergo change. The ideas developed in Youngstown and Pittsburgh during that decade were not unique in American history. On the contrary, they are best understood as a variant of the artisan republicanism espoused in earlier epochs by Thomas Paine and the mechanics of the American Revolution, by the workingmen's parties of the 1820s and 1830s, by the local labor parties associated with the Knights of Labor in the 1880s, and by (less well known) local labor parties active between 1929 and 1936.[5] Such movements repeatedly set up economic enterprises, cooperatively organized and locally controlled, wherein rank-and-file working people could act out the possibility of an economic order different from the unrestricted corporate capitalism that has dominated American history. In 1935, for example, the Labor party administration of Berlin, New Hampshire, helped local dairy farmers organize a cooperative dairy and a Forest Products Marketing Association to sell pulpwood from their farms. In 1936, the Labor party candidate for mayor in New Bedford, Massachusetts, promised that if the owners of the city's closed textile mills refused to reopen them, "our idle mills will be taken over by the city and will be operated at cost by the city." Indeed, as young men, John Barbero and Ed Mann, Youngstown trade unionists and key actors in the genesis of the idea of a community right to industrial property, took part in the activity of the United Labor Party of Akron, Ohio. Between 1946 and the early 1950s the candidates of the Akron party advocated city ownership of the transportation system with "full managerial responsibility to be vested in the Transport Workers Union"; provision for adequate housing "under tenant cooperative management"; heavier taxes on absentee-owned corporations; and generally, "industrial democracy with Production for Use," through nationalization or local cooperatives.[6]

Thus the story about to be told is from one point of view a version of a many-times-told tale, in which working people seek relief from control of their lives by autocratic and heartless corporate decision makers. But events in Youngstown and Pittsburgh have added new elements to the drama: particularly a rationale for community intervention that blunts the force of stereotyped objections to public ownership and so opens up new space for creative worker and community initiatives.

Youngstown, 1977–1980

Overview: Three Shutdowns in Three Years. On Monday, September 19, 1977, the Lykes Corporation, conglomerate owner of the Youngstown Sheet & Tube Company, abruptly announced the immediate closing of most of the area's largest steel mill, the Campbell Works. The first group of permanently laid off workers left the mill for the last time that week. As they crossed the Mahoning River on the footbridge that led to the clock house, many threw into the river, as a gesture of protest, their hard hats and metatarsal shoes.[7]

September 19 proved to be only the beginning. In November 1977 Lykes announced an intention to merge with the LTV Corporation, conglomerate owner of Jones & Laughlin Steel. The merger was approved by the stockholders of the two corporations in December 1978. A few days later the merged company announced its intention to close the other mill owned by Lykes in the Mahoning Valley, the Brier Hill Works. Almost a year later, on November 27, 1979, the Board of Directors of U.S. Steel announced the closing of all its Youngstown-area facilities, the Ohio Works where the steel was made and the McDonald finishing mills.

Thus, in less than three years, all steelmaking in what had once been the second steelmaking city of the nation, next to Pittsburgh, came to an end. Approximately ten thousand steelmaking jobs were lost: five thousand at the Campbell Works, fifteen hundred at Brier Hill, and thirty-five hundred at the U.S. Steel mills. The ripple effect on other employment was dramatic. In the Youngstown-Warren metropolitan statistical area, a chain of communities running north and south along the Mahoning River, between 1976 and 1982 total employment fell an estimated 26.2 percent.[8]

Response to the shutdowns took the form of a campaign to reopen one or more of the mills under worker or community ownership. The effort was led by certain affected local unions, particularly two United Steelworkers of America (USWA) locals, Local 1462 at the Brier Hill Works, and Local 1330 at the Ohio Works of U.S. Steel, together with a coalition of church groups known as the Ecumenical Coalition of the Mahoning Valley. The campaign failed when the Economic Development Administration of the federal Department of Commerce refused to provide the grants and loan guarantees required to reopen the Campbell and Brier Hill works, and when, following U.S. Steel's refusal to negotiate with union and community representatives, the courts declined to require the company to offer its mills for sale.[9]

Employee ownership of a steel mill is not, in itself, a very radical idea. So long as the current owner of a piece of property is willing to sell it, the resulting transaction is legally commonplace, even if the prospect of workers owning the common stock of so large a facility as a steel mill has considerable novelty. The hundreds of employee-owned enterprises in the United States have no perceptible effect on the larger social scheme of things. At Weirton, West Virginia, in 1982, the conglomerate owner of a steel mill actually proposed that workers buy the mill to save the firm the costs of a plant shutdown, with associated pension and severance payouts.

A Wall Street investment firm accordingly organized an Employee Stock Ownership Plan. The Weirton Steel Corporation, the "employee-owned" company that resulted, has a board of directors dominated by outside corporate representatives and presents no threat whatever to the right to exclusive private ownership and management of property.[10]

The worker-community ownership proposed in Youngstown was more controversial, because the owners of each of the three mills were initially unwilling to sell. Eventually Lykes, the owner of the Campbell and Brier Hill mills, was induced to offer the mills for sale when Senators Edward Kennedy and Howard Metzenbaum threatened to hold up the merger of Lykes and LTV if it did not. U.S. Steel, however, remained intransigent. Chairman of the Board David Roderick refused to negotiate with the would-be worker-community owners because, he explained, "We are not interested . . . in creating subsidized competition for ourselves," or, as he testified on the witness stand in Youngstown, because

> it is our policy . . . to dispose of property that the United States Steel Corporation owns in the best interests of the corporation [and because] I believe very strongly in the right of private property, I believe very strongly in a competitive system, and I believe very strongly in opposing those things that would distort the competitive system.

Thus in Youngstown, unlike Weirton, the issue of whether a community has some inherent right to take industrial property from an unwilling current owner was squarely posed.[11]

"Why Don't We Buy the Damn Place?". The day Lykes announced that it would close most of its Campbell Works, area union leaders met to discuss what to do. One of the participants, Gerald Dickey, recording secretary of Local 1462 (the Brier Hill Works local union), suggested nationalization of the steel industry.

> That's all I could think of that first day. I put it, "I think it's coming anyway. Five, ten years down the road. Like the railroads: when you finally milk it to the point that you can't get any more, you give it to the government." I said, "Well hell, let's go get it now."

Dickey's proposal was brushed aside by the Steelworkers' district director. Instead the meeting drafted a petition to Washington along conventional lines.

SAVE THE MAHONING VALLEY
We Need Jobs, Not Welfare
We, the undersigned, petition the President . . . and the Congress to give
Immediate Relief to the American Steel Industry by Imposing Emergency
Import Quotas, Relaxing the E.P.A. Standards, and Allowing the Steel Indus-
try to EARN A FAIR PROFIT.

In three days more than one hundred thousand signatures were collected on this petition, which buses of steelworkers then took to Washington, without apparent result.[12]

Worker-community ownership was first suggested six days after the
shutdown announcement, at a meeting in the Campbell, Ohio, city
council chambers. A local attorney and member of the city board of education said, "Why don't we all put up five thousand bucks and buy the
damn place?" Dickey, who was present, seized on the idea. During suc-
ceeding weeks it was also endorsed and elaborated by the Ecumenical
Coalition and by John Barbero, another officer of Local 1462.[13]

The religious leaders who formed the Ecumenical Coalition were
convened on September 26 by James Malone, bishop of the Youngstown
Diocese of the Roman Catholic Church (and later president of the
National Conference of Catholic Bishops), and by John Burt, bishop of
the Episcopal Diocese of Ohio. A statement issued that day declared:

> As religious leaders we are committed to studying the moral dimensions
> of this problem. What is the responsibility of an industry to the citizens of the
> community in which it is located? What is the moral responsibility of man-
> agement to labor, and labor to management, and of both to the community?

Three days later another statement said:

> [We] have a serious moral concern about an economic system and the
> laws which regulate it that would allow and even necessitate good men ago-
> nizing over a decision directly affecting an entire community in the isolation
> and secrecy of a board room. We feel that the system is inadequate and there
> must be a re-definition of the relationship between a corporation or an
> industry and the community in which it transacts business.

A Steel Crisis Conference at the end of October authorized issuance of
a pastoral letter. That document, *A Religious Response to the Mahoning Valley Steel Crisis*, serves as a convenient benchmark of community attitudes
at an early stage of the struggle.[14]

The Youngstown pastoral letter sidestepped the question of *why* the Campbell Works were closed. But the letter was unambiguous in asserting that decisions like the closing of the Campbell Works have catastrophic social consequences and are therefore public, not private, decisions.

> Some maintain that this decision is a private, purely economic judgment which is the exclusive prerogative of the Lykes Corporation. We disagree. This decision is a matter of public concern since it profoundly affects the lives of so many people as well as the future of Youngstown and the Mahoning Valley.

And again:

> Economic institutions, although they have their own purposes and methods, still must serve the common good and are subject to moral judgment.

The letter proposed an alternative to ordinary corporate decision making: "We believe that industrial investment decisions ought to take into account the needs and desires of employees and the community at large. . . . Human beings and community life are higher values than corporate profits."[15]

It followed that, other things being equal, new investment should be made in existing facilities, with the object of retaining "basic steel and associated jobs in communities steelworkers live in."[16] The idea that for social reasons the steel industry should be modernized in the communities where it already had roots came to be known as "brownfield" development. It contrasted with the practice of moving on every few years to begin all over again in a new, "greenfield" site.

The brownfield idea meshed with the belief that when companies fail to make socially needed investments, the public should step in and do the job itself. The most articulate exponent of brownfield development in Youngstown was John Barbero, then vice-president of Local 1462. Almost a year before the closing of the Campbell Works, Barbero had written to the local paper that "steel communities, like steelworkers, must not be scrapped after they are used up." He later found the brownfield versus greenfield nomenclature in a speech by Stewart Udall, a former secretary of the interior. After the Campbell Works closed, Barbero wrote in the Local 1462 newspaper:

Our Union must provide leadership to the mayors of steel towns where
the steelworkers already are. . . . Our Union must not allow steelworkers to
become the gypsies of the next ten years similar to the miners of Appalachia.
And our steel communities must not be discarded like so many strip mines.[17]

Youngstown, in Barbero's view, was being treated like a "leper
colony." If the Youngstown area were to be struck by a tornado, he wrote,
the president of the United States and the governor of Ohio would vie
with each other to pledge rebuilding loans. (Niles, near Youngstown,
was in fact devastated by a tornado in 1985.) But there was no such
response to the man-made disaster in Youngstown, where company,
union, and government appeared to stand by "as eager undertakers
wishing to dispose of the plague-ridden bodies in a hurry." Barbero was
determined to break the silence. He told two interviewers what William
Saroyan had written about the response to the Turkish massacre of
Armenians. Saroyan "said that ever since that time you never hear an
Armenian speaking in a quiet voice." Barbero went on, "They're afraid
that if they're quiet, people will forget what happened to them. That's
how I feel about Youngstown. Every place we go we should shout,
'Youngstown!'"[18]

The idea of brownfield development won acceptance in Local 1462
and in the Youngstown movement for worker-community ownership. By
the spring of 1979, as Local 1462 was fighting to save its own mill, the
Brier Hill Works, the local was firmly committed to the brownfield perspective. A pamphlet produced by the local stated:

The steel industry must be modernized in traditional steelmaking areas.
Instead of "greenfield" plants, we need "brownfield" plants. Open hearths
and blooming mills must be replaced by Basic Oxygen Furnaces, electric furnaces, and continuous casters. A national steel policy must be developed that
would not only preserve the industry, but . . . also protect steel communities and steelworkers. Modernization is the answer, not abandonment.[19]

Youngstown advocates of brownfield development lacked any means
to compel steel companies, or the federal government, to invest in
brownfield modernization. There was some attempt to persuade steel
company decision makers that brownfield development was in their self-
interest. When U.S. Steel proposed to build a new supermill only ninety
miles from Youngstown in Conneaut, Ohio, Locals 1462 and 1330 joined

with Local 1397 (U.S. Steel Homestead Works) and environmentalists in a lawsuit seeking to stop the project, or at least to require more thorough consideration of alternative sites under provisions of the Environmental Protection Act. To all such arguments the companies responded that their legal duty to their stockholders was to maximize profits and that concern for workers and communities affected by company decisions took second place. As U.S. Steel chairman Roderick put it to Congressman Peter Kostmayer: "We're here to make money. You guys can't get that through your heads." The hope for brownfield development of the Campbell and Brier Hill mills under worker-community auspices died in March 1979 when the federal government denied the project financial support. Documents later brought to light by a local reporter suggest that, even under Democrat Jimmy Carter, the federal bureaucracies never seriously considered so radical a move.[20]

The failure of the campaign to reopen the Campbell and Brier Hill works left U.S. Steel the only company in the Mahoning Valley that, in the spring and summer of 1979, still ostensibly planned to make steel there.

"A Property Right Arises from a Long-established Relation between a Company and a Community". U.S. Steel's announcement in November 1979 that it would close all its Youngstown-area operations provoked the first assertions that the community had, not just a moral claim, but a legal right to the soon-to-be-closed mills.

Rank-and-file steelworkers under the leadership of the local (but not the national) union briefly occupied U.S. Steel's Pittsburgh headquarters and, later, the company's Youngstown administration building. News photographs showed the demonstrators carrying signs that said:

Save Our Valley
U.S. Steel Kills Communities
The Year of the Child; How About Ours?
U.S. Steel Says, 'Promises Are For Breaking'
I Gave My Life to USS; They Gave Me the Shaft
Profits Before People Again
Who's Next?
The Mahoning Valley Needs A Marshall Plan
From Steel City To Cobweb City
People First Profits Second

Save Youngstown! Save the Plant!
Keep Our Mills Open
Jobs Not Welfare
U.S. Steals Jobs! Family! and Life!
Steel Companies Kill Communities
Youngstown Ghosttown USA
U.S. Steel Adds 13,000 Hostages
Job Justice
Human Rights for Brier Hill
Is Hunger And Lost Jobs Progress?

Perhaps the best summary of the ideology of the Youngstown resistance in 1979–1980 was offered by Bob Vasquez, president of Local 1330, just before hundreds of workers followed him down the hill from the union hall to occupy the U.S. Steel administration building. "If U.S. Steel doesn't want to make steel in Youngstown," Vasquez said, "the people of Youngstown will make steel in Youngstown."[21]

To make steel in Youngstown in steel mills owned by U.S. Steel, however, the people of Youngstown needed title to the facilities. U.S. Steel would not voluntarily sell them the property, so they needed to find a legal way to take it. Such a theory of legal right evolved along two lines.

On December 21, 1979, less than a month after U.S. Steel's shutdown announcement, a lawsuit against U.S. Steel was filed in federal court. The suit was a joint effort by incumbent Republican Congressman Lyle Williams and the local unions at the U.S. Steel mills, assisted by Northeast Ohio Legal Services. Plaintiffs included the congressman, the U.S. Steel locals, the Brier Hill local (based in a plant just across the river from U.S. Steel's Ohio Works and so conceivably part of an integrated plan of redevelopment), the Lordstown local of the United Auto Workers (which claimed to be interested in a nearby source of steel for making automobiles), sixty-five individual U.S. Steel workers, and the Tri-State Conference on Steel, successor to the Ecumenical Coalition. I was lead counsel.

The theory of the lawsuit was suggested by my Legal Services colleague Jim Callen. The complaint alleged that U.S. Steel had promised to keep its Youngstown mills open if the mills could be made profitable; that workers relying on those promises had agreed to a variety of concessions; that the concessions made the mills profitable but that U.S. Steel, in breach of its promises, closed the mills anyway. The complaint rested on a *contract* theory. Its premise was that U.S. Steel, however absolute its otherwise unrestricted control over its own property, could limit its freedom to manage that property by entering into a contract. The suit expressed feelings deeply held by Youngstown-area workers: they had all their lives been required to live up to contractual commitments; now, when the employers were in trouble, workers wrote, "We want every cent of what we earned under our contract agreement by a life time of labor, toil, and sweat."[22]

A second and more radical theory laid claim to the U.S. Steel mills on the basis of a community *property* right. That theory was suggested by the judge in the federal lawsuit, Thomas D. Lambros. In January 1980 Judge Lambros set a trial date of March 17. A few weeks later U.S. Steel brazenly announced that it would close its Youngstown mills on March 11, six days before the plaintiffs' claim that the company was contractually committed to keep the mills open was to be tried. Plaintiffs accordingly sought an injunction directing U.S. Steel to keep its mills open. On February 28, 1980, counsel for the plaintiffs (former Attorney General Ramsey Clark and I) and the defendant argued the propriety of that unprecedented injunction before the judge.

At the beginning of the hearing, Judge Lambros unexpectedly spoke for about half an hour. He said in part:

> We are not talking now about a local bakery shop, grocery store, tool and die shop or a body shop in Youngstown that is planning to close and move out. . . .
>
> It's not just a steel company making steel. . . . Steel has become an institution in the Mahoning Valley. . . .
>
> Everything that has happened in the Mahoning Valley has been happening for many years because of steel. Schools have been built, roads have been built. Expansion that has taken place is because of steel. And to accommodate that industry lives and destinies of the inhabitants of that community were based and planned on the basis of that institution: Steel.

Up to that point Lambros had repeated the rationale of Youngstown exponents of brownfield development, stressing the social consequences of a shutdown decision. Then he broke new ground:

> But what has happened over the years between U.S. Steel, Youngstown and the inhabitants? Hasn't something come out of that relationship . . . [?]

. . . it seems to me that a property right has arisen from this lengthy, long-established relationship between United States Steel, the steel industry as an institution, the community in Youngstown, the people in Mahoning County and the Mahoning Valley in having given and devoted their lives to this industry. Perhaps not a property right to the extent that can be remedied by compelling U.S. Steel to remain in Youngstown. I think the law could not possibly recognize that type of an obligation. But I think the law can recognize the property right to the extent that U.S. Steel cannot leave that Mahoning Valley and the Youngstown area in a state of waste, that it cannot completely abandon its obligation to that community, because certain vested rights have arisen out of this long relationship and institution.

At the end of the day Judge Lambros granted the requested injunction, to remain in effect until the pending trial.[23]

After trial, however, Judge Lambros denied both the contract and the property claims. Dismissing the property claim that he himself had suggested, the judge said:

. . . the lives of 3500 workers and their families and the supporting Youngstown community cannot be dismissed as inconsequential. United States Steel should not be permitted to leave the Youngstown area devastated after drawing the life-blood of the community for so many years.

Unfortunately, the mechanism to reach this ideal settlement, to recognize this new property right, is not now in existence in the code of laws of our nation. . . . this Court is not a legislative body and cannot make laws where none exist. . . . this Court can determine no legal basis for the finding of a property right.[24]

The U.S. Steel struggle, like the struggle to save the Campbell and Brier Hill works, thus ended in defeat. At the few remaining steel facilities in the Mahoning Valley, LTV made sure that future concession agreements were in writing and were insulated against contract claims like those made in the U.S. Steel suit.[25] The idea of a community property right had been articulated, but it had also been found visionary, without apparent lodgment in existing law.[26]

Pittsburgh, 1981–1985

"The Eminent Domain Laws Can Be Used by Communities to Defend Themselves". The idea of eminent domain gave the movement against plant

shutdowns a strategy for defending itself, even for going on the offensive. One Pittsburgh organizer quoted the language of the United States Constitution, that a purpose of government is to "provide for the common defense and promote the general welfare." We believe, he wrote, that the eminent domain laws "can be used by communities to defend themselves; to legally seize abandoned industry for the common good." Eminent domain, declared another, "opens up the door to the political stage, for working people and their allies. . . . It allows them to stand squarely on center stage and become active participants, instead of passive bystanders."[27]

Eminent domain was proposed in Youngstown, but so late in the day that it was not possible to try to give the idea practical application. In the spring of 1980, as the struggle against U.S. Steel was winding down, Arthur Bray, a city planner, suggested that the city's power to condemn blighted inner-city land for urban renewal could also be used to acquire steel mills. Bray argued that if the present owner declined to operate a plant on the ground that the plant was technically obsolete, the community should not only take the plant, but take it at scrap value. The idea applied to the U.S. Steel situation, where Judge Lambros based his decision partly on "the obsolescence . . . of the Mahoning Valley plants."[28]

At almost the same time, the idea of using eminent domain to acquire industrial facilities abandoned by their owners was proposed in Pittsburgh.[29] Frank O'Brien, a former president of Local 1843, USWA, at the Jones & Laughlin mills in Pittsburgh, had also served in the Pennsylvania state legislature. There he noticed the frequent use of a provision in the Pennsylvania Municipal Authorities Act that permitted a city to form a development authority, which, by means of its eminent domain power, could acquire private property for such purposes as the construction of shopping centers. On reflection he realized that Jones & Laughlin had also used the eminent domain power to expand its Pittsburgh landholdings. O'Brien advocated using the eminent domain power to acquire steel mills and put them back in production.

O'Brien explained his ideas at a father-and-son communion breakfast at Saint Stephen's church in Hazelwood, a Pittsburgh neighborhood, in the spring of 1981. The Jones & Laughlin hot strip mill in Hazelwood had closed a few weeks before. Speaking to an audience that included the mayor of Pittsburgh, O'Brien described how the companies had used the eminent domain law for their own purposes. "In the

1950s J & L used it to evict people from their homes in Scotch Bottom at Hazelwood. They said they needed the land to expand, but when they had evicted the people and gotten the land they didn't expand. They just let the land sit there and stored raw materials on it." He was thinking, O'Brien continued, that "the law can be used in reverse."

> I said the Mayor had better start worrying now about the U.S. Steel mills, that when they built that plant in Conneaut they're going to shut down every plant up and down the river.
>
> He said, "Well, what would you do?" I told him: "You, and the County Commissioners, sit down and form an authority. We can run the plants ourselves."[30]

The spring of 1981 was a good time to bring forth the eminent domain scenario in Pittsburgh. During the 1970s, primary metals employment in the nine-county area including Pittsburgh had dropped by over 22 percent, with a loss of over twenty-five thousand jobs.[31] As O'Brien told his Hazelwood hearers, in 1981 U.S. Steel was still considering the proposed supermill at Conneaut, Ohio, which was intended to take over the production of semifinished steel from the company's Edgar Thomson Works in Braddock, Pennsylvania, and the production of structural steel from the Homestead Works. The closing of the Jones & Laughlin hot strip mill in Hazelwood was the first shutdown of an entire steel mill in the Pittsburgh area. Although the closing might have been dismissed as an isolated incident in other times, Pittsburgh steelworkers, with the example of the serial destruction of all steelmaking in Youngstown before them, were open to a more pessimistic forecast. In the event, pessimism was fully justified. Between 1980 and 1983, in Allegheny County alone, steel facilities closed by U.S. Steel terminated fifteen thousand workers. Year by year, as Pittsburgh's version of the Youngstown tragedy unfolded, those who prophesied hard times and urged new remedies to deal with them were listened to more and more attentively.

Eminent domain offered the movement against plant shutdowns a version of constitutional rhetoric as ancient and deeply rooted as the appeal to due process in defense of private property. Eminent domain is the power of government to take private property for a public purpose without the owner's consent.[32] No more than the right to private property is eminent domain expressly set forth in the United States Constitution, but it is implied to the same extent, and indeed by the same clause of the Fifth Amendment, which states: "nor shall private property be taken for public use, without just compensation." In subsequent Pittsburgh-area litigation the proponents of eminent domain invoked Hugo Grotius, who appears to have coined the term "eminent domain." They also pointed to the use of eminent domain to acquire land for public roads, mill sites, and railroad rights-of-way in the eighteenth and nineteenth centuries; to a recent decision of the Supreme Court of the United States, approving the use of eminent domain to transfer large landed estates in Hawaii to tenant farmers; and to Pennsylvania authority for the proposition that all private owners hold their property subject to the state's "reserved right" to reclaim it.[33]

In Youngstown and Pittsburgh, advocates of eminent domain have argued that *if* a private owner refuses to operate a socially needed enterprise, *then* the community may properly step in, acquire the facility, and ensure its continued operation under alternate management. That approach can be criticized as "lemon socialism," whereby the public acquires only what private enterprise has stripped of usefulness and is ready to scrap. However, a facility can often be viable on a low-profit or not-for-profit basis when private owners, demanding a 20 percent rate of return, wish to abandon it.[34] Moreover, it is doubtful whether middle American workers, who only a few years ago showered rivets on anti–Vietnam War demonstrators while building the U.S. Steel headquarters in Pittsburgh, would have supported the idea of public ownership in any other circumstances.[35] Workers in Youngstown and Pittsburgh, in my experience, are both scornful of management personnel as nonproducers (hence the widely expressed belief that the mill runs better on the midnight shift when there are few foremen around) and uncertain whether they could run the plant themselves. They will try to do so only if default by the owners makes a takeover by workers seem necessary to preserve their jobs.

The TriState Conference on Steel. The social composition of the coalition that formed to advocate use of eminent domain in Pittsburgh was much the same as that of its Youngstown predecessor, the Ecumenical Coalition of the Mahoning Valley. In Youngstown advocates of worker ownership and brownfield development had been steelworkers active at the local union level and clergy led by a Catholic bishop. The sources of support reflected characteristics of the local work force. Local unions, whose very existence was threatened by the shutdown of a particular mill, tended to be more iconoclastic than a national union with many constituencies and better prospects for survival. The Catholic Church in Youngstown and Pittsburgh, although far from exclusively working-class, was still closer to the cities' working-class ethnic neighborhoods than any Protestant church.[36]

In Pittsburgh, too, local-level trade unionists and Catholics came together to promote the idea of eminent domain. Working through an organization with the unlikely name of TriState Conference on Steel, they were a handful of persistent advocates whose influence grew as the steel industry crumbled.[37] The core group included Frank O'Brien; Ron Weisen, elected president of the historic Homestead Works local (USWA, Local 1397) in the spring of 1979, and later a candidate for district director and national president of the union; Monsignor Charles Owen Rice, ordained in 1934 and still vigorously active as a labor priest in the 1980s; Mike Stout, a grievance committeeman at the Homestead Works, who composed songs that he performed on the electric guitar and was TriState's principal stump speaker; Charley McCollester, a Ph.D. in philosophy from the University of Louvain, but in Pittsburgh a machinist and chief steward at a plant that made railway equipment; Father Garrett Dorsey, TriState's chairperson, and pastor of Saint Stephen's Church (where O'Brien had spoken to the communion breakfast); Father Rich Zelik, a Capuchin and treasurer of TriState; and two young steelworkers who had been laid off, Jim Benn from U.S. Steel's Duquesne Works, and Jay Weinberg from the Homestead Works.[38]

As in the Youngstown movement, some had grown up in the community; others were outsiders. Father Dorsey once remarked that his father's gravestone in a cemetery overlooking the Homestead Works would have less red iron oxide on it now that the mills were closed. Stout and McCollester, on the other hand, were young men from other parts of the country who became industrial workers because of political conviction, married working-class women, and stayed in Pittsburgh by choice. The TriState nucleus was perhaps most significant as a small-scale representation of the encounter of Catholicism with secular radicalism that was occurring during the same years in the creation of Polish Solidarity (August 1980) and in Latin America.

TriState developed a movement culture that reflected its component parts. McCollester designed the group's letterhead, where the name of the organization appeared between carved figures of a miner and a machinist that McCollester had noticed on a local bridge. Two gala events at the Local 1397 hall further suggest the TriState ambience. On Labor Day 1981 master of ceremonies Weisen introduced a program including: convocation by Father Bernard Costello, pastor, Saint Mary Magdalen Church, Homestead; a slide show, "Homestead We're Not Dead Yet"; a speech by a congressman; scenes from a historical novel about Pittsburgh steelworkers, *Out of This Furnace,* presented by a local theater group called "The Iron Clad Agreement"; a speech on the implications of the 1981 Clean Air Act amendments; a song by Stout commemorating John Barbero, who had died on July 4, 1981; and finally a presentation on TriState's plans for the fall.[39]

Even more elaborate was the presentation of the Thomas Merton Center's annual award to "The People of Poland." After Weisen's welcome and an invocation, the evening included the singing of "Solidarity Forever," led by Stout; the Polish Falcon Choir; a dance by the Polish Women's Alliance of Pittsburgh; and presentation of the award by McCollester. The printed program offered a rationale for the award in words that also applied to anti-shutdown activity in Youngstown and Pittsburgh:

> By using non-violent means and stressing mass organization, they have [organized workers]. . . . They have asserted the workers' right to participate in economic planning and decision-making on every level of society, including the right of workers to remove incompetent or oppressive management. They have fought for increased economic rights. . . . They have actively and consistently struggled for human rights.[40]

McCollester's speech set forth the ideas of Polish workers organized in Solidarity that had meaning for steelworkers of Polish descent in the Mon Valley. Polish Solidarity, McCollester stated, defined the core of the Polish crisis as a disappearance of democratic institutions that gave a free hand to what the Solidarity draft program of July 1981 called a "class of rulers not subject to control by those whom they rule." Is this a peculiarly Polish problem? asked McCollester. Not at all. "The destruction of a major steelmaking center in Youngstown, Ohio, the radical reduction of steel and other industrial jobs in our own Mon Valley were decided by no vote, no consultation with any public body." The movement to prevent plant shutdowns had no hope of winning unless, like Polish Solidarity, it recognized itself as a movement for economic democracy.[41]

"The Threat Is Real From U.S. Steel." Inevitably, TriState faced off with the corporate leadership of Pittsburgh-based U.S. Steel. In 1979 and 1981 U.S. Steel alternately promised to modernize its Mon Valley facilities and backed away from its words. In May 1979, board chairman Roderick hailed a consent decree negotiated with the Environmental Protection Agency, stating: "U.S. Steel is committed to remaining in the steel business in the Monongahela Valley. . . . U.S. Steel can now act aggressively to revitalize our Pittsburgh-area operations." But U.S. Steel's 1980 annual report stated that the economics of required environmental investments might dictate "that certain facilities be closed instead of modified to comply with the requirements." In March 1980 Roderick told the Allegheny County Commissioners that the company was "reviewing plans to install a modern basic oxygen shop or other new steelmaking technology here in the Mon Valley to replace the present open hearth steelmaking facilities at Homestead Works." At the shareholders' meeting the next spring, however, Weisen asked Roderick from the floor whether there were plans to modernize the Homestead Works, and the company chairman said no. In December 1980 and again in its 1980 annual report U.S. Steel stated that it planned to build a new continuous caster at its Edgar Thomson Works in Braddock. But at the shareholders' meeting in 1981, Roderick stated that the company was reviewing the prospect for the sale of flat-rolled steel, and that the review might lead to changes in its previously announced plan to install a continuous caster at "E.T."[42]

Efforts to induce U.S. Steel to modernize its Mon Valley steel mills reached a climax in the summer of 1981. Company spokespersons lobbied for changes in the federal tax law (to permit accelerated depreciation of new investment) and the Clean Air Act (to permit decelerated compliance with environmental goals if the money saved were used in modernization).[43] The area's congressional representatives voted for both amendments. The amendments passed.

In 1980 and 1981 TriState repeatedly warned that U.S. Steel might have no intention of modernizing. The company, Stout wrote in the local union paper, blamed layoffs and plant closings on imports. But "if U.S. Steel wanted us to stay ignorant, they should never have let Carnegie build libraries and give us library cards." U.S. Steel was letting its mills rot and become outdated "while reinvesting the profit they made off the mills back into cement, chemicals, fertilizers, etc." Thus the problem was not just that steel companies were building new steel mills in greenfield sites away from the rust belt. The problem was that steel companies were "disinvesting" from steel altogether, putting their capital in more profitable investment opportunities. In May 1981 U.S. Steel held its annual shareholders' meeting in downtown Pittsburgh. TriState members carried coffins through the streets to the meeting hall, each coffin bearing the name of a U.S. Steel mill. Shareholders entering the meeting were handed a "Counter Annual Report." The cover featured the picture of a preschool-age boy carrying a lunch bucket (actually, the son of Gerald Dickey, photographed when Dickey was leading the fight to save the mills in Youngstown) with the caption, "Will he have a future in the Mon Valley?" In reply to the bland bumper sticker distributed by the companies, which read The Threat Is Real From Foreign Steel, demonstrators carried signs that said The Threat Is Real From U.S. Steel.[44]

U.S. Steel's announcement in November 1981 that it would use a war chest of $6 billion to buy the Marathon Oil Company, rather than to modernize its steel mills, sent shock waves up and down the Mon Valley. Overnight, TriState's interpretation of events became plausible, and TriState representatives began to be quoted in the media. As Weisen told the Associated Press, "Six billion dollars would modernize and update every U.S. Steel facility in the country."[45] The delegitimation of U.S. Steel, its chairman of the board David Roderick, and the corporate ideology of maximizing profit, however, had not yet yielded agreement about what should be put in their place. There was still no widespread endorsement of TriState's plan for reindustrialization through a regional development authority, using the eminent domain power.

The Movement to Save Dorothy and the Creation of the Steel Valley Authority. TriState's first public opportunity to propose the use of eminent domain to save a steel mill came when Colt Industries announced the closing of its Crucible Steel mill in Midland. Monsignor Rice suggested that Midland use its eminent domain power to acquire the mill and arranged a public meeting at the parish hall of the local Catholic church. The withdrawal of a possible buyer, Cyclops Corporation, and the fears of city councilmen and their attorneys blocked action, but the potential uses of eminent domain had been put before the public.[46]

In the fall of 1982 the threat of an eminent domain taking helped prevent the closing of a large Nabisco plant in Pittsburgh. When the company announced its intention to close the plant, an ad hoc Save

Nabisco Action Coalition convened a rally of twelve hundred people at a high school across the street from the factory, at which the mayor of Pittsburgh said he would learn to bake his own cookies if the plant were closed. TriState members met with the city Urban Redevelopment Authority and presented the eminent domain strategy. A vocal member of the Pittsburgh City Council publicly endorsed the idea. Just before Christmas Nabisco announced that it would keep the plant open after all.[47]

In the spring and summer of 1983, TriState proposed eminent domain for a third time in connection with the closing of the Mesta Machine plant in West Homestead, which made heavy machinery for the mills. A majority of the borough council approved the creation of a West Homestead Municipal Authority, with power to use eminent domain. But the mayor vetoed the council's action, and the council lacked the votes to override the veto.[48]

TriState drew some important lessons from the Mesta campaign. The agitation had been kicked off with a standing-room-only meeting at a high school gymnasium, addressed by Mesta workers, TriState attorneys, local clergy, and the mayor of West Homestead. Thereafter, however, as the borough council (of which TriState's Ron Weisen was a member) took the legal steps to create a municipal authority, popular support had not seemed essential and was not solicited. When the mayor unexpectedly interposed his veto, TriState concluded that "the borough has by now been flooded with so much confusing and negative information about the Authority" that a referendum campaign might not succeed. Pointing to apparent ties linking Mayor John J. Dindak and the council members who supported him to the Mellon Bank Corporation, which as Mesta's largest creditor had foreclosed on Mesta's mortgage and had its own plans for the property, the TriState newsletter observed that in the future, TriState would have to do a better job of acquainting the public with its eminent domain strategy. Town meetings would not be enough. Political leaders in Mon Valley boroughs could be expected to have a stronger allegiance to the Mellon Bank than to any worker-community plan to save their basic industries. They should be expected to engage in campaigns of distortion to discredit such a plan. TriState's efforts were likely to fail unless it could generate "a groundswell of grass roots support to overwhelm that opposition."[49]

TriState was not the only group that helped generate the desired ground swell. A group of Protestant ministers formed a Denominational

Ministry Strategy (DMS) that sought to spotlight the role of Mellon Bank in the valley's deindustrialization. Residents with accounts at Mellon's downtown and neighborhood banks were told that "your money is being used against you" when Mellon invested their savings outside the region and overseas. They were urged to transfer their money to other banks. An early focus for this strategy was some five hundred thousand dollars in wages owed to Mesta Machine workers when the company went bankrupt. Mellon Bank, as principal creditor, sought to prevent payment of the wages. DMS and TriState induced the United Steelworkers of America; the United Mine Workers; United Electrical Workers, Local 610 (where McCollester was a chief steward); the entire Pittsburgh City Council; the Allegheny County Commissioners; and several state legislators to pledge withdrawal of their accounts from Mellon unless the wages were released. Mellon released the wages. Later DMS turned to confrontational tactics, such as depositing dead fish in branch bank safety deposit boxes, dropping rolls of pennies on bank floors, and disrupting the services of suburban churches attended by U.S. Steel and Mellon Bank executives.[50]

Important, too, were the Mon Valley Unemployed Committee and the Save Our Neighborhoods Action Coalition (SNAC), an outgrowth of the Nabisco campaign. The Mon Valley Unemployed Committee organized steelworkers for direct action. By appearing en masse at foreclosure proceedings, 1930s-style, committee members saved many steelworkers' homes. TriState sponsored a "resumes for Reagan" campaign in response to the rhetoric that retraining was the answer to plant shutdowns. Unemployed workers who had taken retraining courses but could not find jobs mailed their resumes to the president. Finally, SNAC presented a draft ordinance to the Pittsburgh City Council that required employers of more than fifty employees to notify the city one year in advance of the proposed closing or relocation of an enterprise when the planned action would result in loss of employment for at least 15 percent of the work force. The council, after reducing the notification period, making it 90 to 270 days long, depending on the size of the enterprise, passed the ordinance, only to have it held unlawful on appeal to the courts.[51]

Meantime, TriState set about to refine and build support for its eminent domain strategy. A conference at the Local 1397 union hall in October 1983 brought together rank-and-file steelworkers and national experts on the steel industry and the labor movement to discuss a first draft of the plan written by Robert Erickson, a sociology professor at a local college. The same proposals were visually portrayed in a film by California Newsreel called *The Business of America,* released, and attacked by the *Wall Street Journal,* early in 1984. In midsummer 1984 after widespread community discussion of drafts or summaries, TriState released its plan in a pamphlet entitled *Steel Valley Authority: A Community Plan to Save Pittsburgh's Steel Industry.*[52]

A new opportunity to apply TriState's ideas soon presented itself. In spring 1984 U.S. Steel closed the steelmaking end of its Duquesne Works, including a blast furnace named Dorothy 6, for the wife of a U.S. Steel executive. In September, there fell into the hands of TriState activists a brochure of the U.S. Steel Realty Division that listed among other projects the "USS Industrial Park of Duquesne, Pa." Inquiry revealed that, without public announcement, U.S. Steel was planning to dynamite the blast furnace in December in order to convert about 100 acres of the 260-acre site into an industrial park.[53]

The projected demolition of a facility that had only recently set production records upset people more than the closing itself. A meeting of area activists and legislators called on the company to postpone the demolition pending a study. After a first feasibility study found that a reopened Dorothy could be profitable, the campaign swelled. U.S. Steel, arrogant unilateral decision maker par excellence, on four separate occasions postponed the publicly announced destruction.[54]

The threat to Dorothy engendered a breadth and depth of community support that the area typically produces only for incumbent presidents and football teams. On May 18, 1985, an extraordinary parade brought together the different constituencies seeking to reopen the mill. Marchers assembled at the Polish Hill Softball Field on a hill overlooking downtown Duquesne. Amid a carnival atmosphere, school bands, drum and bugle corps, fire engines, and ambulances from the towns of the Mon Valley proceeded down Grant Street to the Duquesne Plaza. Veterans of the Youngstown struggle carried a banner in a place of honor toward the front of the march. At the plaza marchers were greeted by a wall of placards of support held by steelworkers from Philadelphia. Dorothy T-shirts, sweatshirts, mugs, lapel pins, key rings, buttons, and bumper stickers were sold in large numbers. Endorsing persons and organizations included the USWA, which put an estimated $1 million into the Dorothy campaign; Saint Stephen's Church in Hazelwood (Father Dorsey's church); other churches and religious figures;

the Pennsylvania American Federation of Labor-Congress of Industrial Organizations; the Mon Valley Unemployed Committee; the Homestead Unemployment Center; and a variety of other unions, legislative bodies, and individual legislators. Not surprisingly, two weeks later the mayor and city council of Pittsburgh endorsed the proposal to create a Steel Valley Authority (SVA) that could acquire Dorothy by using its eminent domain power and also pledged fifty thousand dollars toward the SVA's initial budget.[55]

The creation of the SVA was the crowning achievement of TriState's more than five years of agitation. Nine city councils in the Mon Valley—those governing the boroughs of Homestead, Munhall, Rankin, East Pittsburgh, Turtle Creek, Swissvale, Glassport, and McKeesport and the city of Pittsburgh—took all the legal steps necessary for final incorporation of the authority in January 1986. It was a prodigious organizing achievement. Appropriately, Frank O'Brien became the SVA's first chairperson, and Charley McCollester and Mike Stout were named to the board as representatives of Pittsburgh and Munhall, respectively. The SVA remains in existence despite the ultimate failure of the project to reopen Dorothy.[56]

Youngstown and Pittsburgh, 1986–1987

Solidarity USA. In advocating the use of eminent domain to buy and to run abandoned industrial plants, Youngstown and Pittsburgh steelworkers were motivated, not by a belief in the intrinsic virtue of public enterprise, but by their desperate need for jobs. In 1986–1987, as the crisis reached beyond jobs to the pension and medical benefits that had been promised to retirees, steelworkers and their spouses came to advocate a national public corporation that would acquire at least portions of the American steel industry. They did so because the conduct of corporate executives who treated loyalty to workers, products, factories, communities, and even the nation as expendable convinced them that only public ownership could guarantee their benefits.[57]

On July 17, 1986, the LTV corporation, the second largest steel company in the United States, declared bankruptcy.[58] At the same time that it filed its bankruptcy petition the company unilaterally stopped payment of medical and life insurance benefits to approximately eighty thousand hourly and salaried retirees, eleven thousand of them in the Mahoning Valley. The results were catastrophic. One retiree in

Struthers, Ohio, south of Youngstown, decided not to go to the hospital when he experienced a recurrence of heart symptoms because he did not know how his treatment would be paid for. He died a few hours later. The response to LTV's actions made clear that whatever residual confidence in private steel company management remained in the community was dramatically eroding. Clergymen and congressmen spoke of "industrial terrorism," of conduct no different from "a mugging," of "one of the most unconscionable corporate acts in this century." The probusiness *Youngstown Vindicator* editorialized, "We think the whole situation stinks."[59]

Delores Hrycyk, a lector at her local Catholic church and wife of a retiree who had worked thirty-six years for Republic Steel, telephoned radio talk shows and called a protest rally in downtown Youngstown on July 26. One thousand people attended. A few weeks later Youngstown-area retirees, under Hrycyk's leadership, formed an organization that they named Solidarity USA. Between August 1986 and March 1987 the group took busloads of retirees to New York City (where LTV had filed its bankruptcy petition), to Washington, D.C. (where emergency legislation temporarily restored the retirees' benefits), to sympathetic city councils in Pittsburgh and Cleveland, and to downtown Aliquippa, Pennsylvania, where retirees blocked access to the mill. On January 31, 1987, more than two thousand retirees from LTV plants in northeastern Ohio and western Pennsylvania met in Youngstown's largest auditorium to plan further mass action.[60]

Solidarity's ideas, like the ideas of the Ecumenical Coalition and of TriState, developed in response to the crisis. After the July 26 rally veterans of the decade-long campaign met to assess the new situation. Participants included Mann and myself from Youngstown; Stout, McCollester, O'Brien, and other TriState activists; and steelworkers from Cleveland, Warren, and Aliquippa. For the first time discussion moved beyond acquisition of particular plants or the rebuilding of steel in a particular region. LTV's bankruptcy was felt to require public acquisition of the entire LTV Steel company, including the company's profitable plants in Cleveland, Ohio; Indiana Harbor, Indiana; and Hennepin, Illinois. When LTV abruptly terminated its pension plans in January 1987, TriState and Solidarity publicists pointed out that the plans were underfunded by a sum greater than the total market value of LTV Steel, and that under the federal pension law the federal government thus had an arguable right to acquire the whole company, free.[61]

The evolution of the idea of a community right to industrial property thus led to a proposal not entirely dissimilar to nationalization. There were important differences: Solidarity and TriState members were still speaking of the acquisition of one company, not the entire industry; the rationale was still basically that facilities should be acquired when private owners no longer wished to run them; and the alternative management was envisioned as decentralized and community-controlled, not as a Washington bureaucracy. Above all, the development of ideas had been gradual and in response to felt needs, rather than dominated by ideological reasons.

An event encapsulating the Catholic and working-class constitutionalism of the intellectual history described in this article took place on April 12, 1987, outside the plant gate in Aliquippa, Pennsylvania. It was Palm Sunday. It was also the fiftieth anniversary of the United States Supreme Court's decision in *National Labor Relations Board v. Jones & Laughlin Steel Corporation* (1937), holding the Wagner Act constitutional. As the *Wall Street Journal* described the scene:

> On Palm Sunday, hundreds of LTV Corp. pensioners reunited outside the steelmaker's nearly deserted mill here to play out a symbolic crucifixion—their own. Anchoring a makeshift pine cross outside the plant gates, the gray-haired throng chanted, "Who owns the pensions? The workers!"[62]

My wife and I were among those who walked from Saint Titus's Catholic Church to the mill gate, carrying palms. The gate had been the scene of daily demonstrations by retirees seeking guarantees for their pension and medical benefits. At the gate, a former tractor operator explained in broken English that he was one of those, discharged by the company in the mid-1930s, who had filed the National Labor Relations Board (NLRB) charge that initiated the *NLRB v. Jones & Laughlin* case. We also heard from Monsignor Rice of TriState, from Delores Hrycyk of Solidarity USA, and from an acoustic band and chorus who sang "Christ the Worker." As the mass ended, rolls were distributed, Easter embraces exchanged, and the hat passed to gather funds for the next demonstration.

Conclusion

Youngstown has become a symbol of how unilateral corporate decision making can lay waste a community. A photograph of the dynamited blast furnaces at U.S. Steel's Ohio Works, crumbling as they fell, was used to introduce a *New York Times* article, "Collapse of Our Industrial Heartland." The *New Yorker* put Youngstown in grim company in 1985 when it alluded to the "news from yet another hopeless, sorry corner of the world. Youngstown. Chile. Ethiopia. South Africa."[63]

But the story of Youngstown and Pittsburgh in the decade when the mills closed is also a tale of new beginnings. For example, a direct line of ideological descent leads from the November 1977 pastoral letter of the Ecumenical Coalition of the Mahoning Valley (an organization cochaired by Youngstown's Catholic bishop, James Malone) to the November 1986 pastoral letter on economic justice of the National Conference of Catholic Bishops (chaired by the same bishop). The Youngstown pastoral letter argued that although some maintained that the decision to close the Campbell Works was a private, purely economic judgment and the exclusive prerogative of the Lykes Corporation, the decision was "a matter of public concern since it profoundly affects the lives of so many people." Similarly, the bishops' 1986 pastoral declared:

> Decisions must be judged in light of what they do *for* the poor, what they do *to* the poor, and what they enable the poor to do *for themselves*. The fundamental moral criterion for all economic decisions, policies, and institutions is this: They must be at the service of *all people, especially the poor*.[64]

As the Ecumenical Coalition's letter had, the pastoral letter went on from that abstract pronouncement to express advocacy of public ownership on a case-by-case basis, and even of eminent domain. "The common good may sometimes demand that the right to own be limited by public involvement in the planning or ownership of certain sectors of the economy," the bishops stated. No one has the right to unlimited accumulation of wealth. No one "is justified in keeping for his exclusive use what he does not need, when others lack necessities." The letter quotes Pope John Paul II's advice that the duty to serve the common good places a "social mortgage" on all private property, so that "one cannot exclude the socialization . . . of certain means of production." And the limits on the private accumulation and control of wealth are the basis of "society's exercising the right of eminent domain."[65]

Such ideas are beginning to be applied in other parts of the United States. In 1984 in New Bedford, Massachusetts, where a Labor party candidate had called for public ownership of the textile mills in the 1930s, the city threatened to use eminent domain if the conglomerate owner of the Morse Cutting Tools plant refused to sell it to a company prepared to keep the plant in operation. Gulf and Western backed down, and the plant stayed in business. Three years later the plant went bankrupt under its new ownership. In bankruptcy proceedings the judge ordered the assets sold to a bidder whose offer was slightly lower than the highest bid but who was willing to keep the plant operating in New Bedford. Union organizer Ron Carver commented that the judge's decision "established a principle that a plant that has been around for all these years is a community resource."[66]

The most important contribution of the Youngstown and Pittsburgh effort may have to do with the way in which the state (and with it, the Constitution and the language of rights) is viewed by advocates of fundamental social change. One historian expressed such advocates' ambivalence:

> Beginning in the 1890s the state took on more and more the role of coordinator of the socioeconomic order. . . . Faced with a practically irrevocable leviathan, radicals were forced into new but no less difficult choices. . . . If to abandon politics meant to risk being hemmed in by leaving the state's powers in the hands of labor's enemies, to pursue the state-oriented strategy meant to risk assimilation and the taming of the movement that had launched it.

A second scholar concluded that at most American workers and their organizations have been able to gain through the state only a "counterfeit liberty."[67] The dilemmas present themselves specifically in the case of the steel industry. Only the federal government appears to be a practical source for the massive investment required to rebuild America's steel mills. Yet workers and communities who have been battered by the decisions of absentee bureaucracies—corporate bureaucracies, government bureaucracies, and union bureaucracies—are understandably hesitant to turn to Washington for solutions to their problems.

The Youngstown and Pittsburgh experience offers a model combining massive federal investment with decentralized administration by workers and consumers. The key ideas are, first, that means of production should be acquired from their present owners only when those owners are not willing to operate them, and second, that management should be locally controlled. Those ideas have made something akin to socialism acceptable to middle American working people. The vision of public authorities acquiring abandoned industrial facilities by the power of eminent domain and operating them, or delegating their operation, on a not-for-profit or low-profit basis in the manner of Amtrak or the Tennessee Valley Authority, has won wide popular support.[68]

This recasting of the rationale for community ownership of industrial property avoids a dichotomous choice between the public world of the state and a nonpublic world based on the exclusive private ownership and management of property. A variety of public-and-private patterns are possible. Public ownership can coexist with the virtues of voluntarism, spontaneity, and popular participation usually associated with private ordering.

Emergence of a community right to industrial property also has implications for the accepted ordering of relations between employers and employees. Since the passage of the Wagner Act, it has generally been supposed that if workers were encouraged to form unions and to bargain with management as to their wages and hours, management could retain its prerogative to make investment decisions without posing a threat to workers or the community. The experience of plant shutdowns in Youngstown and Pittsburgh suggests otherwise. Where management retains the unilateral right to determine whether an enterprise shall continue to operate at all, the right to bargain about incentives on the second shift has limited meaning. Those who have struggled with the effects of plant shutdowns in Youngstown and Pittsburgh throughout the decade 1977–1987 would argue that workers and communities must come to have a voice in *all* management decisions, by becoming the managers themselves. Through the elaboration and practical implementation of this belief it may yet be possible, as John Barbero hoped, to "shout Youngstown."

11

The Internationalization of Capital and Labor's Response

How do we deal with the fact that at a time when most of those gathered here are taking the merest first steps toward a new kind of labor movement, are necessarily working at a local level and in a very preliminary manner, are barely scratching the surface of a huge collective task that involves rethinking the assumptions on which the labor movement of the United States has proceeded at least since the 1930s, and in some respects, since the 1880s—that just at this moment, when our work is properly so tentative and decentralized, capital has reorganized itself on a scale ever more far-flung and internationalized? Doesn't the scope and power of capital's reorganization make our work, by comparison, almost grotesquely irrelevant?

Like each of you, in approaching these questions I can only draw on my own experience.

Let me quickly sketch three groups of working people in Youngstown whom I represent, and how each group views the future of the labor movement.

A talk at the Second Annual Conference on Workers' Self-Organization, Minneapolis, May 4–6, 1990. Later published in expanded form as *Solidarity Unionism* (Chicago: Charles H. Kerr, 1992).

First, there are workers in non-union shops. Many of these persons worked in steel mills before the mills in Youngstown shut down. Others are Blacks and women trying to get a foothold in the labor force. Wages are typically $4, $5, $6 an hour. Safety and health conditions are atrocious. Yet these workers, who it would seem have every reason to belong to unions, have been disillusioned by the performance of big existing unions as they have experienced it, or been told about it. After one concession contract too many, the non-union workforce in the Mahoning Valley is looking for something other than joining the Steelworkers, or the Teamsters, or the Auto Workers.

Second, there are persons who belong to existing unions. In some cases the union's headquarters is an hour and a half away in Cleveland or three hours away in Columbus; the union never holds meetings in Youngstown, and members do not even know the name of the union to which they belong. In these situations I find myself working with elected shop stewards who in effect run a parallel union on the shop floor. The largest unionized workplace in the area is GM Lordstown. Workers there *do* know the name of their union. They also know the name of GM's Chairman of the Board. Recently GM gave each Lordstown worker a profit-sharing check in the amount of $50, as compared with thousands of dollars received by workers at other auto companies. Lordstown workers responded by circulating, first, a picture of three $50 bills with Roger B. Smith's face in the middle and, second, a leaflet ending with the words: "when . . . you really feel you'd like to quit, don't come to me, I don't give a shit. ROGER SMITH." GM management replied with an information bulletin to the effect that Shop Rule #29 had been modified to cover "the making or publishing of malicious statements concerning any employee, the company or its products." The UAW locals at Lordstown have done nothing to challenge this shop rule, just as they did nothing to challenge the previous management practice of requiring employees to get leaflets approved by the GM labor relations director before passing them out in the plant parking lot.

Finally, there are former members of unions who are retired or disabled. These may be the most alienated of all. For example, in the case of LTV Steel there are 13,800 active workers and 46,000 hourly retirees. The retirees are not union members, do not vote for union officers, and have no voice in the formation or ratification of contracts that change their pension and medical benefits. In the LTV Steel contract just negotiated, and ratified by the active workers alone, active workers received an average of $7.25 in contract improvements for every $1 received by the average retiree. There is a company-wide retiree protest movement. Among its demands are:

1. All Retirees [should] have the right to vote on a contract that directly affects their Benefits and Pensions.
2. Retirees must have the opportunity to take part in negotiations concerning Retiree Benefits. One Delegate should be elected to serve on the negotiation committee from each Local Union Retirees Organization.
3. Copies of Union Demands should be sent to each Retiree Organization.

Youngstown-area workers have created some interesting organizations during the last several years.

One is the Workers' Solidarity Club of Youngstown, which has existed since 1981. It can best be described as a parallel central labor union, to which rank-and-file workers, unemployed persons, and retirees can come when they need support for their various struggles.

Another is Solidarity USA, an organization of retirees. Solidarity USA was formed in 1986 when LTV Steel declared bankruptcy and stopped paying medical insurance benefits to retirees. Although at first made up almost entirely of retirees from this one company and their spouses, Solidarity USA has absorbed retirees from several other steel companies, and is on its way to becoming a central labor body for retirees of all descriptions. The retirees who make up Solidarity USA, lacking any voice in the union, have no alternative to direct action. They join each other's picket lines in struggles with particular companies, and join together to demand national health insurance.

It is a commentary on the present state of the labor movement that nowhere have I seen such life as among retirees. They are not forced to belong to retiree organizations; hence they come to meetings gladly. Each local retiree organization makes its own decisions. Meetings have a social as well as an economic character. Participants sustain each other through the trials of growing old, as well as confronting together the latest modification in benefits they had supposed to be guaranteed.

Workers Against Toxic Chemical Hazards (WATCH) was formed in 1988. Again the core consisted of persons from a particular plant, in this case chemically poisoned workers from GM Lordstown. They too are no longer members of the union and can only make themselves heard by imaginative direct action. And as in the case of Solidarity USA, WATCH has been sought out by chemically injured workers from other places of work beside GM Lordstown. It has broadened its focus to the point that a week ago it sponsored the first celebration of Workers' Memorial Day in the Mahoning Valley. Indeed Youngstown had a Workers' Memorial weekend: on Saturday WATCH sponsored a citizens' hearing on toxic chemicals, and on Sunday the Workers' Solidarity Club scattered ashes of Joe Hill.

These three overlapping networks also have a hand in organizations like the local chapter of the American Civil Liberties Union, whose president and secretary are a utility lineman and a steelworker from the Workers' Solidarity Club, and which concerns itself not just with government repression, but with free speech fights against private employers.

Thus my experience and that of my associates in Youngstown is an experience on the edge of the organized labor movement. Sometimes our activities are sponsored and supported by local unions or by AFL-CIO central labor bodies. More often they are not. Countless threads of shared experience bind us to the official labor movement. Retirees, for example, built the CIO in the Youngstown area, often served as grievance representatives and officers of their local unions, and still have personal relations with active workers, officers, and staff representatives. Yet they, and I, are profoundly disillusioned with the organized labor movement as it exists in our area. We are a valley of brokenhearted lovers.

I know they would want me to say one more time, before continuing, that neither they nor I are anti-labor or anti-union.

Capital, not labor, is the main enemy and always will be. When a union exists at the workplace where any of us is employed, he or she should join that union. When there are union elections, we should vote, just as most of us choose to vote in elections outside the workplace. While I am extremely critical of the actions of the government of the United States, especially in foreign policy, I have never ceased to consider myself a good citizen. In the same way, I believe we can be good union members at the same time that we criticize, not just incumbent union officers, but also the basic assumptions of existing unions in the United States: their acceptance of collective bargaining agreements that prohibit strikes during the life of the contract; the one-party government that exists in all major unions in the United States, causing incumbent union officers to view dissent as a sort of treason; the insipid union press, which reports only victories and in which critical and independent voices are almost never heard; in a word, the culture of domination and conformity that makes the internal life of unions in the United States considerably less free than life in the Soviet Union, while at the same time, in their relations to management, even those unions that are rhetorically most militant in fact play the role of junior partner, suppressing spontaneous activity on the shop or office floor in the name of carrying out contract obligations, and ensuring the survival of the union treasury.

I want to suggest, as a hypothesis to be tested by us all in the course of our collective work, that the time has come to break with the forms of organization of the existing labor movement: not necessarily to work outside of existing unions, but, if we work within them, self-consciously to seek the emergence of new forms. I want to suggest that trade unions as they have come to be in the United States—and I mean even the best trade unions, in their most heroic moments of struggle, like the United Mine Workers under the leadership of Richard Trumka—are part of the problem, rather than part of the solution: that, far from prefiguring the kind of society we wish to create, these unions are centralized, bureaucratic, life-deadening institutional dinosaurs, that resemble the capitalist corporations with which they purport to do battle and are inherently and structurally incapable of changing the economy that those corporations command. I want to suggest that the internationalization of capital, far from proving that such centralized unions are needed more than ever, has, on the contrary, demonstrated their impotence: that while CIO unions were created precisely to try to deal with the national scale of corporate organization, the new international scale of corporate organization has shown that something qualitatively different is required, something horizontal rather than vertical in its organizing strategy, something that breaks down the barriers between crafts and industries rather than institutionalizing them—in a word, that the increased quantitative scope of capital's organization makes clear the need for a decisive qualitative change in labor's response.

In illustration of this thesis, I look, first, at the historical origins of CIO business unionism and then at the alternative forms of organization suggested by movements like the IWW. Finally, I comment briefly on the spirit in which we build these new forms.

The Historical Origins of CIO Business Unionism

The Committee for Industrial Organization, or as it later called itself, the Congress of Industrial Organizations, was created in 1935–36 by the presidents of certain AFL unions who saw a need for industrial organization. These union bureaucrats—notably John L. Lewis of the United Mine Workers and Sidney Hillman of the Amalgamated Clothing Workers—seized an opportunity that resulted from a phenomenal upsurge of self-organization by rank-and-file workers in the years 1932–1935.

The rank-and-file struggles of the early 1930s, before the founding of the CIO and the passage of the National Labor Relations Act, or Wagner Act, had two main features. First, they relied on the strike weapon, most successfully in the local general strikes in Minneapolis, Toledo, and San Francisco, and also in the unsuccessful national textile strike, in 1934. Second, they turned to independent labor politics. Between the years 1932 and 1936 local labor parties fielded candidates in Cambridge, New Bedford, and Springfield, Massachusetts; Berlin and Lincoln, New Hampshire; Danbury and Hartford, Connecticut; Buffalo and New York City; Allentown and Philadelphia, Pennsylvania; Akron, Canton, and Toledo, Ohio; Detroit, Hamtramck, and Port Huron, Michigan; Chicago and Hillsboro, Illinois; Sioux Falls, South Dakota; Everett and Goldbar, Washington; and San Francisco. In at least ten other communities central labor unions endorsed the idea of a labor party, as did the State Federations of Labor of Rhode Island, Connecticut, Vermont, New Jersey, and Wisconsin. And at the 1935 AFL convention, a resolution endorsing a labor party lost by a margin of only four votes—108 to 104.[1]

Even after the passage of the Wagner Act and the formation of the CIO, the first victories for industrial unionism came from below, through extralegal rank-and-file sit-down strikes at the Akron rubber plants and the General Motors complex in Flint, Michigan. Historians have debated whether the workers who spontaneously occupied their factories wanted anything more than union recognition and collective bargaining. At a minimum, it seems clear, they also wanted increased control over their immediate work conditions. In rubber and auto plants, on the San Francisco waterfront, in steel mills like the Inland Steel mill near Chicago, workers used their new unions to assert control over their work through wildcat strikes, slowdowns, and other kinds of direct action.

But *CIO unions came into being in the context of the National Labor Relations Act as exclusive bargaining representatives certified by the state.* Prior to the 1930s, labor organizations in the United States—whatever their other differences—had jealously guarded the concept of union independence and autonomy. In contrast, the desired objective of CIO unions was to become legal monopolies, complete with enforced membership (union shop) and a source of income independent of any continuing accountability of unions to their members (dues checkoff).

The danger of such state sponsorship for an independent, radical labor movement was clearly perceived at the time. The Industrial Workers of the World (IWW), the Communist Party prior to the Seventh Congress of the Comintern in 1935, the American Civil Liberties Union, and independent radicals like A. J. Muste, for this reason opposed—or expressed grave reservations about—passage of the National Labor Relations Act.

In 1934, when the first version of the Wagner Act was proposed, Mary Van Kleeck of the ACLU wrote to Senator Wagner, advising him that the ACLU would oppose his bill because of the "inevitable trends of its administration." Van Kleeck explained that

> the danger is that the effort to regulate industrial relations by requiring of an employer certain "fair practices," while appearing to impose those obligations upon them, necessarily brings the whole subject within the scope of governmental regulation. This involves a certain assumption as to a status quo. To prevent or discourage strikes which have for their purpose gradual increase in the workers' power in a period when fundamental economic change in the ownership of industry can clearly be envisaged may only serve to check the rising power of the exponents of human rights, and indeed to protect private property rights in exchange for obligations which are likely to be merely the least common denominator of industrial practice.

Van Kleeck concluded by acknowledging that Senator Wagner's bill explicitly protected the right of workers to strike, but insisted "that pressures would inevitably be exerted on the National Labor Relations Board to discourage strikes in favor of less disruptive methods of resolving conflicts."[2] About the same time ACLU president Roger Baldwin, writing to Senator David Walsh, agreed that the machinery proposed by the pending legislation would "impair labor's rights in the long run, however much its authors may intend precisely the contrary."

In 1935, this time in response to the final version of the Wagner Act, Baldwin wrote to Wagner that the ACLU would oppose creation of a National Labor Relations Board

> on the ground that no such federal agency intervening in the conflicts between employers and employees can be expected fairly to determine the issues of labor's rights. We say this from a long experience with the various boards set up in Washington, all of which have tended to take from labor its

basic right to strike by substituting mediation, conciliation, or, in some cases, arbitration.

Baldwin urged Wagner to consider "the view that the pressures on any governmental agency from employers are so constant and determined that it is far better to have no governmental intervention than to suffer the delusion that it will aid labor in its struggle for the rights to organize, bargain collectively and strike."[3]

Thus, even before the Wagner Act had been passed and the CIO had been founded, these critics accurately forecast the domestication and decline of a labor movement sponsored by the government.

Further, *CIO unions were from the outset committed to contractualism, that is, to the regulation of relations between employer and employee by means of a legally binding collective bargaining agreement that (a) forbids strikes for the duration of the contract and (b) cedes investment decisions to the employer.*

The very first contracts between General Motors and the UAW, and between United States Steel and the Steel Workers Organizing Committee, in the spring of 1937, contained clauses prohibiting strikes for the duration of the contract. There was never a time when the leaders of CIO unions opposed such language. Instead, they presented themselves to management as guarantors of labor peace.

Similarly, the "management prerogatives clause" typical in AFL-CIO contracts today was part of the very first collective bargaining agreement with U.S. Steel in 1937. Then the clause stated:

> The management of the works and the direction of the working forces, including the right to hire, suspend or discharge for proper cause, or transfer, and the right to relieve employees from duty because of lack of work or for other legitimate reasons, is vested exclusively in the Corporation.

Essentially the same words appear in the present USX contract:

> The Company retains the exclusive rights to manage the business and plants and to direct the working forces. . . . The rights to manage the business and plants and to direct the working forces include the right to hire, suspend or discharge for proper cause, or transfer, and the right to relieve employees from duty because of lack of work or for other legitimate reasons.

There was an intimate connection between government sponsorship of CIO organization and the fact that CIO unions from the beginning negotiated contracts containing no-strike and management prerogatives clauses. The preamble to the Wagner Act identified its principal objective as labor peace. CIO leaders acted the part they knew to be expected of them if they were to receive ongoing support from the government. Radical labor journalist Len DeCaux wrote in April 1935 that when Lewis and other union officials testified before the Senate committee considering the Wagner Act, the labor leaders said in effect: "Allow the workers to organize, establish strong governmental machinery for dealing with labor questions, and industrial peace will result."[4]

These elements of business unionism that were integral to the CIO from its moment of origin were reinforced and cast in concrete during World War II.

One might ask, why did the rank-and-file trade unionists who organized so effectively from 1932 to 1935 acquiesce in the absorption of their lodges, committees, associations, and local unions by the new, centralized CIO unions? The critical weakness of the rank and file was its inability to organize on a national scale. Clarence Irwin of Youngstown, Ohio, the key figure in pre-CIO organizing in steel, recalled: "Most of us were capable local or district leaders, but we had very little idea what the national picture was like.... We were completely unprepared for a [nationwide] strike. We had no funds, no central leadership, no national organization."[5] I heard the same thing from George Patterson. Before the formation of the Steel Workers Organizing Committee in 1936, Patterson built an independent union of three thousand workers at United States Steel South Works. I remember him showing me Bessemer Park on the South Side of Chicago, and telling me that meetings of the Associated Employees—as they called their independent union— would fill the park. How did you feel about joining the CIO? I asked. Patterson replied that he knew it would be "the end of us as a democratic union. But we had no power; as a single local union, trying to deal with the United States Steel Corporation, about the only decision we could influence was the kind of soap to use in the shower."[6]

I was told the same story by the president of an independent local union at the Du Pont plant in Hammond, Indiana, and by Youngstown bakery workers who affiliated with the Teamsters so as to have some muscle. They were not dummies. They knew they were sacrificing democratic control of their local unions. But they felt that they must belong to a national union in order to stand up to corporations that were organized nationwide.

This is the bargain that has collapsed in the era of multinationalism. National labor unions have shown themselves impotent to protect their members against imports from abroad, against the export of jobs to low-wage economies, against downsizing and restructuring. The centralized, bureaucratic national union has lost its historic reason for existence. There is no longer any rational justification for these unions' pretensions to exclusive status, for their intolerance of internal opposition, for the high-off-the-hog lifestyle of their staff representatives. CIO unionism is an idea whose time has gone.

Alternative Forms of Organization

The inadequacy of one form of organization does not ensure that some other, adequate alternative is available. What can be put in place of the centralized, bureaucratic national union, if labor is to respond effectively to the internationalization of capital?

Most of us trace our labor movement ancestry to the IWW.

Who were the Wobblies? They were what in Latin America would be called "marginalized" workers: bindle stiffs, timber beasts, new immigrants, migratory farm workers, so-called bums. They envisioned One Big Union of working people all over the world. They thought that workers should run the shops in which they labored. At a time when women, Blacks, migratory workers, and newly arrived immigrants could not vote, they cautioned against reliance on electoral politics. They opposed written contracts that inhibited spontaneous shopfloor action and concerted action by workers in different trades and places. Although they led some of the most dramatic strikes in the labor history of the United States, their greater emphasis was on what the Wobblies' enemies called "sabotage" and what the AFL-CIO has recently rediscovered and termed "inside strategies": that is, staying on the job and using direct action in a myriad of forms inside the workplace.

Many historians and trade unionists consider the Wobblies to have been a colorful footnote in the American labor story, lumpenproletarians rather than real workers, romantic and impractical idealists, precursors (but not exemplars) of serious trade unionism.

I propose the very opposite. I think the Wobblies were right. I suggest that the One Big Union, based in local shopfloor committees and local committees of workers from all trades, spontaneously created and re-created by a horizontal process in which workers reach out to their counterparts in other places and other countries, is the organizational form required for effective response to the power of multinational corporations.

Before dismissing this idea as idealistic nonsense, remember recent history. Is what I suggest so much more far-fetched than the way in which Soviet coal miners, operating altogether outside official unions, organized locally and then linked up with each other through improvised coordinating entities? If Polish Solidarity organized an entire national workforce, in the face of government repression, within a period of fifteen months, can we say that the same process cannot go on across national boundaries?

Let me say a bit more about the historical roots of, on the one hand, the shopfloor or stewards' committee, and on the other hand, the coordinating body of all workers in a given locality.

When I speak of a shopfloor or stewards' committee, I mean a committee that may be composed of representatives from different unions. The shopfloor or stewards' committee accordingly breaks with the idea that only one union may represent the workers of a particular workplace. Instead, it embodies the concept familiar in Europe that several unions can co-exist in a plant and send representatives proportionally to a workers' council that bears full responsibility for negotiations with management. This idea, championed by Polish Solidarity, has been accepted by the societies of Eastern Europe but not by labor unions or labor law in the United States. It is an idea that goes far back in labor history.

David Montgomery, for example, has described how in the era of the first World War—under the influence of the Wobblies, but organizationally apart from the Wobblies—workers formed elected committees in individual plants to stand up to the employer through direct action. Thus at the Westinghouse plant near Pittsburgh experience indicated that workers needed an "in-plant organization made up of their own elected delegates" that cut across traditional craft lines. The permanent presence of an active group representative right there on the production floor, "all day every day," augmented the very different kind of representation that a national union could offer. At Westinghouse, as Montgomery tells the story, workers recruited employees of all descriptions (including clerical workers) into an organization marvelously named the Allegheny Congenial Industrial Union. This organization "copied the IWW by devoting itself to organizing struggles around demands, rather than negotiating contracts, ... but it also used a system of departmental delegates inside the plant as its basic structure."[7] The improvised shop committees that Montgomery describes may be compared to the shopfloor activities carried out in industries such as steel, auto, rubber, and electrical equipment during the early years of the CIO at a time when unions had yet to become exclusive bargaining representatives, contracts had not been signed, and, as a result, shop stewards were still free to orchestrate slowdowns and wildcat strikes in support of their constituents' demands.

John Sargent, first president of the CIO union at Inland Steel, tells what happened there in the years between the Little Steel Strike and the beginning of World War II.

John L. Lewis had an agreement with the U.S. Steel Corporation, and they signed a contract. Little Steel—which was Youngstown Sheet and Tube, Republic Steel, Inland Steel, and other independent companies—had no contract with the Steelworkers Union. As a result in 1937 there was a strike called on Little Steel. . . . The strike was not won. We did not win a contract. Neither Youngstown Sheet and Tube, nor Republic Steel, nor Inland Steel won a contract with the company. What we did get was an agreement through the governor's office that the company would recognize the Steelworkers Union and the company union and any other organization that wanted to represent the people in the steel industry. And we went back to work with this governor's agreement signed by various companies and union representatives in Indiana. At Inland Steel we had a company union; we had our own Steelworkers Union. . . . [W]e had no contract with the company. But the enthusiasm of the people who were working in the mills made this settlement of the strike into a victory of great proportions.

Without a contract, without any agreement with the company, without any regulations concerning hours of work, conditions of work, or wages, a tremendous surge took place. We talk of a rank-and-file movement: the beginning of union organization was the best kind of rank-and-file movement you could think of. . . . The union organizers were essentially workers in the mill who were so disgusted with their conditions and so ready for a change that they took the union into their own hands.

. . . Without a contract we secured for ourselves agreements on working conditions and wages that we do not have today [1970], and that were better by far than what we do have today in the mill. For example as a result of the enthusiasm of the people in the mill you had a series of strikes, wildcats, shut-downs, slow-downs, anything working people could think of to secure for themselves what they decided they had to have. If their wages were low there was no contract to prohibit them from striking, and they struck for better wages. If their conditions were bad, if they didn't like what was going on, if they were being abused, the people in the mills themselves—without a contract or any agreement with the company involved—would shut down a department or even a group of departments to secure for themselves the things they found necessary.[8]

Equally deep-rooted in labor history is another kind of committee: the council in which local unions or rank-and-file groups from different places of work make contact with each other, broaden one another's consciousness, and take common action.

The official AFL-CIO central labor body purports to be such an entity, and there are situations in which it will actually function as such. (Montgomery tells of a period in Schenectady when metal workers organized by the IWW were permitted to send delegates to the AFL trades assembly.) In other circumstances workers will have to organize new entities—parallel central labor bodies like the Workers' Solidarity Club of Youngstown—to perform this function. Montgomery describes how at the Westinghouse plant, when a key organizer was dismissed, two thousand men and women walked out. By the next morning, thirteen thousand striking workers linked hands to form a huge human chain around the Westinghouse complex. Giant processions of strikers and supporters gradually closed down the whole valley. On May 1, a parade bedecked with red flags and led by a Lithuanian band, invaded steel mills, chain works, and machinery companies, bringing out thirty-six thousand workers. "The ethnic antagonisms that have absorbed the attention of most historians studying the region's workers seemed to melt away, as the angry and joyous tide of humanity poured through the streets."[9] Essentially the same thing happened in the local general strikes in Minneapolis, Toledo, and San Francisco in 1934. And by whatever name, such as "district assemblies" in the era of the Knights of Labor, or "soviets" in the Russian Revolutions of 1905 and 1917, or local branches of Polish Solidarity, the bodies that coordinate such actions rely on the solidarity of all workers in a particular locality.

Again the 1930s prove to be a storehouse of alternatives. The Los Angeles Labor Notes Committee, in a paper called "The Failure of Business Unionism and the Emergence of a Rank and File Alternative," gives the following example.

Out of a sitdown strike in the Hormel plant at Austin, Minnesota, in 1933 emerged the Independent Union of All Workers (IUAW). It contained meat-packing workers, grocery clerks, butchers, waitresses, bartenders, and many more. All who were employed could join. Like most rank and file organizing efforts at that time, the IUAW was deeply rooted in both workplaces and the general community. It made substantial headway in south-central Minnesota. The IUAW affiliated with the CIO as soon as the new federation came out of the AFL. Representatives of CIO President John L. Lewis immediately split the IUAW into several parts and redistributed them into different international union organizing committees. (How valuable an IUAW-type structure would have been to Local P-9 forty-two years later when its 4,000 members were individually forced to take permanent wage cuts in order to loan Hormel the money to build an automated plant nearby which eliminated over 2,500 jobs.)[10]

We are not speaking of some organizational chart that anyone will impose on the wonderful variety of workers' self-organization. The point is just the reverse: these two kinds of committee—the committee formed at the individual workplace, with its elected delegates or stewards, and the committee of all kinds of workers in a given locality—recur and recur whenever working people organize for themselves, without somebody telling them how to do it.

One sees this again in the 1960s. First came groups of students in different towns where there were colleges for Blacks, sitting in, taking on the local power structure. Then these local committees reached out to one another and, under the guidance of Ella Baker, refused to join the Southern Christian Leadership Conference; instead they formed their own organization, the Student Nonviolent Coordinating Committee (SNCC).

When SNCC reached Mississippi, the second kind of committee became necessary. Rank-and-file activists in that state were connected with different organizations. Some of the most seasoned, like E. W. Steptoe in Amite County and Aaron Henry in Clarksdale, belonged to the NAACP. The Congress of Racial Equality (CORE) had its cadres also, such as Mickey Schwerner and Dave Dennis. And as Bob Moses of SNCC started to organize, first in the southwestern part of the state, in and around McComb, and then in Greenwood and the Mississippi Delta, young men and women, such as Curtis Hayes, Hollis Watkins, Brenda and Jimmie Travis, and Willie Peacock, emerged as SNCC organizers. Wisely, Moses chose not to engage in a struggle for organizational hegemony but instead formed the Council Of Federated Organizations, where, as in a European works' council, many organizations—so to speak, many unions—worked together.

Whether we are in or out of existing trade unions, these are the forms we should be building: shopfloor committees, on the one hand, and parallel central labor bodies, on the other. We must be ready to recognize these forms in different guises. In Youngstown, Solidarity USA is a central labor body for retirees, and WATCH is a central labor body for disabled workers. Thus there can be more than one central labor body: there can be different entities, responding to different constituencies or problems, but with the common feature of cutting across workplace and industry boundaries. Solidarity USA and WATCH recognize their kinship, and fraternally support one another. We are stronger because we have two such bodies, rather than just one.

In times of crisis, shopfloor committees and parallel central labor bodies will reach out to make contact with their counterparts elsewhere. Dockers in Great Britain, nurses in France, miners in the Soviet Union, meatpackers in the United States, have all done so: we don't need more proof of this phenomenon to know that it can happen. We are a little scared to believe that the same process can happen across national boundaries. But of course it can. The key is an attitude of solidarity nurtured and practiced at the local level, as when, in one Polish city, steelworkers went on strike on behalf of teachers' demands while teachers stayed on the job to teach everybody's children.

The Spirit in Which We Build New Forms

For some time to come, the actions we may be able to take on behalf of a new kind of labor internationalism will be very small. We are at that stage in organizing when what we are really doing is meeting people, making friends, building community in the one-on-one manner memorably described by Ignazio Silone in *Bread and Wine*, or by Stan Weir and Bob Miles in their image of the "singlejack" miners, one holding the spike, the other swinging the sledge, who after a time change places.

This means somehow finding the time and money physically to take ourselves to other countries, as Stan did in coming to know the "coordinadora" movement on the Spanish docks, or as eight of us from Youngstown, Aliquippa, and Pittsburgh did in 1988 when we spent two weeks at a Nicaraguan steel mill.

I want to say a few more words about the spirit in which we take these first small steps.

We speak of a "horizontal" as opposed to a "vertical" style of organization. We all know what we mean by this, but the word "horizontal" is very clinical, very two-dimensional, very cold. Horizontal organizing is organizing on the basis of labor solidarity: it is relying not on technical expertise, nor on numbers of signed-up members, nor yet on a bureaucratic chain of command, but on the spark that leaps from person to person, especially in times of common crisis. It is solidarity unionism.

And solidarity unionism is unionism in the spirit not only of the Wobblies and the rank-and-file organizers of the early 1930s and the early 1960s and of our heroic brothers and sisters at Hormel and Pittston: solidarity unionism is unionism re-created and rediscovered in the spirit of the feminist movement. One of the reasons why the labor movement is so dead, and so dull, is the degree to which it is dominated by males, and by masculine values of fighting, dominating, and ranking people one above the other. If it is true, as I have argued, that innovation will come from the margins, from the unorganized, from the disregarded, this means among other things that the new will come from women and will be led by women. In Youngstown, the charismatic leader who founded Solidarity USA was a woman whose husband was a steelworker, and the chairperson of WATCH is a woman. The feminization of the workforce is a good and hopeful thing, and I believe we will find, as we come to meet our counterparts in other countries, that very often the convenors of base communities and the spokespersons for shopfloor committees— although less often those who go to international conferences—will be women. We should cherish this feminization of the labor movement, we should recognize the kinship in spirit between solidarity and feminism, and those of us who are males should self-consciously seek to step back from conventional leadership roles and learn to lead by serving.

There is also a religious dimension to what we will be doing. I know it's a scandal to say this among unreconstructed Wobblies, but it's true nonetheless. During the Pittston strike, people who for generations have had very quick trigger fingers in those cricks and hollers of Appalachia acted out nonviolent civil disobedience to a degree unknown in the United States since the 1960s. I am aware that nonviolence was not all that went on. Still, if it is true that Cecil Roberts and others were influenced by Taylor Branch's *Parting of the Waters,* a book about Martin Luther King and his times, that strikes me as extraordinary.

We will find the same thing in Latin America. After years of feeling that in this country I was too Christian for the Marxists and too Marxist for the Christians, I went to Nicaragua and felt that everyone I met was like myself.

There is a scene in the movie *Romero* that I cannot get out of my mind, and with which I would like to close. A young Hispanic woman is taken to a garbage dump to be shot by a right-wing death squad. She is slight, black-haired. There is blood all over her white dress, and she presumably has been repeatedly raped. Later we are told that her tongue has been cut off. She is directed to kneel. Instead she remains standing, and, tottering, turns to face those who are about to kill her.

She is from the Third World, that garbage dump for United States imperialism. She is a woman. Beginning as a Christian who took religion seriously, she has become a revolutionary. I think she is saying to us that although we are few, and are just beginning, and feel overwhelmed by the forces arrayed against us, nothing on earth can prevent us from prevailing in the end.

> In our hands there is a power greater than their hoarded
>   gold,
> Greater than the power of armies multiplied a thousandfold,
> We can bring to birth a new world from the ashes of the
>   old,
> For our union [our solidarity] makes us strong.

12 The Webbs, Lenin, Rosa Luxemburg

In *The Communist Manifesto,* Marx and Engels pictured a working class that would be radicalized in the course of its own self-activity. The contradictions of capitalism would deepen. Workers would engage in conflict with employers on a broader and broader scale. This widening conflict would necessarily become political as the state intervened on the side of the employers: "[E]very class struggle is a political struggle," they wrote.[1]

Marx and Engels were at pains to disavow the notion that Communists brought ideas into the workers' movement from without.

> The Communists . . . have no interests separate and apart from those of the proletariat as a whole.
>
> They do not set up any sectarian principles of their own, by which to shape and mould the proletarian movement. . . .

Paper delivered at the North American Labor History Conference, October 1995.

The theoretical conclusions of the Communists are in no way based on ideas or principles that have been invented, or discovered, by this or that would-be universal reformer.

They merely *express, in general terms, actual relations springing from an existing class struggle, from a historical movement going on under our very eyes.*[2]

Believing that radical working-class consciousness would develop on the basis of experience made necessary by life itself, Marx affirmed throughout his life that "the emancipation of the working class would be the act of the workers themselves."[3]

The theory of working-class radicalization set forth in *The Communist Manifesto* is a powerful engine of explanation. It was exemplified in the United States by the experience of Eugene Debs. Debs, initially associated with a railroad workers' craft union, first organized an industrial union of all railroad workers, and then, when the federal government crushed the Pullman strike, he became a socialist.[4]

The Webbs and Lenin

A very different sequence of events—if anything, a deradicalization rather than a radicalization of labor—unfolded in Great Britain. In 1894, the year of the Pullman strike, Sidney and Beatrice Webb published *The History of Trade Unionism*. The Webbs found that the "revolutionary period" in the history of the British labor movement was in the beginning, in 1829–1842.[5] Surveying the emergent business unionism in Great Britain, the Webbs found it good, or at any rate inevitable. They concluded in their *Industrial Democracy*, published in 1898, that

in spite of crude ideas of democracy suited only to little autonomous communities, and in spite of a strong prejudice in favor of local exclusiveness, the Trade Union world has, throughout its whole history, manifested an overpowering impulse to the amalgamation of local trade clubs into national unions, with centralised funds and centralised administration.... The Trade Union of the future will, therefore, be co-extensive with its craft, national in its scope, centralised in its administration, and served by an expert official staff of its own.[6]

Even in 1920, when an updated edition of *The History* was published, the Webbs concluded—after the formation of the British Labor Party, after the shop stewards' movement in Great Britain during the first World War, and after the Russian Revolutions of 1905 and 1917—that the principal deficiency of the British labor movement was the absence of a sufficient core of properly chosen and trained full-time staff representatives.[7]

In just those same years that Debs was becoming a socialist and the Webbs were publishing what amounted to a rationale for business unionism, in 1894–1895, Lenin began his own work as a labor organizer in St. Petersburg. He and other Russian Marxists of that time used as the basis of their work a pamphlet called *On Agitation*. *On Agitation* was written by Alexander Kremer and Lenin's future Menshevik opponent, Julius Martov. It generalized the experience of organizers in Poland, where industrialization was further advanced than in Russia, and echoed the basic thesis of *The Communist Manifesto*.[8]

According to *On Agitation*, "the task of Social Democrats is one of constant agitation among factory workers on the basis of their everyday needs and demands." The workers' awareness of their social situation develops progressively in the course of clashes with the powers that be. "Spreading out as it progresses, embracing entire industries instead of separate factories, the movement collides with government authorities at every step. Thus their consciousness matures. . . . The ground is now prepared for political agitation. This agitation finds a class *organized by life itself*."[9]

The distribution of a series of leaflets exposing factory conditions, as recommended by *On Agitation*, was very successful.[10] The leaflets invariably concluded with a call to strike until the offending conditions were corrected. When a general strike of more than thirty thousand St. Petersburg textile workers erupted in the summer of 1896, the utility of the new method seemed to have been proved by experience.[11]

Although arrested in December 1895, and then imprisoned, exiled, and out of contact with Russian workers until 1900, in his writings through at least 1897 Lenin embraced the organizing method set forth in *On Agitation*. For example, in 1896 Lenin drafted in prison a program for the Social Democratic party. There Lenin wrote of the desirable relationship between workers and intellectuals:

> The Russian Social Democratic party declares as its task to *help* this struggle of the Russian working class by developing labor's class-consciousness, assisting its organization, and showing it the real goals of the struggle. . . . The task of the party is not to invent in its head some fashionable methods of

helping the workers, but to *join* the labor movement, to illuminate it, to *help* the workers in the struggle which they have begun to wage themselves.

As Richard Pipes comments, "The whole tenor of this definition is quite un-Bolshevik insofar as it places emphasis on assisting, not leading, labor." Further, with regard to the priorities of the party, Lenin wrote that Social Democrats should give their "main attention" to the struggle of workers for their daily needs. And finally, economic struggle was perceived to lead naturally to radical political consciousness in exactly the manner predicted by *The Communist Manifesto*.

> This struggle develops the political consciousness of the workers. The mass of workers live in conditions which give them neither the leisure nor the opportunity to think about any political problems. But the struggle of the workers with factory owners for their daily needs confronts them *of itself and inevitably* [*sama soboi i neizbezhno*] with problems of state and politics, showing them what Russia's political system is, how laws and ordinances are issued, and whose interests they serve. Every conflict in the factory inevitably brings the workers in conflict with laws and with the representatives of state power.

Pipes rightly concludes, "These statements are, of course, merely a restatement of the thesis that Kremer and Martov outlined in *Ob agitatsii*."[12]

But in those very same years, according to fellow organizers, Lenin was consistently "against any sort of autonomous workers' organizations, . . . against allowing the workers any function of control," and insisted that funds should be in the hands of Social Democratic intellectuals rather than workers.[13] The strategy of *On Agitation*, which drew more and more workers into conflicts from which they learned for themselves how to interpret their social world, conflicted head-on with the belief that a cadre of self-selected professional revolutionaries should control the agitation. By the time he wrote *What Is to Be Done?* in 1902, Lenin had scrapped the organizing method so as to ensure that control remained in the hands of professional revolutionaries.

A telling detail in this connection is Lenin's insistence on taking militant workers out of the shop. "A workingman who is at all talented and 'promising,' *must not be left* to work eleven hours a day in a factory. We must arrange that he be maintained by the party, that he may in due time go underground, that he change the place of his activity, otherwise he will not enlarge his experience, he will not widen his outlook, and he will not be able to stay in the fight against the gendarmes for several years."[14]

This transformation in Lenin's outlook was influenced by Sidney and Beatrice Webb. Lenin translated the Webbs' *Industrial Democracy* while in Siberian exile in 1898 and accepted the findings of the Webbs with regard to the development of trade unions.[15] Thus Lenin wrote in *What Is to Be Done?*: "The history of all countries shows that the working class, exclusively by its own effort, is able to develop only trade-union consciousness." Socialist consciousness could only be brought to workers "from without," by Marxist intellectuals. The spontaneous labor movement, Lenin wrote elsewhere in the same pamphlet, "is pure and simple trade unionism." Hence the task of socialists is "to *divert* the labour movement, with its spontaneous trade-unionist striving," and bring it under the wing of revolutionary Social Democracy.[16]

Lenin set forth his views about the limits of trade-union consciousness as a prelude to his argument for a centralized vanguard party of professional revolutionaries. In *What Is to Be Done?* Lenin quoted with approval the Webbs' condemnation of trade union "primitive democracy":

> In Mr. and Mrs. Webb's book on trade unionism, there is an interesting section on "Primitive Democracy." In this section, the authors relate how, in the first period of existence of their unions, the British workers thought that in the interests of democracy all the workers must take part in the work of managing the unions; not only were all questions decided by the votes of all the members, but all the official duties were fulfilled by all the members in turn. A long period of historical experience was required to teach these workers how absurd such a conception of democracy was and to make them understand the necessity for representative institutions on the one hand, and of full-time professional officials on the other.[17]

Lenin contrasted to such an "absurd" state of affairs the efficiency of full-time functionaries who specialized in particular tasks. Lenin now viewed himself as a full-time (revolutionary) functionary and looked back on the time he had spent with individual workers in the era of *On Agitation* as a waste of time.

> In collecting illegal material from workers . . . we waste a lot of the efforts of revolutionists. . . . I very distinctly remember my "first experiment," which

I am not going to repeat. I spent many weeks "examining" a workingman, who came to visit me, about the conditions prevailing in the enormous factory at which he was employed. True, after great effort, I managed to obtain material for a description (of just one single factory!), but at the end of each interview the workingman would wipe the sweat from his brow, and say to me smilingly: "I would rather work overtime than reply to your questions!"[18]

The Webbs also misled Lenin to expect that Russian workers would organize themselves in national trade unions, so that "in order that this work may be carried out, we must have a single, All-Russian organisation of revolutionists capable of undertaking the leadership of the All-Russian trade unions."[19] In fact, during the years when Lenin was developing his ideas on organization, St. Petersburg workers repeatedly created city-wide central bodies made up of representatives from a variety of industrial trades, districts, and workplaces.[20] In 1905 and 1917 workers all over Russia would organize, not through all-Russian trade unions, but through local central labor bodies that came to be called soviets.

The activity of the soviets in 1917 occasioned a final chapter in the relationship between Lenin and the Webbs. During the summer of 1917 Lenin wished to discredit the Russian national government, including its parliament, and to enhance the legitimacy of factory committees and soviets. Reversing what he had said in *What Is to Be Done?* about the absurdity of "primitive democracy," Lenin wrote in *State and Revolution:*

> One of the "founders" of modern opportunism, Eduard Bernstein, has more than once indulged in vulgar bourgeois jeers at "primitive" democracy. . . .
>
> In his renegade book, *The Premises of Socialism,* Bernstein wars against the ideas of "primitive" democracy, and against what he calls "doctrinaire democracy": binding mandates, unpaid officials, impotent central representative bodies, etc. To prove that this "primitive" democracy is unsound, Bernstein refers to the experience of the British trade unions, as interpreted by the Webbs. Seventy years of development "in complete freedom," he avers . . . , convinced the trade unions that primitive democracy was useless, and they replaced it with ordinary democracy, i.e., parliamentarism combined with bureaucracy.
>
> As a matter of fact, the trade unions did not develop "in complete freedom" *but in complete capitalist slavery,* under which, it goes without saying, "we do not get along" without a number of concessions to the prevailing evil, to violence, falsehood, and exclusion of the poor from the affairs of the

"higher" administration. Under socialism much of the "primitive" democracy will inevitably be revived since, for the first time in the history of civi-
lized societies, the *mass* of the population will rise to take an *independent* part,
not only in voting and elections, *but also in the everyday administration.*[21]

But the Bolsheviks viewed the party rather than the soviets (or factory committees) as the basic vehicle of revolution. The workers' self-
activity celebrated by Lenin in these passages did not long survive the
November Revolution.[22]

A Third Path: Rosa Luxemburg

For roughly the past century, labor historians in the United States
have used the explanatory paradigms created by the Webbs and by
Lenin. The first such paradigm might be termed *bureaucratic business
unionism.* Originating in the work of the Webbs, it has been replicated
by Selig Perlman and associates in the 1920s, and more recently by David
Brody. A second position, set forth by Lenin, accepts the Webbs' labor
history but asserts that radical ideas can nonetheless be injected into the
labor movement from without by socialist intellectuals. Historians who
emphasize the positive work of Leftist leaders in the early CIO, especially
in promoting racial equality, provide latter-day variants of this second
paradigm. We might call this the *political vanguard* view of labor history.

Rosa Luxemburg exemplifies a third interpretive paradigm. This
third view is consistent with the emphasis of recent labor studies on history from the bottom up and on oral history; on the history of workers,
not just of trade unions; on the development of working-class culture
and consciousness; and on the critical contribution of women. I propose
the awkward English term "self-activity" as the term that may best indicate where Luxemburg's ideas originated and to which contemporaries
she was most closely connected.[23]

Luxemburg's self-activity analysis can be understood as a dialectical
synthesis of Marx's vision of working-class *Selbsttätigkeit,* or "self-activity"
(thesis), and the Webbs' understanding of the natural tendencies of
trade unions in a capitalist society (antithesis). As Marx had revised his
view of state and revolution by observing the Paris Commune of 1871, so
Luxemburg elaborated the concept of working-class self-activity on the
basis of her encounters with German trade unionism and with the Russ-

ian Revolution of 1905. Also during the first quarter of the twentieth century, but at different times and in both cases only for a certain period of years, Alexandra Kollontai and Leon Trotsky set forth similar ideas, using the Russian term *samodeyatelnost*, or "spontaneous, self-directed activity."[24]

Luxemburg developed her doctrine after reading the Webbs[25] and in conscious opposition to Lenin. She agreed with Lenin that *trade unions* operate within the logic of the capitalist system and have no interest in transforming capitalism into socialism. Unlike Lenin in *What Is to Be Done?*, however, she believed that *workers* would in the course of their own self-directed activity come into fundamental opposition to existing institutions and be radicalized in the process. Unorganized workers, outside the trade unions, would have a central role. And intellectual radicals like herself would also play an essential part, not by injecting political ideas into working-class consciousness from the outside, but by accompanying workers and helping to articulate the goals implicit in their struggle.

Lenin's *What Is to Be Done?* appeared in 1902, and his *One Step Forward, Two Steps Back*, a discussion of the Russian Social Democratic Party congress of 1903, in 1904. In 1904 Luxemburg replied to Lenin's views on party organization with a pamphlet that prefigured what she would begin to write about labor strategy two years later. In "Organizational Questions of the Russian Social Democracy," Luxemburg said that the question before Russian Social Democracy was

> [h]ow to effect a transition from the type of organization characteristic of the preparatory stage of the socialist movement—usually featured by disconnected groups and clubs, with propaganda as a principal activity—to the unity of a large, national body, suited for concerted political action over the entire vast territory ruled by the Russian state?[26]

This was a description of the primitive democratic stage in the development of a political party strikingly similar to the Webbs' description of the primitive democratic phase of trade unionism.

Lenin's solution to the question facing Russian socialists was, in Luxemburg's phrase, "pitiless centralism." Lenin's thesis, she went on, "is that the party Central Committee should have the privilege of naming all the local committees of the party. . . . It should also have the right to impose on all of them its own ready-made rules of party conduct. It should have the right to rule without appeal on such questions as the dissolution and reconstitution of local organizations. . . . The Central Committee would be the only thinking element in the party. All other groupings would be its executive limbs."[27]

Luxemburg conceded that in Russia, as in Germany, there must be a single, nationwide socialist party, not a federation of local groups. But the issue was "the degree of centralization necessary" inside such a party, she insisted. Lenin's critical error was to allow no space for "the direct, independent action of the masses."[28] Along with the "blind subordination" of all party organs to the party center, Lenin advocated "[t]he necessity of selecting, and constituting as a separate corps, all the active revolutionists, as distinguished from the unorganized, though revolutionary, mass surrounding this elite."[29]

Luxemburg opposed the domination of professional revolutionaries over class-conscious workers. Social Democratic centralism could not be the centralism of a handful of conspiratorial leaders, whose tactics could "be decided on in advance and took the form of a ready-made plan." Except for general principles of the struggle, "there do not exist for the Social Democracy detailed sets of tactics which a Central Committee can teach the party membership in the same way as troops are instructed in their training camps." Rather, socialist centralism is "so to speak, the 'self-centralism' of the advanced sectors of the proletariat."[30]

Lenin, Luxemburg wrote, "glorifies the educative influence of the factory, which, he says, accustoms the proletariat to 'discipline and organization'." The kind of discipline Lenin had in mind "is being implanted in the working class not only by the factory but also by the military and the existing state bureaucracy—by the entire mechanism of the centralized bourgeois state." Luxemburg rejected a "discipline" that was "the regulated docility of an oppressed class." To it she counterposed *self*-discipline, "the spontaneous co-ordination of the conscious, political acts of a body of [human beings]," a freely assumed self-discipline that resulted not from the discipline imposed by the capitalist state but by extirpating, "to the last root," old habits of obedience and servility.[31]

In reality, said Luxemburg, the most fruitful changes in the tactical policy of Russian Social Democracy during the previous decade had "not been the inventions of several leaders and even less so of any central organizational organs. They have always been the spontaneous products of the movement in ferment."

[T]he first stage of the proletarian movement . . . began with the spontaneous general strike of St. Petersburg in 1896. . . . [The following period
was] introduced by the spontaneous street demonstrations of St. Petersburg
students in March 1901. The general strike of Rostov-on-Don, in 1903, mark-
ing the next great tactical turn in the Russian proletarian movement, was
also a spontaneous act. "All by itself," the strike expanded into political
demonstrations, street agitation, great outdoor meetings, which the most
optimistic revolutionist would not have dreamed of several years before.[32]

Moreover, "the initiative and conscious leadership of the Social
Democratic organizations played an insignificant role in this development." Had there been such a guiding center, it "would probably have
increased the disorder of the local committees by emphasizing the difference between the eager attack of the mass and the prudent position
of the Social Democracy." Experience shows—and here Luxemburg
almost took the step from party history to labor history—"that every time
the labor movement wins new terrain, [the directing organs of the
socialist party] work it to the utmost. They transform it at the same time
into a kind of bastion, which holds up advance on a wider scale."[33] Thus:

If the tactics of the socialist party are not to be the creation of a Central Committee but of the whole party, or, still better, of the whole labor movement,
then it is clear that the party sections and federations need the liberty of
action which alone will permit them to develop their revolutionary initiative
and to utilize all the resources of a situation. The ultra-centralism asked by
Lenin is full of the sterile spirit of the overseer. It is not a positive and creative spirit. *Lenin's concern is not so much to make the activity of the party more fruitful as to control the party—to narrow the movement rather than to develop it, to bind
rather than to unify it.*[34]

In conclusion, Luxemburg asserted that Russian Social Democracy
required "the co-ordination and unification of the movement and not its
rigid submission to a set of regulations." For, as she wrote in words that
have immortalized this essay, "the errors committed by a truly revolutionary movement are infinitely more fruitful than the infallibility of the
cleverest Central Committee."[35]

It is easy to see what would happen when this believer in workers'
self-education[36] confronted the practices of a German labor movement

thoroughly committed to bureaucratized business unionism. Already in 1899, in her *Reform or Revolution,* Luxemburg had shredded the notion that the daily struggle of the working class through trade unions would gradually bring about a socialist society. Trade unions, she insisted, were necessary but defensive institutions. The indispensable struggle of trade unions merely to maintain the worker's share of capitalist profits was "a sort of labor of Sisyphus."[37] This was a phrase for which German trade union leaders are said never to have forgiven her.[38] Also in 1899, at the party congress, she said about English trade unions what she already thought about German ones: "From a school of class solidarity and socialist ethics, the trade union movement became a business, a commerce, . . . a highly complex work of art, a comfortable home erected for permanence, and in the whole working class world of that period a *spirit of prudent,* if somewhat *restricted* statesmanship reigned."[39]

And then came Luxemburg's visit to Russia in the throes of its 1905 revolution, "the central experience of her life."[40]

The Revolution of 1905 and Luxemburg's Theory of the General Strike

Luxemburg described the self-activity of Polish and Russian workers in the 1905 revolution in words that, with a change in place-names, would equally describe the early 1930s in the United States or the time of the creation of Solidarity in Poland. Writing in Finland during the summer of 1906 after her release from a Polish prison, at the request of the Social Democratic branch in Hamburg where the biggest German strike of 1905–1906 had occurred,[41] Luxemburg grouped her observations around the phenomenon of the *Massenstreik,* in English "the general strike."

The all-important first point was the same made in her reply to Lenin: a general strike is not the product of leadership decisions. The general strike had not been "propagated" or even "discussed" in Russian political circles before it happened.

> If . . . the Russian Revolution teaches us anything, it teaches above all that the mass strike is not artificially "made," not "decided" at random, not "propagated." . . . If anyone were to undertake to make the mass strike generally, as a form of proletarian action, the object of methodical agitation,

and go house-to-house canvassing with this "idea" in order to gradually win the working class to it, it would be . . . idle and profitless and absurd.[42]

No, "the mass strike in Russia displays such a multiplicity of the most varied forms of action that it is altogether impossible to speak of 'the' mass strike, of an abstract schematic mass strike. All the factors of the mass strike, as well as its character, are not only different in the different towns and districts of the country, but its general character has often changed in the course of the revolution."[43]

Luxemburg then plunged into a history of Russian general strikes from 1896 to 1906. The 1896 general strike in St. Petersburg was a strike of textile workers. Spinners and weavers in St. Petersburg worked thirteen, fourteen, fifteen hours a day at miserable piecework rates. On the occasion of the czar's coronation in 1896, textile employers required their workers to take three days off work without pay. A meeting of three hundred workers put forward the demands of payment for the "holidays," a ten-hour day, and higher piece rates. In a week forty thousand workers were on strike. The strike began over a relatively minor matter; it was outwardly a mere struggle for economic demands; and the strike was brutally suppressed. But these indicia were misleading. The next January "the textile workers of St. Petersburg repeated the general strike [and achieved] the legal introduction of a working day of eleven hours throughout the whole of Russia." And these strikes were entered into "without a trace of organization or of strike funds."[44]

The general strike in the Caucasus in 1902 likewise was triggered by an apparently accidental and wholly economic issue: the proposed transportation of four hundred unemployed petroleum workers to their respective home districts in March 1902. At Rostov in November 1902 the inciting event was a dispute about pay rates in the railroad shops. Again the strike demands were seemingly nonpolitical, for "a nine-hour day, increase of wages, abolition of fines, dismissal of obnoxious engineers, etc." All work in Rostov stopped, and "every day monster meetings of fifteen to twenty thousand were held in the open air, sometimes surrounded by a cordon of Cossacks." Again the strike ended in massacre and apparent defeat.[45]

But in May, June, and July of 1903 the whole of South Russia was ablaze. Here again, "the movement did not arise on any preconceived plan." Thus in Tiflis, "the strike was begun by 2000 commercial employees who had a working day from six o'clock in the morning to eleven at night. On the fourth of July they all left their shops and made a circuit of the town to demand from the proprietors of the shops that they close their premises," very much as in David Montgomery's description of the Westinghouse strike of 1916 in East Pittsburgh. In Odessa the movement began with a wage struggle by a so-called Zubatov union, the equivalent in early twentieth-century Russia to the company unions of the early 1930s in the United States. In Kiev the strike began when two delegates of the railwaymen were arrested, and at the station all the strikers with their wives and families sat down on the tracks to stop trains from leaving town. When police fired into the crowd, killing thirty to forty persons, the whole of Kiev went on strike. "The movement was soon at an end. But the printers had won a shortening of the working day by one hour and a wage increase of one ruble; in a yeast factory the eight-hour day was introduced; the railway workshops were closed by order of the ministry; other departments continued partial strikes for their demands."[46]

One could go on and on; Rosa Luxemburg does. She was at particular pains to stress that the seemingly anarchistic, chaotic actions of the 1905 general strike had produced tangible gains in working-class life throughout Russia. Reflecting her broader conclusion that Russia was now leading the proletariat of western Europe, she wrote: "At the present time the actual working day in Russian industry leaves behind not only Russian factory legislation (that is, the legal working day of eleven hours) but even the actual conditions of Germany."[47] She emphasized as well the widespread formation of trade unions and, in passing, the creation in St. Petersburg of "a 'central bureau,' that is, a trade-union council": the celebrated St. Petersburg soviet.[48]

Even in detail the style and forms of self-organization in the Russian Revolution of 1905 prefigured participatory democracy of the early 1930s in the United States. Like workers at the Westinghouse plant in East Pittsburgh in the mid-1930s, St. Petersburg workers in October 1905 decided to inform the bosses of the conditions on which they would continue to work. As Luxemburg tells it:

> That means that on the appointed day all the workers in Petersburg should inform their employers that they were not willing to work more than eight hours a day, and should leave their places of work at the end of eight hours. The idea was the occasion of lively agitation, was accepted by the proletariat with enthusiasm and carried out, but very great sacrifices were not thereby

avoided. Thus for example, the eight-hour day meant an enormous fall in wages for the textile workers who had hitherto worked eleven hours and that on a system of piecework. This, however, they willingly accepted. *Within a week the eight-hour day prevailed in every factory and workshop in Petersburg.*[49]

Workers in Russia in 1905–1906 like workers in the early 1930s in the United States also preferred to share work in a spirit of solidarity rather than practice strict seniority. Luxemburg wrote to Karl and Luise Kautsky:

Workers everywhere are, by themselves, reaching agreements whereby, for instance, the employed give up one day's wages every week for the unemployed. Or, where employment is reduced to four days a week, there they arrange it in such a way that no one is laid off, but that everyone works a few hours less per week.

The same letter told of the formation of factory committees remarkably like those that surfaced everywhere in 1932–1935 in the States. "[I]n all factories, committees, elected by the workers, have arisen 'on their own,' which decide on all matters relating to working conditions, hirings and firings of workers, etc. The employer has ceased being 'the master of his own house.' "[50]

The work of one such committee, that of the Moscow printers, is described in an article Luxemburg wrote in October 1906. She quoted the following excerpts from the "wage agreement between the Moscow printers and the bosses":

1. The question as to how the factory is to be subdivided for the election of the workers' representatives shall be decided in the general assembly of the factory workers. The assembly for this purpose shall be convened upon the wish of one-tenth of the workers employed in the factory, and shall be held in the absence of the management and chaired by a freely elected chairman.

3. Every factory department shall elect its own representatives, one for each 50 workers (or fraction thereof).

4. All workers of eighteen years of age or over, without regard to sex or length of employment, shall be eligible to stand for election and to vote in the election of delegates.

8. The factory management shall not have the right to discharge the elected representatives of the workers prior to the expir[ation] of their term of office (one year). In the event that the factory management intends to discharge a delegate immediately upon the expir[ation] of his term of office, it shall be obliged to communicate its intention to all the workers one month prior thereto.

9. The workers' representatives must be gainfully employed. They shall be free to depart from the general working regulations in the event that the duties of their office so require. The factory management may not make any wage deductions for such activities.

10. The workers' representatives shall attend all meetings between the workers and the factory management, except in such cases as the representatives permit the factory management to deal directly with the workers.

11. The workers' representatives shall decide collectively on the question of hiring and firing each worker after the factory management has submitted to them the pertinent facts. Where the owners are not satisfied with the decision of the representative commission, they may appeal to the general assembly of factory workers.

12. The workers' representatives shall decide the maximum number of apprentices permissible for each department and for the whole factory.

13. The workers' representatives shall ensure the strict mutual adherence of the last agreement between the workers and the factory directorate.

16. The workers shall be obliged to support their representatives with all their power. In the event of disciplinary punishment they must support the same wage demands, strikes, boycotts etc., as their representatives.

17. The delegates of the workers shall function as the factory's representatives in relations with other labour organizations. They shall be obliged to remain in the closest contact with the latter, and shall inform all the workers of their factory on the state of the workers' struggle in other enterprises.[51]

The Revolutionary Role of Unorganized Workers

Rosa Luxemburg returned from Russia to Germany late in 1906 with a *self-activity* paradigm fully formed in her mind. From then until she died in 1919 she agitated for the general strike as the basic form of labor struggle appropriate in a mature capitalist society such as Germany. In the latter sections of her pamphlet on the general strike, she argued against the idea that the Russian Revolution of 1905 was a passing phase of labor development soon to be superseded or that it was "solely the product of specifically Russian conditions which need not be taken into account by the German proletariat."[52]

According to Luxemburg, the apparent differences between Russia and Germany were exaggerated, especially when one considered the unorganized workers who made up the majority of each country's working class. Beyond the quarter of a million German trade union members were the mine workers, the textile workers, the homeworkers, the ready-made clothing workers, the electricity workers, the railway and postal employees, and workers on the land. These were social spheres "in which there is a great deal of 'Russian' absolutism in its most naked form, and in which economically the most elementary reckonings with capital have first to be made." Even among trade unionists, she contended, the Russian demands for the eight-hour day, for the introduction of workers' committees into all the factories, for the abolition of piecework and of homework in handicraft, for the complete observance of Sunday rest, and for recognition of the right to organize had not been achieved in Germany.[53]

Luxemburg rejected the "attitude of many trade-unionists" in Germany that one had first to organize the rest of the working class into trade unions and only *then* think about such a hazardous trial of strength as a general strike. Luxemburg viewed this as a "rigid, mechanical-bureaucratic conception" which "cannot conceive of the struggle save as the product of organization at a certain stage of its strength." Such an approach would end by dividing the proletariat into a labor aristocracy organized in trade unions, and a great mass of marginalized unorganized workers. Luxemburg argued that

> even in Britain, which has had a whole century of indefatigable trade-union effort without any "disturbances"—except at the beginning in the period of the Chartist movement—without any "romantic revolutionary" errors or temptations, it has not been possible to do more than organize a minority of the better-paid sections of the proletariat.

Russia pointed to a better way. Rather than struggle arising from organization, "the living, dialectical explanation makes the organization arise as a product of the struggle. We have already seen a grandiose example of this phenomenon in Russia, where a proletariat almost wholly unorganized created a comprehensive network of organizational appendages in a year and a half of stormy revolutionary struggle."

Luxemburg concluded that "the plan of undertaking mass strikes as a serious political class action with organized workers only is absolutely hopeless. If the mass strike, or rather, mass strikes, and the mass struggle are to be successful they must become a real *people's movement*, that is, the widest sections of the proletariat must be drawn into the fight." A strategy of class struggle which does not reckon with the cooperation of the entire labor community, "which is based upon the idea of the finely stage-managed march out of the small, well-trained part of the proletariat, is foredoomed to be a miserable fiasco." Generally, in German Social Democratic discourse there was an overestimate of the role of organizations and an "underestimate of the unorganized proletarian mass and of their political maturity."

The class consciousness evident in Russia was the product of "direct revolutionary mass action." Six months of a revolutionary period would educate the as yet unorganized masses of Germany more than could "ten years of public demonstrations and distribution of leaflets." When Germany came to such a time, "the sections which are today unorganized and backward will, in the struggle, prove themselves the most radical."[54]

Luxemburg closed her pamphlet on the general strike with a critique of those very full-time functionaries that the Webbs (and in his own way, Lenin) ardently advocated. The rapid growth of the German trade-union movement had brought with it the "necessary evil" of a regular trade-union officialdom. But at a certain point this necessary means would become an obstacle to further development. The specialized activity of trade-union leaders all too naturally produces "bureaucratism and a certain narrowness of outlook."

Such functionaries tend to "the overvaluation of the organization, which from a means has gradually been changed into an end in itself, a precious thing, to which the interests of the struggles should be subordinated. From this also comes that openly admitted need for peace which shrinks from great risks and presumed dangers to the stability of the trade unions." In labor newspapers edited by such bureaucrats, only the positive side of the daily struggle is emphasized. "Fulsome flattery and boundless optimism are considered to be the duty of every 'friend of the trade-union movement'."

Likewise the appearance of full-time functionaries brings about "a revolution in the relations of leaders and rank and file. In place of the direction of colleagues through local committees, with their admitted inadequacy, there appears the businesslike direction of trade-union officials." Initiative and the power of making decisions become the tasks of trade-union specialists, while for the mass of members there remains "the more passive virtue of discipline." The working masses of social democracy, in and out of trade unions, must therefore "learn how to express their capacity for decision and action, and therewith to demonstrate their ripeness for that time of great struggles and great tasks in which . . . the directing bodies . . . will only be the interpreters of the will of the masses."[55]

That time of great struggles and great tasks was not far distant. In her earliest debates with Bernstein's revisionism, Luxemburg had insisted that capitalism was *not* stabilizing itself, that the contradictions of capitalism would in the end produce wider and deeper catastrophe than anything yet experienced.[56] The First World War seemed to prove her right all too abundantly.

Against War and Violence

Rosa Luxemburg was passionately opposed to militarism, imperialism, and war. She wrote in 1912 that "no thinking proletarian woman can help being a deadly enemy" of militarism.[57] On September 16, 1913, she made a speech in Frankfurt in which she touched on the question of whether Social Democrats would permit themselves to be dragged helplessly into a war. After shouts of "Never" in the body of the hall, she is supposed to have said, "If they think we are going to lift the weapons of murder against our French and other brethren, then we shall shout: 'We will not do it'."[58] These are the words that caused her to be tried, convicted, and, after the war began the next August, imprisoned. Meantime Luxemburg toured the country, denouncing the brutal treatment of recruits in the German army. The Minister of War asked for her indictment "in the name of the entire corps of officers and non-commissioned officers of the German army." An appeal was published for defense witnesses to come forward and testify about maltreatment of recruits. After one thousand former conscripts presented themselves, the indictment was dropped.[59]

The outbreak of the first World War caused Luxemburg and other female leaders of the Second International, such as Clara Zetkin, Angelica Balabanoff, and Alexandra Kollontai to draw together in protest. Kollontai, who happened to be in the Reichstag on the day that the Social

Democratic deputies voted for war taxes, wrote that the silence and passivity of German workers in the face of war was the result of their years of silence and passivity in the German Social Democratic movement.

> If the working masses are to be capable not only of grasping the significance of current political events but also of responding actively to them without having to wait for the word from above, it is necessary to cultivate a tradition of open activity, to foster faith in one's own strength and to allow for what we can call "revolutionary experience." It was this experience that was avoided in Germany. The party leaders grew to resemble old-fashioned pedagogues: on the one hand they developed class thinking, but on the other, they held back and impeded manifestations of revolutionary will or mass action in every way. . . .
>
> Take, for example, the sphere of trade-union struggle. The amazing successes of German industry over the past twelve years have created a situation which favours the increasingly frequent application of compromise tactics. The employers, in order to avoid open struggle, . . . were willing to offer the workers certain minimal handouts; the union centres would rush to accept and arrange a "peaceful compromise." Is it not significant that at a time when the total number of industrial conflicts was rising the number ending in strike action was decreasing relatively?[60]

From Sweden, Kollontai addressed a passionate declaration to women in which she called on them to unite in a "war on war."[61]

Luxemburg sent telegrams to three hundred German officials who were considered to be oppositionist, inviting them to Berlin for an emergency conference. Only Clara Zetkin immediately cabled support. Through the journal *Gleichheit*, which she edited, Zetkin tried to unite women against the war under the slogan, "If men are killing, it is women's duty to come forward for life."[62] Early in 1915, Rosa Luxemburg was about to leave Germany with Clara Zetkin to attend an international women's conference for peace at the Hague when she was arrested and imprisoned.[63]

That same spring of 1915, Zetkin asked Balabanoff's help in convening a conference in Bern, Switzerland, of working women against the war. Lenin, who directed the Bolshevik women delegates from a nearby cafe, insisted that the conference adopt the slogan of turning the world war into a civil war. Only when Zetkin again and again "appealed to [the Bolsheviks] to withdraw their resolution" was a compromise finally arranged. The conference published a leaflet for women that began:

Where are your husbands, your brothers, your sons? Why must they destroy one another and all that they have created? Who benefits by this bloody nightmare? Only a minority of war profiteers. . . . Since the men cannot speak, you must. Workingwomen of the warring countries, unite![64]

Meantime, imprisoned for most of the next three and a half years, Rosa Luxemburg revealed herself as a person who literally could not hurt a fly. "I feel like a frozen bumble bee," she wrote from prison in 1917.

Did you ever find such a bumble bee in your garden in the first frost of an autumn morning? It lies on its back, quite numb as if it were dead, with its little legs tucked in and its fur covered with hoar frost. Only when the sun warms it through, do the legs slowly begin to stir and stretch. Then the little body rolls over and finally, clumsily, rises into the air with a buzz. I always made it my duty to kneel down by such frozen bumble bees and, with the warm breath from my mouth, bring them back to life.[65]

How was this compulsively compassionate woman to deal with the conclusion of militant Marxists (herself included) that, except perhaps in England and the United States, the transition to socialism would necessarily be violent? Her biographer, J. P. Nettl, speaks of a "Gandhian paradox."

But how did the armed uprising look in practice? First, it would produce its own peculiar weapons—and not necessarily those of history's conventional armed revolts. These were the typical symptoms of bourgeois revolution. What would decide the issue here was the willingness of the masses to make sacrifices. They had behind them the immense energy of historical necessity and enlightenment—far more effective weapons than mere arms. Moreover, the government was weak and incapable of the kind of repression that might cause a physical blood-bath. In the last resort armed uprising thus meant not the willingness to shoot but the willingness to be shot at.[66]

A dramatic example of this Gandhian paradox, which must have been known to Luxemburg at least in outline, took place on International Women's Day in February 1917, when demonstrating women in St. Petersburg appealed to Russian soldiers not to shoot and helped to bring down the czarist regime.

The demonstration was the product of hardships caused by the war. According to a secret police report of January 1917, "mothers of families, exhausted from the endless queues at the shops, suffering from the sight of their sick and half-famished children," were close to revolution. A few days before February 23, the "largely female staff of the Vasilevsky Island trolley-park . . . sent a woman to the neighboring encampment of the 180th Infantry Regiment to ask the soldiers whether they would shoot at them or not. The answer was no."

To an uncanny degree the demonstration that followed fell into the pattern anticipated in Luxemburg's analysis of 1905. The Bolsheviks issued no leaflets on February 23 and in at least one meeting the previous evening, "strongly urged the audience [of women workers] to refrain from action." But on the morning of February 23 women workers in five large textile factories in the Vyborg District held illegal meetings. At the end of their meetings they left work and marched to neighboring factories shouting, "Bread!" They also raised the slogan, "War, High Prices, and the Situation of the Woman Worker." Nevertheless, just as Luxemburg prescribed, the organized Left played a role, too. Faced with the spontaneous general strike of women workers, "experienced activists of the large metal factories joined and assumed leadership of the strike and the demonstration."

When women and soldiers faced each other on the turbulent streets, old women at the head of the demonstration stepped toward the mounted soldiers, pleading: "We have our husbands, fathers, and brothers at the front. But here we have hunger, hard times, injustice, shame. The government mocks us instead of helping us. You also have your mothers, wives, sisters, and children. All we want is bread and to end the war." According to Trotsky, the women went "up to the cordons more boldly than men, [took] hold of the rifles, beseech[ed], almost command[ed]: 'Put down your bayonets—join us'." Again and again the Cossacks refused to ride down the demonstrating women, in the most famous incident disregarding four direct orders.[67]

The German revolution into which Luxemburg emerged from prison in November 1918 posed the question of violence with cruel immediacy. One of Luxemburg's first articles after her release from prison called for the immediate abolition of capital punishment. This "small act of mercy" was a duty of honor, she wrote. Capitalism must be destroyed, "but each tear that might have been avoided is an indictment; and a man who hurrying on to important deeds inadvertently tramples underfoot even a poor worm, is guilty of a crime."[68] In the same spirit, Luxemburg inserted in the Spartacus League program the controversial phrases, implicitly critical of the Bolshevik Revolution: "The proletarian revolution requires no terror for its aims; it hates and despises killing."[69]

In Rosa Luxemburg's speech to the founding congress of the German Communist Party (her last speech, delivered less than three weeks before her assassination), she suggested the possibility that soldiers of working-class background might put down their arms and come over to the workers' side. In so saying, she challenged the view attributed to Engels that modern military technology made it impossible to take power by direct action in the streets. Luxemburg argued that "this assertion is obviously based upon the assumption that anyone who is a soldier is thereby . . . , once and for all, a support[er] of the ruling class."[70] In the same speech Luxemburg also sought to counter the views of those who favored an immediate military insurrection. She did so in exactly the same way that she had protested similar views in her 1904 article against Leninism and in her 1906 pamphlet on the general strike. Over and over again she stressed the need for a prolonged period of struggle in which the revolution would be broadened and deepened "from the depths," in which the political stage of the revolution would give way to a phase in which economic struggle would be "more and more the central focus," in which socialism would be "fought out by the masses, by the masses alone, breast to breast against capitalism, in every factory, by every proletarian against his employer." As before, so now she declared: "Socialism will not and cannot be established by decrees; nor can it be established by any government, however socialistic. . . . Where the chains of capitalism are forged, there they must be broken." The external form of this struggle would be the strike. I ask you, she pleaded, "to direct your attention not to the leadership, not above, but to the base."[71]

The Bolshevik Revolution and the Workers' Opposition

Rosa Luxemburg produced a prophetic libertarian critique of the Bolshevik Revolution when it was less than a year old. She wrote the manuscript in prison, and parts of it are mere outlines of what she intended to develop more fully. Because it was critical of a revolution that was then the toast of the international Left, friends persuaded her not to publish it for the time being. It was published in 1922 after her death.

The sentence for which the booklet is most remembered is: "Freedom is always and exclusively freedom for the one who thinks differently."[72] But the *thought* in which this sentence is embedded is the need for widespread working-class discussion which is the "very air" of socialist rule, for a public life in which "the whole mass of the people must take part," for a socialist government that proceeds "step by step out of the active participation of the masses."[73] The words best expressing this thought are perhaps the following:

> Only experience is capable of correcting and opening new ways. Only unobstructed, effervescing life falls into a thousand new forms and improvisations, brings to light creative force, itself corrects all mistaken attempts. The public life of countries with limited freedom is so poverty-stricken, so miserable, so rigid, so unfruitful, precisely because, through the exclusion of democracy, it cuts off the living sources of all spiritual riches and progress. (Proof: the year 1905 and the months from February to October 1917.)[74]

Later Luxemburg used the word "spiritual" again, writing: "Socialism in life demands a complete spiritual transformation in the masses degraded by centuries of bourgeois class rule. Social instincts in place of egotistical ones, mass initiative in place of inertia, idealism which conquers all suffering."[75]

What Luxemburg had regretfully criticized, her Russian colleague Alexandra Kollontai actively resisted after Luxemburg's death. Even in the first days following the Bolshevik victory, Kollontai protested the wholesale arrest of opposition party members, and "petitioned so often for the release of jailed men that the Council of People's Commissars (*Sovnarkom*) issued a strong rebuke to her."[76] As minister of social welfare in the new government, she supported "the extension of soviets to every branch of the commissariat, to provide a mechanism of enabling people at all levels to participate in the decision-making process."[77]

Then in the early 1920s, Kollontai became a spokesperson for the Workers' Opposition. The Workers' Opposition sought to rescue free speech from blind subordination to Party superiors and to place the administration of the economy in the hands of autonomous trade unions. In a pamphlet fifteen hundred copies of which she printed and distributed to delegates at the 1921 Party Congress, Kollontai wrote that all the Bolshevik leaders spoke of unions as "schools for communism."

"But all these systems of 'education' lack provisions for freedom of experiment, for . . . the expression of creative abilities by those who are to be taught. In this respect all our pedagogues are behind the times." Continuing, she argued:

> The administrative economic body in the workers' republic during the present transitory period must be a body directly elected by the producers themselves. . . . All else is goosestepping, that shows distrust toward the creative abilities of the workers, distrust which is not compatible with the professed ideals of our party, whose very strength depends on the perennial creative spirit of the proletariat.[78]

Kollontai asked in her speech at the Party Congress: "Is it to be bureaucracy or self-activity of the masses?" This was a conflict between two diametrically opposed principles, she said. Bureaucracy is a direct negation of mass self-activity, she argued, as life in the young Soviet Union proved only too well.

> Every comrade [Kollontai wrote] can easily recall scores of instances when workers themselves attempted to organise dining-rooms, day nurseries for children, transportation of wood, etc. Every time a lively, immediate interest in the undertaking died from the red tape, interminable negotiations with the various institutions that brought no results, or resulted in refusals, new requisitions, etc. Wherever there was an opportunity under the impetus of the masses themselves—of the masses using their own efforts—to equip a dining-room, to store a supply of wood, or to organise a nursery, refusal always followed refusal from the central institutions. . . . How much bitterness is generated among working men and women when they see and know that if they had been given the right, and an opportunity to act, they could themselves have seen the project through.

The revival of self-activity required freedom of thought. "There can be no self-activity without freedom of thought and opinion." Also needed was a "complete realisation of all democratic principles." The central committee of the party must become one that workers felt to be their own, wherein representatives of the "lower layers connected with the masses" were something more than figureheads. In making these demands, Kollontai concluded, the Workers' Opposition was only saying "what has long ago been printed in *The Communist Manifesto* by Marx and Engels: the building of communism can and must be the work of the toiling masses themselves."[79]

Conclusion

Barely five feet tall, walking with a perpetual limp because of a childhood hip disorder, a Jew, a woman, and, during her adult political life and at her death, a refugee: Rosa Luxemburg may well be the most significant theorist of the twentieth-century labor movement.

Luxemburg was released from prison in the midst of revolution, and thrust into leadership of a movement she had not known firsthand for many years. She opposed the transformation of the Spartacus League into the German Communist Party, and was outvoted. She opposed immediate armed insurrection, but was undone by the impulsiveness of Karl Liebknecht.[80]

As events slipped beyond her ability to influence them, Rosa Luxemburg chose imagery that betrayed her sense of what was to come. Her pamphlet on the program of the Spartacus League ended with the imagined cry to "crucify" the Spartacists by capitalists, military officers, anti-Semites, and Social Democratic politicians in government, "who, like Judas Iscariot, have sold the workers to the bourgeoisie and are trembling at the thought of losing [their] pieces of silver." In her address to the founding congress of the German Communist Party, Luxemburg said: "The proletarian revolution can reach full clarity and maturity only by stages, step by step, on the Golgotha-path of its own bitter experiences."[81] I believe Luxemburg foresaw that the German Revolution might prove a Golgotha, a place of the skull, for herself and others (who, in the event, included Liebknecht and Luxemberg's long-time comrade and lover Leo Jogiches). I think that in her choice of imagery, she was suggesting—perhaps unconsciously—that their humiliating deaths, like the crucifixion of an obscure Jewish carpenter in the first century, might only seemingly be a failure.

Of the models of labor organizing described in this essay, two (bureaucratic business unionism and the political vanguard party) have been tried and found wanting. The third has barely begun to be explored. The working-class self-activity that Rosa Luxemburg chronicled, praised, and advocated has recurred since her death in the United States, Spain, Germany itself, Hungary, Poland, and elsewhere, usually on a local level, and perhaps especially among women.[82] No one can be sure what the future significance of such activity will be. But we can certainly nurture in quiet times the horizontal, decentralized organizational forms based on solidarity, which, as Luxemburg showed, explode from within the working class in moments of crisis.

Notes

INTRODUCTION: THE ONCE AND FUTURE MOVEMENT

1 Helen Garvy to Staughton Lynd, February 17, 1996.

2 Barbara Deming wrote that those in nonviolent rebellion "are able at one and the same time to disrupt everything for [the adversary], making it impossible for him to operate within the system as usual, and to temper his response to this, making it impossible for him simply to strike back without thought and with all his strength. They have as it were two hands upon him—the one calming him, making him ask questions, as the other makes him move." Barbara Deming, "On Revolution and Equilibrium," in *Nonviolence in America: A Documentary History*, ed. Staughton Lynd and Alice Lynd, rev. ed. (Maryknoll, N.Y.: Orbis Books, 1995), p. 416.

3 Charles M. Payne, *I've Got the Light of Freedom: The Organizing Tradition and the Mississippi Freedom Struggle* (Berkeley: University of California Press, 1995), p. 102.

4 Ibid., p. 121.

5 SNCC founding statement, quoted in Gregory Nevala Calvert, *Democracy from the Heart: Spiritual Values, Decentralism, and Democratic Idealism in the Movement of the 1960s* (Eugene, Oregon: Communitas Press, 1991), p. 71.

6 Leonardo Boff, introduction to *Relentless Persistence: Nonviolent Action in Latin America*, ed. Philip McManus and Gerald Schlabach (Philadelphia: New Society Publishers, 1991), p. ix.

7 Payne, *I've Got the Light*, pp. 3, 4.

8 Ibid., p. 101.

9 Mary E. King, "Women and Civil Rights—A Personal Reflection," paper presented in the 12th Annual Fannie Lou Hamer Lecture Series, Dept. of Political Science, Jackson State University, October 5, 1995, pp. 3, 6.

10 See Daniel Perlstein, "Teaching Freedom: SNCC and the Creation of the Mississippi Freedom Schools," 30 *History of Education Quarterly* (Fall 1990), pp. 297–324.

11 Perlstein, "Teaching Freedom," pp. 306–8; Payne, *I've Got the Light*, pp. 68–76 (citizenship schools), 302–6 (freedom schools).

12 The deep convergence of Movement educational theory and the educational theory of Freire is demonstrated in Myles Horton and Paulo Freire, *We Make the Road by Walking: Conversations on Education and Social Change* (Philadelphia: Temple University Press, 1990). In the 1980s and 1990s, former SNCC organizer Bob Moses developed an Algebra Project in which the same approach to learning was given new form. "The program is built on the egalitarian, non-hierarchical values that informed the organizing tradi-

tion, and it was developed in that tradition's step-by-step, bottom up fashion. Like any good organizer, the program started where children are, taking things students understand intuitively—a trip on the subway, trading possessions, playing musical chairs—and helping them see the mathematics inherent in these activities. Teachers are more facilitators than teachers in the traditional sense. They are expected to not give direct answers to students' questions but to help students find questions that will lead them to discover their own answers. Teachers are also expected to present themselves as learners, as people who don't always know the answers." Payne, *I've Got the Light*, p. 410.

13 The two preceding sentences draw on Helen Garvy's letter cited in note 1.

14 Archbishop Oscar Romero, *Voice of the Voiceless: The Four Pastoral Letters and Other Statements* (Maryknoll, N.Y.: Orbis Books, 1985), pp. 127, 139, 147, 155–56.

15 See Essay 10, as well as Jane Slaughter, "An Interview with Staughton Lynd," 58 *The Progressive* (February 1994), pp. 33–36, reprinted in part in "Our Kind of Marxist: An Interview with Staughton Lynd," 45 *Monthly Review* (April 1994), pp. 48–49.

16 For propositions 1 to 3, see the essays collected in Staughton Lynd, *Class Conflict, Slavery, and the United States Constitution* (Indianapolis: Bobbs Merrill, 1967). A few examples may make the abstractions set forth seem more real. I found that whether tenant farmers along the Hudson River supported or opposed the American Revolution depended on the politics of a tenant's landlord. If the landlord (like those in southern Dutchess County) supported the British, his tenant was likely to be a revolutionary. If the landlord (like the Livingston family in Columbia County) supported independence, the tenant might take part in a pro-British uprising. A tenant's politics depended on how the tenant thought he might best acquire his farm. Whichever side his landlord chose, the tenant tended to make the opposite choice. Ibid., pp. 63–77. Similarly, the politics of city artisans in the Revolutionary period followed from a concern to protect their livelihoods. If politics were based on ideology, it would be difficult to explain how the same ropewalk workers, caulkers, coopers, iron workers, and the like, could be flaming Sons of Liberty before independence and yet, in every seaboard city, parade in enthusiastic support of a conservative United States Constitution in 1787–88. But what mattered to these workers was finding ways to keep imported British goods out of the country. Independence in the 1770s and a strong central government capable of imposing national tariffs on imported manufactures in the 1780s were perceived by city artisans as means to safeguard their jobs. It was a secondary matter if they found themselves in 1787 making common cause with the Alexander Hamilton whom they had reviled as pro-Tory only a few years before. Ibid., pp. 9, 79–108.

17 Karl Marx, instructions to British delegates to the Geneva Congress of the First International in 1866, quoted in Paul Thomas, *Karl Marx and the Anarchists* (London: Routledge and Kegan Paul, 1985), p. 275.

18 See Essay 8 and Staughton Lynd, "A Jobs Program for the 90s," *Social Policy* (Fall 1994), pp. 22–43.

19 Folkways Record Album No. FD5765, *Berkeley Teach-In: Vietnam*, ed. Louis Menashe (1966), quoted in *Nonviolence in America*, ed. Lynd and Lynd, pp. xxxiv–xxxv.

20 One product of Alice Lynd's work was *We Won't Go: Personal Accounts of War Objectors* (Boston: Beacon Press, 1968).

21 Staughton Lynd and Tom Hayden, *The Other Side* (New York: New American Library, 1966).

22 Michael Ferber and Staughton Lynd, *The Resistance* (Boston: Beacon Press, 1971), chaps. 3, 4.

23 S. Brian Willson, *On Third World Legs*, with an introduction by Staughton Lynd (Chicago: Charles H. Kerr, 1992), p. 20.

24 See also Staughton Lynd, *The Fight Against Shutdowns: Youngstown's Steel Mill Closings* (San Pedro, Calif.: Singlejack Books, 1982); and Staughton Lynd, *Solidarity Unionism: Rebuilding the Labor Movement from Below* (Chicago: Charles H. Kerr, 1992), pp. 13–23.

25 During the 1960s Marty Glaberman led a seminar on Marxism in which all seven members of the executive committee of the League of Revolutionary Black Workers took part. James A. Geschwender, *Class, Race and Worker Insurgency: The League of Revolutionary Black Workers* (Cambridge: Cambridge University Press, 1977), p. 171.

26 Sargent's assessment has a good deal of scholarly support. See Robert R. R. Brooks, *As Steel Goes . . . : Unionism in Basic Industry* (New Haven: Yale University Press, 1940), p. 146, and especially Lizabeth Cohen, *Making a New Deal: Industrial Workers in Chicago, 1919–1939* (Cambridge: Cambridge University Press, 1990), pp. 305–7.

27 Lynd, *Fight Against Shutdowns*, pp. 149–159; *We Are the Union: The Story of Ed Mann*, ed. Alice Lynd and Staughton Lynd (Youngstown: Solidarity USA, n.d.), chap. 8.

28 *We Are the Union*, p. 33.

29 Stan Weir, "The Informal Work Group," in *Rank and File: Personal Histories by Working-Class Organizers*, ed. Lynd and Lynd (New York: Monthly Review Press, 1988), pp. 191–92. See Essay 11 for a discussion of shopfloor committees and parallel central labor bodies.

30 Stan Weir, "Unions with Leaders Who Stay on the Job," in *"We Are All Leaders": The Alternative Unionism of the Early 1930s*, ed. Staughton Lynd (Champaign: University of Illinois Press, 1996).

31 In Essay 7 I argue that this was also the point of view of Edward Thompson.

32 Marion Zimmer Bradley, *The Mists of Avalon* (New York: Ballantine Books, 1984), pp. 868, 876.

2. FREEDOM SUMMER

1 Howard Zinn, *SNCC: The New Abolitionists* (Boston: Beacon Press, 1965), p. 187.

2 Mendy Samstein, "Notes on Mississippi," Samstein Papers, State Historical Society of Wisconsin, quoted in Doug McAdam, *Freedom Summer* (New York: Oxford University Press, 1988), p. 38.

3 Charles M. Payne, *I've Got the Light of Freedom: The Organizing Tradition and the Mississippi Freedom Struggle* (Berkeley: University of California Press, 1995), pp. 297–98; Clayborne Carson, *In Struggle: SNCC and the Black Awakening of the 1960s* (Cambridge: Harvard University Press, 1981), pp. 98–100.

4 Payne, *I've Got the Light*, p. 298; Carson, *In Struggle*, pp. 96, 99–100.

5 Taylor Branch, *Parting the Waters: America in the King Years, 1954–1963* (New York: Simon and Schuster, 1988), p. 921.

6 Branch, *Parting the Waters*, p. 921; in agreement, Payne, *I've Got the Light*, pp. 299–300.

7 Payne, *I've Got the Light*, p. 473 n. 21.

8 A letter from a volunteer describing Moses' talk in a very similar way will be found in

Letters from Mississippi, ed. Elizabeth Sutherland (New York: McGraw-Hill, 1965), pp. 31–32.

9 As to the generally warm reception of the volunteers by the black families with whom they lived, see Payne, *I've Got the Light*, pp. 306–15, and McAdam, *Freedom Summer*, pp. 86–93.

10 McAdam, *Freedom Summer*, pp. 93–96.

11 See on the Vine Street project and its manifestos, Carson, *In Struggle*, pp. 191–200.

3. ORAL HISTORY FROM BELOW

1 *I, Rigoberta Menchú: An Indian Woman in Guatemala*, ed. Elisabeth Burgos-Debray (London: Verso, 1984).

2 Donald Katz, *Home Fires: An Intimate Portrait of One Middle-Class Family in Postwar America* (New York: Aaron Asher Books, 1992).

3 S. Brian Willson, *On Third World Legs*, with an introduction by Staughton Lynd (Chicago: Charles H. Kerr, 1992).

4. LIBERATION THEOLOGY FOR QUAKERS

1 Helen Prejean, *Dead Man Walking: An Eyewitness Account of the Death Penalty in the United States* (New York: Random House, 1993), pp. 5–6.

2 Deborah Levenson-Estrada, *Trade Unionists against Terror: Guatemala City, 1954–1985* (Chapel Hill: University of North Carolina Press, 1994), esp. chap. 3.

3 See Phillip Berryman, *The Religious Roots of Rebellion: Christians in Central American Revolutions* (Maryknoll, N.Y.: Orbis Books, 1984), chap. 1, pp. 59–69.

4 *Amanecer* [Dawn] (January–February 1988), p. 20.

5 Quoted in Christopher Hill, *The World Turned Upside Down: Radical Ideas During the English Revolution* (New York: Viking Press, 1977), p. 60, from Ephraim Fagitt, *Heresiography* (5th ed., 1654), p. 136.

6 Christopher Hill, *Society and Puritanism in Pre-Revolutionary England* (London: Secker & Warburg, 1964), pp. 493–94.

7 Larry Ingle, "Quakers and the AFSC: Can We Be Friends?" *Christian Century* (April 19, 1995), p. 413.

8 In *Nonviolence in America: A Documentary History*, ed. Staughton Lynd and Alice Lynd, revised edition (Maryknoll, N.Y.: Orbis Books, 1995), we have collected the experiences of many people who shared these longings and acted on them. Some of these persons, like John Woolman, were Quakers.

9 Alice Lynd, ed., *We Won't Go: Personal Accounts of War Objectors* (Boston: Beacon Press, 1968).

10 Our friend Renate Goepp recalls two other passages from the movie. The first is "the moment when, despondent over the society women who are supporting him, but are really only engaged in a contest of vanities, he [Vincent de Paul] is approached by a peasant girl begging him to let her help. He raises his eyes in prayer, 'Thank you, Lord, for showing me that it is only with the poor that I shall be able to help the poor.' And, finally, the last scene when, knowing himself close to death, he speaks to the last and youngest girl who has joined the sisterhood: 'Never lose your gentleness and your smile; for it is only because of those that the poor will forgive you for helping them'."

11 *Rank and File: Personal Histories by Working-Class Organizers,* ed. Alice and Staughton Lynd (Boston: Beacon Press, 1973).

12 See *Nonviolence in America,* ed. Lynd and Lynd, p. 416.

13 John Dominic Crossan, *The Historical Jesus: The Life of a Mediterranean Jewish Peasant* (New York: HarperCollins, 1991). Our friend Michael Ferber remarks: "The Greek at Luke 17:21 (*entos humon*) almost has to read 'among' when, as here, the object is plural, hence perhaps 'The Kingdom of God is in the midst of you.' At least in this passage Jesus is not advocating an individualistic solution."

14 Crossan offers the following three passages from the Gospel of Thomas as examples:
   (1) Jesus said, "If those who lead you say to you, 'See, the kingdom is in the sky,' then the birds of the sky will precede you. If they say to you, 'It is in the sea,' then the fish will precede you. Rather, the kingdom is inside of you, and it is outside of you."
   (2) His disciplines said to him, "When . . . will the new world come?"
   He said to them, "What you look forward to has already come, but you do not recognize it."
   (3) His disciples said to him, "When will the kingdom come?"
   [Jesus said,] "It will not come by waiting for it. It will not be a matter of saying 'Here it is' or 'There it is.' Rather, the kingdom of the father is spread out upon the earth, and men do not see it."
   Crossan, *The Historical Jesus,* pp. 228–29, quoting Gospel of Thomas 3:1, 51, 113.

15 Crossan, *The Historical Jesus,* p. 341.

16 From notes by Alice Lynd on a workshop held at Kirkridge, Bangor, Pa., on April 21–23, 1995, entitled "The Historical Jesus: A Conversation with John Dominic Crossan."

17 Our daughter Martha reminds us: "Living with the poor is not the only way to challenge oppression. Being a radical artist like Diego Rivera is also a way to challenge oppression. He painted the history of oppression of indigenous people in murals and changed or created space in the Mexican ladino, mainstream consciousness."

18 Our friend Phil Hazelton puts it this way: "What we do must be sustainable. We must hold on to the Kingdom of God long enough for it to settle down, long enough that it can't be blown away."

19 The Little Sisters of Jesus, whom we stayed with in Nicaragua, take a one- or two-day retreat each month and a week-long retreat each year for reflection and inner growth.

20 Barbara Kingsolver, *Animal Dreams* (New York: HarperCollins, 1990), p. 299.

5. THE FIRST NEW LEFT . . . AND THE THIRD

1 Ignazio Silone, "A Note on the Revision of Bread and Wine," prefatory to Ignazio Silone, *Bread and Wine* (New York: New American Library, 1962), pp. vi–vii. The text of the first edition, Ignazio Silone, *Bread and Wine,* trans. from the Italian by Gwenda David and Eric Mosbacher (New York: Harper & Bros., 1937), is to be preferred to the revised edition Silone published after World War II.

2 Silone, *Bread and Wine,* 1937 ed., p. 229.

3 Quoted in Nat Hentoff, *Peace Agitator: The Story of A. J. Muste* (New York: Macmillan, 1963), pp. 99–100.

4 A. J. Muste, "Return to Pacifism" (1936), in *The Essays of A. J. Muste,* ed. Nat Hentoff (Indianapolis: Bobbs-Merrill, 1967), pp. 197–99.

5 Simone Weil, "Are We Heading for the Proletarian Revolution?" reprinted in Simone

Weil, *Oppression and Liberty*, trans. Arthur Willis and John Petrie, introduction by F. C. Ellert (Amherst: University of Massachusetts Press, 1973), pp. 3–4.

6 Ibid., pp. 4–6.

7 Ibid., pp. 6–8.

8 Ibid., pp. 8–9.

9 Ibid., pp. 10–11, 21.

10 Ibid., p. 17.

11 Ibid.

12 Ibid., p. 22.

13 Ibid., pp. 22–23.

14 Ibid., p. 23.

15 Simone Weil, "Reflections concerning the Causes of Liberty and Social Oppression" (1934), reprinted in *Oppression and Liberty*, p. 44.

16 Ibid., pp. 122–23.

17 Weil, "Are We Heading for the Proletarian Revolution?" in ibid., p. 10.

18 Simone Weil, "Fragments, 1933–1938," in ibid., p. 137.

19 Simone Weil, "On the Contradictions of Marxism" (n.d.), in ibid., p. 148.

20 Ibid., p. 153.

21 Ibid., pp. 154–55.

22 "Fragments, 1933–1938," in ibid., p. 129.

23 "Reflections Concerning the Causes of Liberty and Oppression," in ibid., pp. 43–44.

24 Hugh Brand and R. G. Brenneman, "Signs of Renaissance on the Left: The United Labor Party," *Libertarian Socialist* (Winter 1949), p. 16.

6. COMMUNAL RIGHTS

1 Arthur Kinoy, *Rights on Trial: The Odyssey of a People's Lawyer* (Cambridge: Harvard University Press, 1983).

2 See, e.g., Heitzer, "Outline for a Campaign for an Economic Bill of Rights," *Guild Notes* (January–February 1983), pp. 12–13; Fair Budget Action Campaign, "Economic & Social Bill of Rights," in ibid., p. 13; C. Williams, "How the Guild Fights for Economic Rights," paper prepared for the NLG National Executive Committee.

3 See American Civil Liberties Union, "ACLU Legal Director Announces Nationwide Litigation Strategy on Economic Rights," press release May 17, 1983; Burt Neuborne, ACLU Legal Director, to Affiliate Legal Personnel, "Possible Litigation Initiatives in the Area of Economic Rights," memorandum May 1983.

4 See, e.g., Peter Gabel and Paul Harris, "Building Power and Breaking Images: Critical Legal Theory and the Practice of Law," 11 *N.Y.U. Review of Law and Social Change* (1983), p. 369; Joseph William Singer, "The Legal Rights Debate in Analytical Jurisprudence from Bentham to Hohfeld," *Wisconsin Law Review* (1982), p. 975; Mark Tushnet, "An Essay on Rights," 62 *Texas Law Review* (1984), p. 1363.

5 The Declaration of Independence, paragraph 2.

6 Ibid.

7 See Tushnet, "Essay on Rights," pp. 1371–82.

8 Ronald Dworkin, *Taking Rights Seriously* (1977), p. 172.

9 Gary Wills argues that Thomas Jefferson did not share Locke's vision of property as the

basis for all other rights. Hence, Wills contends, Jefferson deliberately wrote "life, liberty, and the pursuit of happiness," rather than "life, liberty, and property." Gary Wills, *Inventing America: Jefferson's Declaration of Independence* (New York: Vintage, 1979), pp. 229–39.

10 See, e.g., Gabel and Harris, "Building Power," p. 376: "A legal strategy that goes beyond rights-consciousness is one that focuses upon expanding political consciousness through using the legal system to increase people's sense of personal and political power."

11 Interview with E. P. Thompson, in New York City, March 1976, reprinted in *Visions of History,* ed. Henry Abelove and others (New York: Pantheon, 1983), p. 9; see also E. P. Thompson, *Whigs and Hunters: The Origin of the Black Act* (London: Allen Lane, 1975), pp. 258–69 (discussing the paradoxical nature of the law as both a defense against arbitrary exercises of power by the ruling class and a means of preserving the existing class structure).

12 Duncan L. Kennedy, "Critical Labor Law Theory: A Comment," 4 *Industrial Relations Law Journal* (1981), pp. 503, 506.

13 Gabel and Harris, "Building Power," p. 377 n. 13.

14 Kennedy, "Critical Labor Law Theory," p. 506. Karl Klare has brought to my attention an eloquent plea to the same effect by Roberto Unger. Unger writes:

> Most of our recognized moral duties to each other and especially those that characterize communities arise from relationships of interdependence that have been only partially articulated [by prevailing legal conceptions]. . . .
>
> These reformed varieties of communal experience *need to be thought out in legal categories and protected by legal rights:* not to give these reconstructed forms of solidarity and subjectivity institutional support would be—as current experience shows—merely to abandon them to entrenched forms of human connection at war with our ideals.

Roberto Unger, "The Critical Legal Studies Movement," 96 *Harvard Law Review* (1983), pp. 563, 598 (emphasis added).

15 G. W. F. Hegel, *The Phenomenology of Mind,* trans. J. Baillie, 2d ed. (London: George Allen & Unwin, 1949), p. 79.

16 Staughton Lynd, *Labor Law for the Rank and Filer* (San Pedro: Singlejack Books, 1982), p. 5.

17 Staughton Lynd, *The Fight Against Shutdowns: Youngstown's Steel Mill Closings* (San Pedro: Singlejack Books, 1982), p. 189.

18 This danger is not limited to labor law. Ronald Garet, for example, has written about the "rights of groups." He considers "communality" to be the rights of groups to maintain themselves and to pursue their distinctive courses. The groups he has in mind include a religious sect and an American Indian pueblo. As Garet sees it, these entities have "group rights" distinct from both individual rights and from the rights of society as a whole. Ronald R. Garet, "Communality and Existence: The Rights of Groups," 56 *Southern California Law Review* (1983), pp. 1001, 1001–4.

19 See Karl E. Klare, "The Public/Private Distinction in Labor Law," 130 *University of Pennsylvania Law Review* (1982), p. 1358.

20 Robert Brousseau has defined "collective rights" in labor law as "those rights, the assertion of which by the individual employee would be ineffective in the long run. . . .

They are the rights which it is necessary to bundle together and vest in a collective representative." Robert Brousseau, "Toward a Theory of Rights for the Employment Relation," 56 *Washington Law Review* (1980), pp. 1, 25–26.

21 29 United States Code section 157.

22 See, e.g., *Rank and File: Personal Histories by Working-Class Organizers,* ed. Alice Lynd and Staughton Lynd (Boston: Beacon Press, 1973).

23 Karl E. Klare, "Judicial Deradicalization of the Wagner Act and the Origins of Modern Legal Consciousness, 1937–1941," 62 *Minnesota Law Review* (1978), p. 265.

24 Cletus Daniel, *The American Civil Liberties Union and the Wagner Act: An Inquiry into the Depression-Era Crisis in American Liberalism* (Ithaca: Cornell University Press, 1980), p. 75 (quoting letter from ACLU director Roger Baldwin to Senator David Walsh, March 20, 1934). Baldwin expressed similar concerns in letters to Secretary of Labor Frances Perkins and Chairman of the Labor Advisory Board, Leo Wollman (p. 34). Mary Van Kleeck, Chairman of the ACLU's subcommittee on labor and policy, wrote Senator Wagner: "I have serious doubts about the inevitable trends of [the Act's] administration" (p. 71).

25 *Visions of History,* ed. Abelove and others, p. 157 (interview with Staughton Lynd).

26 Staughton Lynd, "Government without Rights: The Labor Law Vision of Archibald Cox," 4 *Industrial Relations Law Journal* (1981), p. 495.

27 See generally Klare, "Deradicalization," p. 1420 n. 252 (arguing that the liberal tradition has not placed sufficient value on communal experience).

28 See, e.g., Neal Ascherson, *The Polish August: The Self-Limiting Revolution* (New York: Viking Press, 1982), pp. 145–49.

29 Atkinson, "The Woman behind Solidarity: The Story of Anna Walentynowicz," *Ms.* (February 1984), p. 96. Used by permission.

30 Lynd and Lynd, *Rank and File,* p. 281 (quoting Ed Mann).

31 Thus, within two hours of the Youngstown wildcat described by Ed Mann, "[W]e had a list of thirty demands." Ibid., p. 282.

32 *NLRB v. City Disposal Sys. Inc.,* 104 S. Ct. 1505 (1984), p. 1517 (O'Connor, J., dissenting).

33 *NLRB v. Peter Cailler Kohler Swiss Chocolates Co.,* 130 F.2d 503 (2d Cir. 1942), pp. 505–6. This opinion predated the restriction of so-called secondary activities by the Taft-Hartley Act of 1947 as well as by Board and court decisions. For a brilliant exposition of the unexamined assumption that pecuniary self-interest is a more real and acceptable motive than sympathy strikes and similar activity, see James B. Atleson, *Values and Assumptions in American Labor Law* (Amherst: University of Massachusetts Press, 1983), pp. 67–83. On the other hand, the notion that labor solidarity arises in part from individual self-interest appears to distinguish solidarity from the "altruism" advocated by Duncan L. Kennedy, "Form and Substance in Private Law Adjudication," 89 *Harvard Law Review* (1976), pp. 1717–22, 1771–74.

34 Stan Weir has described such a family-at-work in a General Motors plant where he worked in the 1950s. See Lynd and Lynd, *Rank and File,* pp. 196–98.

35 104 S. Ct. 1505 (1984).

36 Ibid., p. 1509.

37 Ibid.

38 Ibid.

39 Ibid., p. 1508.

NOTES TO PAGES 98-104

40 Ibid., p. 1511.

41 Ibid., pp. 1511–12 (emphasis added).

42 This history is surveyed in Robert A. Gorman and Matthew W. Finkin, "The Individual and the Requirement of 'Concert' under the National Labor Relations Act," 130 *University of Pennsylvania Law Review* (1981), pp. 331–46; Staughton Lynd, "The Right to Engage in Concerted Activity after Union Recognition: A Study of Legislative History," 50 *Indiana Law Journal* (1975), pp. 726–34.

43 Norris-LaGuardia Act, 29 United States Code section 104.

44 National Labor Relations Act, 29 United States Code section 157.

45 Gorman and Finkin, "Requirement of 'Concert'," p. 329.

46 See *Emporium Capwell Co. v. Western Addition Community Org.*, 420 U.S. 50 (1975), p. 62.

47 Gorman and Finkin, "Requirement of 'Concert'," pp. 344–45.

48 *City Disposal*, 104 S. Ct., p. 1511 n. 8.

49 Ibid., p. 1512 (emphasis added).

50 Ibid., p. 1514.

51 Lynd, "Government without Rights," pp. 494–95.

52 Edward Sparer, "Fundamental Human Rights, Legal Entitlements, and the Social Struggle: A Friendly Critique of the Critical Legal Studies Movement," 36 *Stanford Law Review* (1984), p. 527.

53 Ibid., p. 530.

54 See Lynd, "Concerted Activity," p. 734; Lynd, "Government without Rights," pp. 484–85 (articulation of single body of doctrine in section 7 and First Amendment cases); see also Staughton Lynd, "Employee Speech in the Private and Public Workplace: Two Doctrines or One?" 1 *Industrial Relations Law Journal* (1977) (arguing that speech rights of private and public employees have converged).

55 Wills, *Inventing America*, pp. 234–35 (quoting letter from Jefferson to Isaac McPherson, August 13, 1813).

56 United States Constitution, First Amendment.

57 The right to keep and bear arms (U.S. Constitution, Second Amendment), the right to be secure in person, house, papers, or effects (Fourth Amendment), and the right to powers not otherwise expressly delegated (Ninth and Tenth Amendments) are also said to belong to "the people." For an exciting discussion of the Supreme Court's neglect of the communal dimension of the Fourth Amendment, see Donald L. Doernberg, "'The Right of the People': Reconciling Collective and Individual Interests under the Fourth Amendment," 58 *New York University Law Review* (1983).

58 See *Debs v. United States*, 249 U.S. 211 (1919); *Frohwerk v. United States*, 249 U.S. 204 (1919); *Sugarman v. United States*, 249 U.S. 182 (1919); *Schenck v. United States*, 249 U.S. 47 (1919). I should like to express my great indebtedness to David M. Rabban's "The Emergence of Modern First Amendment Doctrine," 50 *University of Chicago Law Review* (1983), pp. 1247–65, with regard to the discussion of post-World War I speech decisions.

59 *Abrams v. United States*, 250 U.S. 616 (1919), p. 624 (Holmes, J., dissenting).

60 See Rabban, "Emergence," pp. 1311–17.

61 Zechariah Chaffee, "Freedom of Speech in War Time," 32 *Harvard Law Review* (1919), p. 934.

62 *Abrams*, 250 U.S., p. 628.

63 274 U.S. 357 (1927), p. 372 (Brandeis, J., concurring); see *Milwaukee Social Democratic*

Publishing Co. v. Burleson, 255 U.S. 407 (1921), p. 417 (Brandeis, J., dissenting); *Gilbert v. Minnesota,* 254 U.S. 325 (1920), p. 334 (Brandeis, J., dissenting); *Pierce v. United States,* 252 U.S. 239 (1920), p. 253 (Brandeis, J., dissenting); *Schaefer v. United States,* 251 U.S. 466 (1920), p. 482 (Brandeis, J., dissenting).

64 *Pierce,* 252 U.S., p. 273 (Brandeis, J., dissenting).

65 *Whitney,* 274 U.S., p. 374 (Brandeis, J., concurring).

66 *Gilbert,* 254 U.S., pp. 337–38 (Brandeis, J., dissenting).

67 Ibid., p. 343.

68 *Whitney,* 274 U.S., p. 374 (Brandeis, J., concurring).

69 The test generally considered most protective of political speech is set forth by the Supreme Court in *Brandenburg v. Ohio,* 395 U.S. 444 (1969) (per curiam). See Staughton Lynd, "*Brandenburg v. Ohio:* A Speech Test for All-Seasons?" 43 *University of Chicago Law Review* (1975); Rabban, "Emergence," pp. 1352–55.

70 See, e.g., Kennedy, "Critical Labor Law Theory," p. 506.

71 Karl Marx, "On the Jewish Question," in *Karl Marx: Early Writings,* trans. and ed. T. B. Bottomore (New York: McGraw-Hill, 1964), pp. 24–25.

72 Ibid., pp. 22–23.

73 Ibid., p. 26.

74 Karl Marx and Friedrich Engels, "Manifesto of the Communist Party," in 6 *Collected Works* (New York: International Publishers, 1976), p. 505.

75 Karl Marx and Friedrich Engels, "Demands of the Communist Party in Germany," in 7 *Collected Works* (New York: International Publishers, 1977), pp. 3–7.

76 Friedrich Engels, "Principles of Communism," in 6 *Collected Works,* pp. 350–51.

77 Marx and Engels, "Demands" (no. 2).

78 Ibid. (no. 3).

79 Ibid. (no. 4).

80 Ibid. (no. 5).

81 Ibid. (no. 12).

82 Ibid. (no. 13).

83 Ibid. (no. 15); Marx and Engels, "Communist Manifesto" (no. 2).

84 Marx and Engels, "Demands" (no. 17); Marx and Engels, "Communist Manifesto" (no. 10); Engels, "Principles of Communism" (no. 8).

85 Marx and Engels, "Demands" (no. 14); Marx and Engels, "Communist Manifesto" (no. 3); Engels, "Principles of Communism" (no. 1).

86 See Karl Marx and Friedrich Engels, "Preface to the 1872 Edition of the Manifesto of the Communist Party," in *The Marx-Engels Reader,* ed. Robert C. Tucker (New York: W. W. Norton, 1972), p. 332.

87 Karl Marx, *Critique of Hegel's Philosophy of Right,* ed. Joseph O'Malley (Cambridge: Cambridge University Press, 1970), pp. 30, 31.

88 See Shlomo Avineri, *The Social and Political Thought of Karl Marx* (Cambridge: Cambridge University Press, 1980), p. 214; Dorothy Thompson, *The Chartists: Popular Politics in the Industrial Revolution* (New York: Pantheon, 1984), pp. 307, 311.

89 Friedrich Engels to August Bebel, March 1875, 24 *Collected Works* (New York: International Publishers, 1989), p. 70; Karl Marx, *Critique of the Gotha Programme,* ibid., pp. 75–99; political demands of the Gotha Programme, ibid., p. 603 n. 100.

90 Gara LaMarche, associate director of the New York Civil Liberties Union, "The ACLU and Poverty: Thoughts on a Public Education Program," unpublished paper.

91 See generally Samuel B. Bowles, David M. Gordon, and Thomas E. Weisskopf, *Beyond the Wasteland: A Democratic Alternative to Economic Decline* (Garden City, N.Y.: Anchor Press/Doubleday, 1983), pp. 261–390; Martin Carnoy, Derek Shearer, and Russell Rumberger, *A New Social Contract: The Economy and Government After Reagan* (New York: Oxford University Press, 1983), pp. 228–31; International Association of Machinists and Aerospace Workers, "Workers' Technology Bill of Rights," in *Let's Rebuild America* (1983), pp. 195–97.

92 John Woolman, "A Plea for the Poor," in *The Journal and Essays of John Woolman,* ed. Amelia Mott Gummere (New York: Macmillan, 1922), p. 403.

93 Thomas Paine, "Preface to Agrarian Justice," in *The Complete Writings of Thomas Paine,* ed. Philip Foner (New York: Citadel, 1945), p. 609.

94 Thomas Jefferson to the Reverend James Madison, October 28, 1785, quoted in Staughton Lynd, *Intellectual Origins of American Radicalism* (Cambridge: Harvard University Press, 1982), p. 83.

95 See ibid., pp. 89–92.

96 Atleson, *Values and Assumptions,* pp. 151–56. See also *First National Maintenance Corp. v. NLRB,* 452 U.S. 666 (1981), p. 676; Staughton Lynd, "Investment Decisions and the Quid Pro Quo Myth," 29 *Case Western Reserve Law Review* (1979), p. 396 (arguing that collective bargaining agreements should provide either that employer will arbitrate investment decisions or that labor has the right to strike over these decisions).

97 William B. Stoebuck, "A General Theory of Eminent Domain," 47 *Washington Law Review* (1972), pp. 580–81.

98 *Poletown Neighborhood Council v. City of Detroit,* 410 Mich. 616, 304 N.W.2d 455 (1981) (holding that eminent domain taking of residential land on which General Motors proposed to build privately owned factory was taking for a "public purpose").

99 *City of Oakland v. Oakland Raiders,* 32 Cal.3d 60, 646 P.2d 835, 183 Cal. Rptr. 673 (1982) (holding that eminent domain power reaches intangible property).

100 *Hawaii Housing Authority v. Midkiff,* 104 S. Ct. 2321 (1984), p. 2329 (holding that "public use" requirement is coterminous with police power).

101 TriState Conference on Steel, "Rebuild Steel: A Program to Reconstruct American Industry" (1984). The Pennsylvania Municipal Authorities Act of 1945, *Pennsylvania Statutes Annotated* (Purdon 1974), sections 301–22, authorizes the creation of municipal authorities "to retain or develop existing industries and the development of new industries" (sec. 306A). The Supreme Court of Pennsylvania has upheld the taking of land on which a business is operating at the time of the taking. *Thompson Appeal,* 427 Pa. 1, 233 A.2d 237 (1967).

102 "Inalienable" rights are discussed in Wills, *Inventing America,* pp. 229–39, and Lynd, *Intellectual Origins,* pp. 43–61. Liberty of conscience may be the only right that is "inalienable," in the sense of being untransferable, by the individual. See Lynd, *Intellectual Origins,* p. 45.

103 Rich Trumka, President of the United Mine Workers of America, speaking at the union's 1983 convention. *New York Times,* December 13, 1983.

7. IN MEMORIAM: E. P. THOMPSON

1 Bryan Palmer, "E. P. Thompson," *In These Times*, September 20, 1993.

2 E. P. Thompson, *Whigs and Hunters: The Origin of the Black Act* (London: Allen Lane, 1975), pp. 260–61.

3 Ibid., p. 261.

4 Ibid.

5 Ibid., p. 263.

6 Thompson uses the term "double service" with regard to Methodism in E. P. Thompson, *The Making of the English Working Class* (New York: Pantheon, 1963), p. 356.

7 Thompson, *Whigs and Hunters*, pp. 263–64.

8 Ibid., p. 266.

9 Ibid., p. 267.

10 Ibid., p. 266.

11 E. P. Thompson, "The State of the Nation," in *Writing by Candlelight* (London: Merlin Press, 1980), pp. 245–46.

12 Ibid., p. 246.

13 Ibid., p. 232.

14 Ibid., p. 236.

15 Susanna Gross, "E. P. Thompson: Defiant Champion of the Working Class," *The Daily Mail*, September 2, 1993 (my friend Alfred Young kindly sent me this obituary); E. P. Thompson, "The Business University" and "A Report on Lord Radcliffe," in *Writing by Candlelight*, pp. 13–37.

16 E. P. Thompson, "Outside the Whale," in *Out of Apathy* (London: Stevens, 1960), p. 184.

17 Thompson, *Making of the English Working Class*, pp. 11–12.

18 The terms "legitimizing notion" and "moral economy" occur in Thompson's description of eighteenth-century food riots in *Making of the English Working Class*, pp. 62–68, and in "The Moral Economy of the Crowd in the Eighteenth Century," *Past and Present* (February 1971), pp. 76–136. Thompson also uses the term "moral economy" in his analysis of the Luddites. *Making of the English Working Class*, p. 521 n. 548. The reference to Trobriand islanders is in "The Moral Economy of the Crowd," p. 131.

19 E. P. Thompson, "The Poverty of Theory or an Orrery of Errors," in *The Poverty of Theory and Other Essays* (New York: Monthly Review Press, 1978), p. 7.

20 Ibid., p. 8.

21 Ibid., p. 152.

22 Ibid., p. 184.

23 Ibid., p. 186.

24 Ibid., p. 189.

25 E. P. Thompson, *William Morris: Romantic to Revolutionary* (New York: Pantheon, 1977), p. 807.

26 Thompson, *Making of the English Working Class*, pp. 157 (Thelwall), 821 (O'Brien).

27 E. P. Thompson, *Witness against the Beast: William Blake and the Moral Law* (Cambridge: Cambridge University Press, 1993), pp. 120–21, 127.

28 Thompson, *Making of the English Working Class*, p. 832.

29 Thompson, *Witness against the Beast*, pp. xiii–xiv.

30 Ibid., p. 86.

[31] Ibid., p. 105.
[32] Ibid., p. 128.
[33] Ibid., p. 221.
[34] Ibid., pp. 228–29.
[35] Thompson, *Making of the English Working Class*, p. 447.
[36] Thompson, *William Morris*, p. 511.

8. TOWARD A PROGRAM FOR PUBLICLY FINANCED JOBS

[1] Transcript of President Clinton's Message on the State of the Union, *New York Times*, January 27, 1994.
[2] "Job Losses Don't Let Up Even as Hard Times Ease," *New York Times*, March 22, 1994.
[3] "Survey: 47% of Companies Reduced Staff in Past Year," *Youngstown Vindicator*, September 23, 1993.
[4] Quoted in "The AFL-CIO and the Jobless," 3 *Labor Educator* (January/February 1994).
[5] "Job Losses Don't Let Up Even as Hard Times Ease," *New York Times*, March 22, 1994.
[6] "Corporate Spending Booms, but Jobs Stagnate," *New York Times*, June 16, 1994.
[7] "In Mississippi, a Clue to Low-Inflation Economics," *New York Times*, May 31, 1994.
[8] Ibid.
[9] "U.S. Corporations Expanding Abroad at a Quicker Pace," *New York Times*, July 25, 1994. According to this article, American companies employ 5.4 million people abroad, 80 percent of them in manufacturing. Gillette, for example, has 62 factories in 28 countries, employing 7,700 workers abroad and just 2,300 in the United States.
[10] According to Gary Chapman, "The High-Tech Gravy Train," *New York Times*, May 31, 1994: "[F]ew people are willing to pay for what really needs doing: a better educational system; crime-free neighborhoods; a healthy environment, and better roads, public buildings, and parks. Governments are supposed to provide these things. But because the Clinton Administration is in thrall to high tech, we're getting flat-panel displays instead."
[11] Irv Ackelsberg and others, "Opportunities for Legal Services Advocacy on Jobs, Employment, Education, and Training Issues," *Clearinghouse Review* (January 1994), p. 984 n. 3, quoting Congressional Budget Office, *Displaced Workers: Trends in the 1980s and Implications for the Future* (Washington, D.C.: Government Printing Office, 1993).
[12] "The official unemployment rate for January was 6.7 percent. The more we focus on it, the less we understand the extent of the problem. A better indicator of prevailing conditions would be a statistic that showed the number of people who wanted a job but could not find one. That number would be astonishingly high." Bob Herbert, "Counting the Jobless," *New York Times*, February 23, 1994.
[13] Ibid.
[14] "U.S. Should Match Europe's Shorter Workweek," *New York Times*, November 5, 1993. Secretary Reich puts the number of part-time workers who would rather be working full-time at six million. Bureau of National Affairs (BNA), *Labor Relations Reporter* (February 14, 1994), p. 176. Worldwide, according to the International Labor Organization, there are 120 million people who are out of work and approximately 700 million who are underemployed. Ibid., p. 181.
[15] "Working Poor Are Among Us," *Youngstown Vindicator*, March 13, 1994.

16 "America's Working Poor Eke Out a Life—Barely," *San Francisco Examiner,* July 17, 1994. Thanks to Doris Walker for this and other clippings.

17 "World's Big Economies Turn to the Jobs Issue," *New York Times,* March 14, 1994. This article and other commentary on the jobs conference convened in Detroit on March 14, 1994, make clear that European industrial countries are experiencing the same problem of structural unemployment that exists in the United States. There is a higher unemployment rate in Europe because these societies provide generous unemployment insurance and for a longer period, as compared with the United States. The United States has created many more jobs than Europe, but only by forcing workers off unemployment insurance into low-paying jobs, "thereby widening the gap between the highest-paid and lowest-paid workers."

18 "President Offers Job Prescriptions," *New York Times,* March 15, 1994.

19 "After the Jobs Went South: A Town Finds Pitfalls in a Retraining Effort," *New York Times,* November 6, 1993.

20 John Judis, "Train in Vain," *In These Times,* January 24, 1994.

21 Ibid., citing articles by Daniel Hecker and Kristina Shelley of the Bureau of Labor Statistics in the June 1992 *Monthly Labor Review.*

22 Examples are Xerox, hailed by both government and AFL-CIO leaders as a showcase for labor-management partnership; Nynex; and General Motors. "Xerox to Fire 10,000 Employees Despite 'Partnership' with Union," 3 *Labor Educator* (January/February 1994).

23 "Wisconsin gets federal OK to test 2-year welfare limit," *Youngstown Vindicator,* November 2, 1993; "Welfare Reform, Done Harshly," *New York Times,* November 8, 1993. See Center for Law and Social Policy, "On, Wisconsin? The Case against the 'Work not Welfare' Waiver" (October 1993), by Mark Greenberg.

24 "Clinton Welfare Planners Outline Big Goals Financed by Big Saving," *New York Times,* December 3, 1993.

25 "Clinton Welfare Planners Facing a Quiet Fight, With Their Friends," *New York Times,* March 18, 1994. Marian Wright Edelman sent a memorandum to the Administration in which she said that forcing people off welfare without jobs would "destroy the safety net," and "violate every standard of decency and fairness."

26 "Eager Democrats Pre-empt Clinton on Welfare Change," *New York Times,* May 12, 1994.

27 John Judis, "No Help Wanted," *In These Times,* November 1, 1993.

28 BNA, Daily Labor Report, October 7, 1993.

29 BNA, *Labor Relations Reporter* (February 7, 1994), quoting Secretary Reich; "The Puzzle of New Jobs: How Many, How Fast?" *New York Times,* May 24, 1994; "Optimistic Report on U.S. Economy," *San Francisco Chronicle,* July 15, 1994.

30 "Jobs: Part-time Issue Moves to Front," *Youngstown Vindicator,* May 31, 1994.

31 "Jobs: Part-time Issue Moves to Front," *Youngstown Vindicator,* May 31, 1994; Deborahann Smith, *Temp: How to Survive and Thrive in the World of Temporary Employment* (Boston: Shambhala, 1994), cited in Steve Burnett, "Recent Effects of the New Role of Temporary Agencies in Mahoning Valley Employment Trends," to which I am indebted throughout this section.

32 Smith, *Temp,* p. 3, and William M. Lewis and Nancy H. Molloy, *How to Choose and Use Temporary Services* (New York: Amacom, 1991), p. 2.

33 "News Watch," *Labor Notes* (August 1994).

34 Burnett, "Temporary Agencies."

35 Manpower Inc., "The Temporary Help Industry and Manpower Temporary Services" (Milwaukee: Manpower, 1988).

36 Lewis and Molloy, *How to Choose and Use Temporary Services,* p. 16. The same source cites the U.S. Chamber of Commerce for the proposition that the hidden cost (benefits, unemployment insurance, recruiting costs, etc.) for an employee who earns $400 a week is $171.18 per week (p. 16).

37 Interview with Kim Straniak, Trumbull Business College, July 1994, in Burnett, "Temporary Agencies."

38 Telephone interview, July 1994, in Burnett, "Temporary Agencies."

39 Interview with Wes Ross, Easco Aluminum, July 1994, in Burnett, "Temporary Agencies."

40 Burnett, "Temporary Agencies."

41 "Survey Predicts Weak Job Market in Both [Mahoning and Shenango] Valleys," *Youngstown Vindicator,* November 30, 1993.

42 Reid Dulberger, "Economy Diversifies; Boasts Positives," *Business Journal* (mid-January 1994), p. 23.

43 Youngstown Warren Regional Chamber, *Four Year Economic Development Plan* (1993).

44 Since the first draft of this essay appeared, the local newspaper has reported in an editorial entitled "Private Sector Takes the Lead" that between thirty and thirty-five companies are being asked by the Chamber of Commerce to pledge at least $40,000 to help finance a plan which has as its goal the creation of *eleven thousand* jobs. No specifics have been provided. *Youngstown Vindicator,* June 19, 1994.

45 Jesse Jackson, "Inman Gives Clinton Opening," *Youngstown Vindicator,* January 24, 1994.

46 Ibid. For specifics, see Ann Markusen and Catherine Hill, *Converting the Cold War Economy: Investing in Industries, Workers, and Communities* (Washington, D.C.: Economic Policy Institute, 1992).

47 "Group Seeks Funds Shift from Military to Cities," *Youngstown Vindicator,* February 9, 1994. See also Lauren Hallinan, "Preserving and Expanding the Rights of the Poor in Communities Where Military Bases Are Closing," *Clearinghouse Review* (February 1994), pp. 1184 ff.

48 Congressional Research Service, *The Employment Effects of Shifting Three Billion Dollars from Defense to State and Local Government-Related Activities* (February 1, 1993), p. 3.

49 Todd Shaffer, *Still Neglecting Public Investment* (Washington, D.C.: Economic Policy Institute, 1993).

50 Carl Davidson, "Clinton's Collapse on Industrial Policy," 5 *Federation for Industrial Retention and Renewal News* (Winter 1993), pp. 5–6.

51 Transcript of President Clinton's Message on the State of the Union, *New York Times,* January 27, 1994.

52 "More Is the Pity at the Pentagon," *New York Times,* February 9, 1994.

53 Ibid.; Lawrence J. Korb, "Shock Therapy for the Pentagon," *New York Times,* February 15, 1994. A memorandum from the Friends Committee on National Legislation, February 11, 1994, compares annual military spending of the United States as compared to that of its "potential adversaries" identified by the Pentagon:

United States	$290.7 billion
Cuba	1.2
Libya	1.5

Syria	1.1
Iraq	8.6
Iran	4.3
N. Korea	5.5

The same memorandum specifies 1994 spending of $14.9 billion on military programs the total cost of which is $420–plus billion "that could be eliminated to generate large savings in the federal budget."

54 Hobart Rowen, "How to Create a Million New Jobs," *Washington Post*, November 26, 1993.

55 Felix Rohatyn, "The American Economy and the Rest of the World: Two Sides of the Same Coin," November 30, 1993. State and local pension funds control one-third of the nation's total pension fund assets. BNA, *Labor Relations Reporter* (January 10, 1994), p. 24. Linda Tarr-Whelan, president of the Center for Policy Alternatives, told a conference in 1994: "If state public employee pension systems alone invested just 2 percent of their portfolios in economically targeted investments, this would yield 100 billion dollars' worth of investment capital to create jobs and growth in capital-starved neighborhoods." BNA, *Labor Relations Reporter* (February 21, 1994), p. 212. Pension fund investment in housing was announced in "Two Big Pension Funds Will Back Housing for Low-Income Families," *New York Times*, March 15, 1994.

56 See also Bernard Sanders, "Here's a Plan to Create Jobs and Rebuild America," *Labor Notes* (October 1994), p. 10.

57 Holly Sklar, "Disposable Workers," *Z Magazine* (January 1994), p. 40.

58 Congressional Research Service, *Unemployment, Dislocated Workers, and Job Creation* (July 6, 1992), p. 9.

59 Joni Rabinowitz, "Copping Out on Human Services," 21 *Allegheny Socialist* (December 1993–January 1994), pp. 1–2.

60 "Lawmakers submit fund requests to state," *Youngstown Vindicator*, February 14, 1994.

61 Bob Herbert, "America's Job Disaster," *New York Times*, December 1, 1993.

62 Sklar, "Disposable Workers," pp. 40–41.

63 Linda Mills, "An Escape from Welfare *and* Poverty" (Center for Law and Social Policy, August 1993), pp. 7–9.

9. THE POSSIBILITY OF RADICALISM IN THE EARLY 1930S

1 C. Wright Mills, *The New Men of Power: America's Labor Leaders* (New York: Harcourt Brace, 1948), p. 224.

2 Mark Naison, "The Southern Tenant Farmers' Union and the CIO," *Radical America* (September–October 1968), p. 53. The present essay attempts to carry a step further the argument of Naison's splendid article.

3 Art Preis, *Labor's Giant Step: Twenty Years of the CIO* (New York: Pathfinder Press, 1972), chap. 4.

4 Jeremy Brecher, *Strike!* (San Francisco: Straight Arrow Books, 1972), chap. 5 et passim.

5 Staughton Lynd, "Prospects for the New Left," *Liberation* (Winter 1971), p. 20.

6 Carroll Daugherty, Melvin de Chazeau, and Samuel Stratton, after stating, "What the actual membership strength of the Association was at different times under the Steel Code—how much the total number of fully paid-up and partially paid-up members came to—apparently no one knows," estimate the total membership in February 1934

at 50,000. 2 *The Economics of the Iron and Steel Industry* (New York: McGraw-Hill, 1937), p. 947n. Vincent D. Sweeney, a Pittsburgh reporter in the early 1930s and later public relations director for SWOC (which would have had no reason to exaggerate the achievements of the Amalgamated), states: "No official figure of the growth of the union in that campaign has ever been made public. The peak was probably around 200,000." *The United Steelworkers of America Twenty Years Later, 1936–1956* (n.p.: n.d., but obviously 1956), p. 7. The rank-and-file leaders claimed 150,000 signed up as of April 1934 (Harvey O'Connor in Federated Press dispatch, April 30, 1934, Columbia University).

7 Harvey O'Connor, "Personal Histories of the Early CIO," *Radical America* (May–June 1971).

8 My authority for this statement is a novel written by a steelworker that very closely follows the events of the 1930s and includes extracts from the minutes of the company union at the Edgar Thomson Works. Thomas Bell, *Out of This Furnace* (New York: Liberty Book Club, 1950), p. 290.

9 Walter Galenson, *The CIO Challenge to the AFL: A History of the American Labor Movement, 1935–1941* (Cambridge: Harvard University Press, 1960), p. 75.

10 Ibid., p. 94.

11 David J. McDonald, *Union Man* (New York: E. P. Dutton, 1969), pp. 93 ff.

12 This account of the captive mine strike of 1933 is based on almost-daily dispatches of reporters for the Federated Press, July–December 1933; Harvey O'Connor, *Steel—Dictator* (New York: John Day, 1935), chap. 14; Irving Bernstein, *Turbulent Years: A History of the American Worker, 1933–1941* (Boston: Houghton Mifflin, 1971), pp. 49–61; and Muriel Sheppard, *Cloud by Day: The Story of Coal and Coke and People* (Chapel Hill: University of North Carolina Press, 1947), chap. 10. Bernstein appears in error both in saying that "the UMW struck the Frick mines" (p. 50) and in giving the impression that the settlement was a solid victory (pp. 60–61). As to the latter point, see not only O'Connor, *Steel—Dictator*, pp. 162 and 192–95, where the strike is termed a "defeat" for the Frick miners, but also Daugherty and associates, 2 *Economics of Iron and Steel*, p. 1008n.: ". . . the recognition of the United Mine Workers by certain steel companies in their Illinois captive mines, where recognition has existed for decades and where recognition, unlike the diluted sort given under the Recovery Act to the union in the captive coal mines of Pennsylvania, is real and complete."

13 Harold Ruttenberg, "Steel Labor, the NIRA, and the Amalgamated Association," a detailed narrative of the rank-and-file movement of 1934, Ruttenberg Papers, Pennsylvania State University. Unless otherwise indicated, statements about the 1934 movement are based on this source.

14 Robert R. R. Brooks, *As Steel Goes . . . : Unionism in a Basic Industry* (New Haven: Yale University Press, 1940), chap. 3. This is an extraordinary interview, but must be used with care. Brooks interviewed Clarence Irwin, for Mrs. Irwin remembers the occasion. But the text of the so-called interview as published in *As Steel Goes . . .* draws on several sources, including Ruttenberg's narrative, as Brooks explicitly acknowledges (p. 262n).

15 Interview with Heber Blankenhorn, Columbia University Oral History Project, pp. 437a and 438a. According to the minutes of the AFL executive council meeting of February 12, 1935, Lewis told this body: "You have to utilize the services of these young men in the steel industry. They have no training, no background in trade unionism, no experience in the labor movement." Carroll Moody kindly called this statement to my atten-

tion. I should like to thank Carroll Moody of Northern Illinois University for his remarkable scholarly generosity during my work on rank-and-file movements in steel. He permitted me to examine not only a first draft of a study on the rank-and-file movement in the Amalgamated Association of Iron, Steel, and Tin Workers, but the notes on which that study is based. I have made clear in the footnotes those few cases in which a statement in the present essay is made on the authority of Professor Moody's research. In general, however, his research makes it possible for me to advance more confidently conclusions which I had reached independently on the basis of personal recollections of steelworkers and of documents they had saved.

16 Daugherty and associates, 2 *Economics of Iron and Steel*, p. 959n.

17 The rank and file in the United Steelworkers of America, AFL-CIO, have repeatedly attempted to modify the USWA constitution in these same three ways—referendum vote on new contracts, election of staff men, local right to strike—and repeatedly failed.

18 O'Connor, "Personal Histories of the Early CIO."

19 This account of the SMWIU is based on Horace B. Davis, *Labor and Steel* (New York: International Publishers, 1933), especially pp. 257–58 and 264, and on interviews with three SMWIU organizers.

20 Address by Leon Callow, former SMWIU organizer in Youngstown, at Youngstown State University, April 14, 1972.

21 SMWIU, "Steel Workers! Organize and Prepare to Strike!," leaflet, O'Connor Papers, Wayne State University, n.d. but obviously May or early June 1934. Carroll Moody kindly made this document available to me.

22 Clarence Irwin to Harold Ruttenberg, May 17, 1934, Exhibit 10 attached to Ruttenberg's narrative.

23 Blankenhorn interview, p. 444a. In Daugherty and associates, 2 *Economics of Iron and Steel*, p. 1059, the statement is made that one or more of the Big Four persuaded the rank-and-file leaders to "turn down united-front offer from Left-wing Steel and Metal Workers" on May 20. Since Ruttenberg was a student of Daugherty's and did research for this study, we can be sure that this statement reflects Ruttenberg's views.

24 The quoted words are identical to words that Ruttenberg, in his narrative, has himself saying to Forbeck: "Number 3 (Ruttenberg) told Forbeck that they wanted to institutionalize the whole affair," and so forth.

25 Cecil Allen, Open Letter to "Fellow Steel Workers," undated but around July 1, 1934, Exhibit 34 attached to Ruttenberg's narrative. The Weirton leaders had been to Washington prior to May 1934 to testify in their own behalf before the National Labor Board. As early as April, Bill Spang stated, "We're tired of sending delegations to Washington and of the endless run-around we get there." Federated Press dispatch, April 18, 1934.

26 Statement by James Egan to Harold Ruttenberg on June 5, 1934, Ruttenberg narrative, p. 23. On the same day an SMWIU delegation in Washington stated this criticism to the press. Federated Press dispatch, June 5, 1934.

27 Harold Ruttenberg to George Soule, July 6, 1934, Ruttenberg Papers.

28 Arthur S. Weinberg interview with Ruttenberg, May 12, 1968, and Don Kennedy interview with Ruttenberg, April 24, 1969, Pennsylvania State Oral History Project.

29 The statement about strikebreakers is made on the basis of an interview with John Morris, March 30, 1972. Morris was hired by the Calumet Protective Association at its office on the fifth floor of the Hotel Gary, issued a uniform and a gun, and housed in the

Youngstown Sheet and Tube Mill in East Chicago, Indiana, for three days before the Amalgamated special convention in mid-June 1934.

30 Harold Ruttenberg, "The Special Convention . . ." Carroll Moody kindly made this document available to me.

31 Bell, *Out of This Furnace*, pp. 323–24.

32 Clarence Irwin to "Dear Brother," November 19, 1934, NSLRB files. This was an invitation to the secret meeting of representatives from several districts of the Amalgamated with SMWIU representatives in Cleveland on November 25. Carroll Moody kindly made this document available to me.

33 Clarence Irwin to Harold Ruttenberg, January 23, 1935, Ruttenberg Papers, and Harvey O'Connor to Clarence Irwin, February 12, 1935, O'Connor Papers. Carroll Moody kindly made the latter document available to me.

34 *Youngstown Vindicator,* February 8, 1935, Irwin scrapbook.

35 *Pittsburgh Post Gazette,* February 4, 1935, Ruttenberg Papers.

36 Prior to the Amalgamated convention of 1935, the rank and file asserted that they represented between 75,000 and 90,000 expelled members. At the convention a careful check was made, and the figure was scaled down to 50,000. Bill Spang claimed that of the 150,000 steelworkers in District 1 of the Amalgamated, the Pittsburgh area, a majority belonged to the union. He offered the following figures for membership in the Amalgamated at particular large mills: 3,800 of 4,200 in Duquesne, 3,300 at the U.S. Steel mill in Braddock, 2,200 at the U.S. Steel mill in Homestead, almost 6,000 at the Jones and Laughlin mill in Aliquippa. Large mills such as these can be assumed to have supported the rank-and-file movement. See Federated Press dispatches, March 28 and April 2, 29, and 30, 1935.

37 Federated Press dispatch, February 5, 1935.

38 *Daily Worker,* April 15, 1935. Carroll Moody kindly made this document available to me.

39 Federated Press dispatch, March 28, 1935.

40 Federated Press dispatches, April 1 and 2, 1935.

41 Harold Ruttenberg, "A Rank-and-File Strike," Ruttenberg Papers; Federated Press dispatches, May 29 and 31 and June 3, 4, and 5, 1935. Clarence Irwin was fired as a result of the strike and thenceforth worked full-time, first for the rank-and-file movement and then for SWOC. Brooks, *As Steel Goes* . . . , p. 70.

42 Federated Press dispatches, June 3 and 14, July 1, 5, and 29, and August 22, 1935.

43 Federated Press dispatch, April 2, 1935.

44 Blankenhorn interview, p. 475a; Federated Press dispatches, April 19 and May 4, 1935.

45 A group of rank-and-file steelworkers confronted Lewis when he spoke at Greensburg, Pennsylvania, on April 1, 1936, and demanded that he make good on his rhetoric about organizing steel. Lewis invited a committee of three to meet with him and the CIO executive committee in Washington the next week. The result was the decision to offer $500,000 to the Amalgamated convention, meeting in Canonsburg, Pennsylvania, on April 28. There are three accounts of the April 1 encounter: by Irwin, in Brooks, *As Steel Goes* . . . , pp. 71–72; by Albert Atallah, in an interview with Alice Hoffman, September 20, 1967, Pennsylvania State Oral History Project; and by George Powers, in *Monongahela Valley: Cradle of Steel Unionism* (East Chicago, Ind.: Figueroa Press, 1972). My statement about the connection of the Communist Party with this event is based on an interview with a participant.

46 "Foster, who should know, wrote later that 60 of the first organizers hired by SWOC
    were members of the Communist Party." Len DeCaux, *Labor Radical: From the Wobblies to
    CIO* (Boston: Beacon Press, 1971), p. 279.
47 Brooks, *As Steel Goes* . . . , pp. 157, 177, and DeCaux, *Labor Radical*, p. 280.
48 Statements made to Harvey O'Connor at the February 3, 1935, meeting, Federated
    Press dispatch, February 5, 1935.
49 *Daily Worker,* March 2 and July 24, 1935. Carroll Moody kindly made these documents
    available to me.
50 Press clippings, March 31, 1936, and May 21, 1939, Irwin scrapbook.

10. GENESIS OF THE IDEA OF A COMMUNITY RIGHT TO PROPERTY

1 Morton J. Horowitz, *The Transformation of American Law, 1780–1860* (Cambridge: Harvard University Press, 1977), pp. 101–8; William E. Forbath, "Ambiguities of Free Labor:
   Labor and the Law in the Gilded Age," *Wisconsin Law Review* (1985), pp. 768–817; James
   B. Atleson, *Values and Assumptions in American Labor Law* (Amherst: University of Massachusetts Press, 1983).
2 Nationwide employment in basic steel dropped from more than 400,000 in 1977 to less
   than 150,000 in 1987. *New York Times,* July 7 and 14, 1987. The cause of the American
   steel industry's collapse is "disinvestment," that is, investment of money earned within
   the steel industry outside the industry where a higher rate of profit can be earned.
   Helen Shapiro and Steven Volk, "Steelyard Blues: New Structures in Steel," 12 *NACLA
   Report on the Americas* (January–February 1979), pp. 2–40; "Big Steel's Liquidation," *Business Week,* September 17, 1979, pp. 78–96.
       In the Youngstown, Ohio, area, three major steel mill closings between 1977 and
   1980 cost 10,000 jobs in basic steel. Staughton Lynd, *The Fight Against Shutdowns:
   Youngstown's Steel Mill Closings* (San Pedro: Singlejack Books, 1982), pp. 6–9. Between
   1977 and 1987 manufacturing production jobs in the Youngstown-Warren metropolitan
   statistical area fell from 63,600 to 38,200. Ohio Bureau of Employment Services, *Labor
   Market Review* (May 1987), p. 43. In January 1987 it was reported that about 51,000 persons in Mahoning County, or one out of six persons, were believed to have annual
   income below the federally defined poverty level of $5,360 a year for a single person or
   $11,000 a year for a family of four. *Youngstown Vindicator,* January 21, 1987.
       In Pittsburgh and its surrounding region, the loss of jobs was on a larger scale.
   Between 1982 and January 1987 the number of steel industry jobs declined from 90,000
   to 22,000. *New York Times,* January 21, 1987. That decline included a reduction in the
   number of jobs at Pittsburgh-area United States Steel Corporation mills from 22,554 in
   1980 to 5,133 in 1985 and at Jones & Laughlin Steel Corporation's Aliquippa Works
   from 10,000 in 1980 to 3,500 in 1984. United Steelworkers of America, *New Hope for Steel*
   (Pittsburgh, 1985); testimony of James V. Cunningham, professor of Social Work, University of Pittsburgh, prepared for the Special Committee to Investigate Industrial Plant
   Closings, House of Representatives, Commonwealth of Pennsylvania, August 10, 1984.
   See also Department of Engineering and Public Policy, School of Urban and Public
   Affairs, and Department of Social Science, Carnegie-Mellon University, *Milltowns in the
   Pittsburgh Region: Conditions and Prospects* (Pittsburgh, 1983), p. 203. As in Youngstown,
   the loss of steel jobs triggered the loss of a larger number of jobs outside steel. Thus
   from January 1, 1982, to July 1, 1984, at least fifty-two manufacturing plants in the ten-

county southwestern Pennsylvania region permanently closed, throwing 13,280 persons out of work. *Pittsburgh Post-Gazette,* January 15, 1985.

3 Werner Sombart, *Warum gibt es kein Sozialismus in den Vereinigten Staaten?* (Tübingen, Germany, 1906).

4 John Russo, "Saturn's Rings: What GM's Saturn Project is Really About," 9 *Labor Research Review* (Fall 1986), p. 68; *Youngstown Vindicator,* July 31, 1986.

5 On artisan republicanism see, for example, Eric Foner, "Tom Paine's Republic: Radical Ideology and Social Change," in *The American Revolution: Explorations in the History of American Radicalism,* ed. Alfred F. Young (DeKalb: Northern Illinois University Press, 1976), pp. 187–232; Sean Wilentz, *Chants Democratic: New York City and the Rise of the American Working Class, 1788–1850* (New York: Oxford University Press, 1984); and Leon Fink, *Workingmen's Democracy: The Knights of Labor and American Politics* (Urbana: University of Illinois Press, 1983). On local labor parties in the 1930s, see David J. Pivar, "The Hosiery Workers and the Philadelphia Third Party Impulse, 1919–1935," 5 *Labor History* (Winter 1964), pp. 18–23; and Eric Leif Davin and Staughton Lynd, "Picket Line and Ballot Box: The Forgotten Legacy of the Local Labor Party Movement, 1932–1936," 22 *Radical History Review* (Winter 1979–80), pp. 42–63.

6 Davin and Lynd, "Picket Line and Ballot Box," pp. 52–53; report of speech by John D. Connors, *New Bedford Standard-Times,* September 8, 1936; City Committee, United Labor Party of America, "Vote the United Labor Party Ticket to Make Akron a Decent City!" leaflet, Fall 1947; Lewis R. Johnson, "The Future of the United Labor Party," leaflet, September 1947; Provisional National Organizing Committee, "The United Labor Party of America Asks You to Join in Its Forward March," leaflet, 1948; report of speech by Harry Hurtt, *Akron Beacon Journal,* October 16, 1948. John Barbero describes his encounter with the United Labor Party in John Barbero, Ed Mann et al., "A Common Bond," in *Rank and File: Personal Histories by Working-Class Organizers,* ed. Alice and Staughton Lynd (Boston: Beacon Press, 1973), pp. 272–75. Unless otherwise indicated, unpublished materials cited may be found in the Staughton Lynd Papers, Wisconsin State Historical Society, Madison, Wisconsin.

7 Lynd, *Fight Against Shutdowns,* p. 22.

8 Larry C. Ledebur, *A Targeted Industry Strategy for the Mahoning Valley* (Youngstown, 1986), p. 15.

9 Lynd, *Fight Against Shutdowns,* pp. 13–81, 93–127, 131–89.

10 The Weirton Steel Corporation buyout is critically portrayed by Jonathan Prude, "ESOP's Fable: How Workers Bought a Steel Mill in Weirton, West Virginia, and What Good It Did Them," 14 *Socialist Review* (November–December 1984), pp. 27–60, and by Staughton Lynd, "Why We Opposed the Buy-Out at Weirton Steel," 6 *Labor Research Review* (Spring 1985), pp. 41–53.

11 Lynd, *Fight Against Shutdowns,* p. 159; "Trial Proceedings Had Before the Honorable Thomas D. Lambros . . . Commencing on March 17, 1980, Lyle Williams et al. v. United States Steel Corporation," Civil Action No. C-792337-Y (N.D. Ohio 1979), pp. 272–73.

12 Lynd, *Fight Against Shutdowns,* pp. 22–23.

13 Ibid., pp. 26–27.

14 Diocese of Youngstown, press release, September 26, 1977; [Ecumenical Coalition of the Mahoning Valley], statement, September 29, 1977.

15 Ecumenical Coalition of the Mahoning Valley, *A Religious Response to the Mahoning Valley Steel Crisis* (Pittsburgh, November 29, 1977), pp. 1–2, 3, 4.

16 Lynd, *Fight Against Shutdowns*, p. 35.

17 John Barbero and Ed Mann sketch their personal histories as of the early 1970s in Barbero, Mann et al., "A Common Bond," pp. 265–84; John Barbero letter, *Youngstown Vindicator*, February 9, 1977; John Barbero, "Hundreds of Thousands of Steelworker Jobs Are on the Line," *Brier Hill Unionist*, October–November 1977.

18 Unpublished fragment from the papers of John Barbero (the author wishes to thank Miyo Barbero for this reference); John Barbero interview by Carol Greenwald and Dorie Krause, transcript, c. 1981. The leper colony image (reminiscent of the Latin American concept of "marginalization") recurs in the words of another Youngstown retiree, Mike Bibich: "Look at me. You see any rot on me? I keep looking for something wrong with me, everyday in the mirror, but I don't feel any different. What are they tryin' to do, turn this place into a leper colony?" Teresa Anderson, "Mike Bibich and Youngstown, Ohio," *Mill Hunk Herald* (Winter 1985–86), p. 14.

19 Local 1462, USWA, *How Long Will Your Job Last?* (Youngstown, March 1979), p. [3].

20 TriState Conference on Steel, "Environmental Impact of New Industrial Plants: The Case of Conneaut," *Utah Law Review* (1980), pp. 331–53; Ralph Nader and William Taylor, *The Big Boys: Power and Position in American Business* (New York: Pantheon, 1986), pp. 34–35; Lynd, *Fight Against Shutdowns*, pp. 68–69.

21 Lynd, *Fight Against Shutdowns*, pp. 82–89, 155.

22 A detailed recital of the company's promises and the workers' concessions as set forth in the amended complaint is found in *Local 1330, United Steel Workers of America v. United States Steel Corporation*, 631 F.2d 1264 (6th Cir. 1980), pp. 1270–77. The quoted language is from [LTV Corporation retirees], "Public Hearing & Labor Rally; Subjects: Justice, Chapter 11, Plant Closings, Buyouts & Mergers, Community Impacts, Quality of Life," leaflet, January 1987.

23 "Proceedings Had before The Honorable Thomas D. Lambros . . . on . . . Feb. 28, 1980, Lyle Williams et al. v. United States Steel Corporation," Civil Action No. C-792337-Y (N.D. Ohio 1979), pp. 6–7, 9, 11–12, quoted in part in *Local 1330*, 631 F.2d, pp. 1279–80.

24 *United Steel Workers of America, Local No. 1330 v. United States Steel Corporation*, 492 F.Supp. 1 (N.D. Ohio 1980), p. 10. The court of appeals affirmed that portion of the district court's decision for similar reasons. *Local 1330*, 631 F.2d, pp. 1279–82.

25 In 1981 Jones & Laughlin Steel, an LTV Corporation subsidiary, negotiated an agreement with the local union at the Campbell Works coke plant, one of the few parts of that facility still in operation. The agreement provided that if the company announced a decision to rebuild the coke plant, it could implement a variety of concessions. Soon thereafter, the LTV board of directors approved an expenditure of $150 million to rebuild the coke plant and began to implement the concessions contained in the agreement. In fact, as the company later admitted, the decision to rebuild was contingent on Environmental Protection Agency approval of certain extensions of environmental compliance deadlines. Within six months of signing the agreement, the company knew that it would probably not receive the desired extensions. Even after that, the CEO stated publicly that "[w]e will spend 150 million dollars on this project over the next three years," and the chairman of the board declared that the company did not intend

to close any of its Mahoning Valley facilities. In January 1983, having taken advantage of the concessions contained in the agreement for eighteen months, the company announced the permanent closing of the Campbell Works coke plant. When coke plant workers sued for fraud and breach of contract, the court dismissed the suit because the preamble to the 1981 agreement contained the phrase, "without intending any limitation on Management's rights under the terms of the" Basic Steel Contract. *Joseph Serrano et al. v. Jones & Laughlin Steel Co.,* 790 F.2d 1279 (6th Cir. 1986).

26 Law review commentators agree that the U.S. Steel case was decided wrongly under existing contract law, quite apart from the community property right claim. Daniel A. Farber and John H. Matheson, "Beyond Promissory Estoppel: Contract Law and the 'Invisible Handshake'," 52 *University of Chicago Law Review* (Fall 1985), p. 939; Jay M. Feinman, "Critical Approaches to Contract Law," 30 *UCLA Law Review* (April 1983), p. 859; Duncan L. Kennedy, "Distributive and Paternalistic Motives in Contract and Tort Law, with Special Reference to Compulsory Terms and Unequal Bargaining Power," 41 *Maryland Law Review* (1982), p. 630.

27 Charley McCollester, "Proposal on Program," memorandum, n.d.; Mike Stout, "Eminent Domain and Bank Boycotts: The TriState Strategy in Pittsburgh," 1 *Labor Research Review* (Summer 1983), p. 22.

28 *United Steel Workers of America, Local No. 1330 v. United States Steel Corporation,* 492 F.Supp., p. 10; Arthur Bray, conversation with Staughton Lynd, Spring 1980.

29 Minutes of the TriState Conference on Steel for May 1, 1980, relate, "After Msgr. Rice raised the question of eminent domain the discussion returned to that topic several times. . . . It was decided to take this possibility very seriously."

30 Frank O'Brien interview by Joseph S. Hornack and Staughton Lynd, June 4, 1981. A transcribed and edited version appears in TriState Conference on Steel, *What Can We Do About Plant Closings?* (Pittsburgh, 1981).

31 Mellon Bank Economics Department, *The Pittsburgh Economy: Review and Outlook* (Pittsburgh, 1981), p. 6.

32 See P. Nichols, 1 *The Law of Eminent Domain* (New York, 1985), pp. 1–13 to 1–735.

33 The litigation was *Steel Valley Authority v. Union Switch and Signal Division, American Standard, Inc. et al.,* Civil Action No. 86-625 (W.D. Pa. 1986). Plaintiffs cited Hugo Grotius's *De Jure Belli et Pacis* (1625) as paraphrased by P. Nichols: "It was the theory of Grotius that the power of eminent domain was based upon the principle that the state had an original and absolute ownership of the whole property possessed by the individual members of it antecedent to their possession of it, and that their possession and enjoyment of it was derived from a grant by the sovereign and was consequently held subject to an implied reservation that it might be resumed, and that all individual rights to such property might be extinguished by a rightful exertion of this ultimate ownership by the state." Nichols, 1 *Law of Eminent Domain,* pp. 1–14. Eminent domain has been described as "the one truly explosive legal 'time bomb' in all antebellum law." Horwitz, *Transformation,* p. 259. On the use of eminent domain to acquire land in the eighteenth and nineteenth centuries, see Horwitz, *Transformation,* pp. 31–62; and William B. Stoebuck, "A General Theory of Eminent Domain," 47 *Washington Law Review* (1972), pp. 553–608. The recent Supreme Court case is *Hawaii Housing Authority v. Midkiff,* 467 U.S. 229 (1984). On Pennsylvania's apparently idiosyncratic doctrine, see Phil H. Lewis, "Eminent Domain in Pennsylvania," 26 *Pennsylvania Statutes Annotated* (Purdon 1958),

p. 4. On varieties of public or common property rights recognized in American law, see Harry Scheiber, "Public Rights and the Rule of Law in American Legal History," 72 *California Law Review* (March 1984), pp. 217–50; and Carol Rose, "The Comedy of the Commons: Custom, Commerce, and Inherently Public Property," 53 *University of Chicago Law Review* (Summer 1986), pp. 711–81.

34 David M. Roderick of U.S. Steel told California Newsreel in 1982 that the company's new investments must have at least a 20 percent rate of return. "Is USS Getting Out of Steel? An Interview with USS Chairman, David M. Roderick," 2 *TriState Conference on Steel Newsletter* (November–December 1982), pp. 11–12. On Roderick's attitude toward company investment, see also Nader and Taylor, *Big Boys*, pp. 60–61.

35 The incident was described to the author by a participant in the demonstration who is now a faculty member in Flint, Michigan.

36 The national Steelworkers union's opposition to the campaign for worker-community ownership in Youngstown is described in Lynd, *Fight Against Shutdowns*, pp. 49–62. The ties between the Catholic Church and working-class Youngstown are suggested by Bishop James Malone's recital at a retiree rally in Youngstown of how during the Little Steel Strike of 1937 his father came home bloody and bruised from a skirmish with strikebreakers. *Youngstown Vindicator*, February 1, 1987.

37 The TriState Conference on Steel derived its name from a conference organized by persons active in the Ecumenical Coalition of the Mahoning Valley early in 1979. Thereafter it turned into a continuing organization that existed only in Pittsburgh.

38 Together with Frank O'Brien, Msgr. Charles Owen Rice was TriState's link to earlier phases of Pittsburgh's labor and religious history. See *New York Times*, June 7, 1982; and Charles Owen Rice, "The Tragic Purge of 1948," 29 *Blueprint for the Christian Reshaping of Society* (February 1977), p. 1. The author wishes to thank Charley McCollester for this reference. In the 1980s Rice wrote a weekly column in the *Pittsburgh Catholic*, wherein he stated, "The more I study this, the more I am convinced that nationalization of the basic steel industry is the only way to save it." *Pittsburgh Catholic*, May 22, 1981.

39 "Celebrate Labor Day!" leaflet [August–September 1981].

40 Thomas Merton Center, "Spirit of Solidarity: The Thomas Merton Award Proudly Presented to the People of Poland," printed program, February 10, 1982. The Thomas Merton Center promotes radical Catholic activism in the Pittsburgh area. One of its leading personalities, Molly Rush, became a member of the board of directors of the TriState Conference on Steel.

41 Charley McCollester, "To the Spirit of Solidarity," typescript. The draft program of Polish Solidarity was printed in the *Militant*, July 24, 1981. Like TriState in its plans for the Steel Valley Authority, Solidarity advocated: "The participation of society in the planning process and in control over planning should be ensured by open discussion and decision-making through the medium of the [parliament] and through social organizations, local self-government bodies, and the trade unions.... This social control should also safeguard the autonomous socialized enterprises.... Socialized concerns should be given the freedom to determine their production plans and methods." Ibid. The author wishes to thank Charley McCollester for this reference.

42 U.S. Environmental Protection Agency, *Environmental News*, May 22, 1979; U.S. Steel, *1980 Annual Report* (Pittsburgh, 1981), pp. 10, 29; *Pittsburgh Post-Gazette*, December 3, 1980; *Wall Street Journal*, May 5, 1981.

43 For an example of U.S. Steel agitation on behalf of the legislation enacted in 1981, see David M. Roderick, *Is There an OSEC in Our Future?* (Houston, 1979).

44 TriState Conference on the Impact of Steel, *Counter Annual Report* (Homestead, May 1981); Mike Stout, "The Layoffs—Who Is to Blame?" *1397 Rank and File,* July 1980.

45 The dismay of Pittsburgh-area congressmen who had voted for tax reform and for amendment of the Clean Air Act on the assumption that it would lead to more investment in steel was expressed by William Coyne, who said he felt "a little double-crossed," and by Joseph Gaydos, who asserted that U.S. Steel's integrity was "on the line." *Youngstown Vindicator,* December 14, 1981; *Braddock Free Press,* November 26, 1981. Rank-and-file steelworkers expressed similar views. See *Pittsburgh Press,* November 20, 1981; *New York Times,* December 7, 1981; and *Warren Tribune,* December 11, 1981.

46 *Youngstown Vindicator,* August 18, 1982; *Pittsburgh Post-Gazette,* August 19, and August 28, 1982. A critical meeting of the Midland City Council and other notables took place at the Midland City Council chambers on August 27, 1982. The school board chairman stated, "Eminent domain scares me," comparing it to William of Normandy's purported belief that everything belongs to the king. Staughton Lynd, notes, August 27, 1982.

47 *Pittsburgh Post-Gazette,* December 17, 1982; *Pittsburgh Press,* December 17, 1982; Save Nabisco Action Coalition to Urban Redevelopment Authority, "Eminent Domain and the Nabisco Closing," memorandum [November 1982]; TriState Conference on Steel, reprint of "Givens to City: Buy Nabisco Plant," *Pittsburgh Post-Gazette,* November 30, 1982, and "Coalition's Muscle Keeps Nabisco Plant Open," *Pittsburgh Press,* December 22, 1982, leaflet.

48 *McKeesport Daily News,* April 23, 1981; "Pennsylvania Town Plans Takeover of Bankrupt Mesta Machine Co.," *Labor Notes,* June 29, 1983; Resolution No. 652 of the Borough of West Homestead, April 12, 1983; Articles of Incorporation of Homestead Steel Authority, typed draft.

49 "The Struggle to Save Mesta," 3 *TriState Conference on Steel Newsletter* (September 1983), p. 8.

50 *Philadelphia Inquirer,* January 22, 1983; *McKeesport Daily News,* April 18, 1983; *Pittsburgh Press,* June 1 and June 7, 1983; *Los Angeles Times,* June 6, 1983; *Pittsburgh Post-Gazette,* June 11, 1983; *New York Times,* July 23, 1984; Stout, "Eminent Domain and Bank Boycotts," pp. 17–19.

51 *Pittsburgh Post-Gazette,* April 12, 1983; Pittsburgh City Ordinance No. 21, July 5, 1983; Kevin C. Forsythe, "National, State and Local Perspectives on the Regulation of Business Dislocations: *Smaller Manufacturers Council v. City of Pittsburgh,*" 45 *University of Pittsburgh Law Review* (Winter 1984), pp. 439–79. A TriState leaflet entitled "Resumes for Reagan" stated: "Dear Mr. President, Please use the resources of my government to match this resume with the jobs you claim exist for me." TriState Conference on Steel, "Resumes for Reagan," leaflet, April 1983.

52 Bob Erickson, "The TriState Program for Revitalizing and Restructuring the Pittsburgh Steel Industry," typed draft, October 29, 1983; *Pittsburgh Post-Gazette,* Nov. 3, 1983; "Ron Weisen, Local 1397 Call for Formation of a TVA-Type Steel Valley Authority," *1397 Rank and File,* March 1984. On "The Business of America," see Bruce Schmiechen, Lawrence Daressa, and Larry Adelman, "Steelworker Revival: Waking from the American Dream," *Nation,* March 3, 1984; and *Wall Street Journal,* April 19, 1984.

53 USS Realty Development, Division of United States Steel, "Realty Development: Quick Reference Guide for USS Managers," leaflet, n.d.

54 *Pittsburgh Post-Gazette,* January 29, 1985; TriState Conference on Steel, "Chronology of Events Leading to Feasibility Study," leaflet, n.d.; *News Bulletin,* June 10, 1985.

55 *New York Times,* January 18, January 30, February 5, and February 13, 1985; "A Brash Bid to Keep Steel in the Mon[ongahela] Valley," *Business Week,* February 11, 1985; Michael Hoyt, "Steelworkers Propose Viable Plan to Revive Dying Plant," *In These Times,* February 20–26, 1985; Michael Hoyt, "How to Make Steel: Agitate and Organize," *Christianity and Crisis,* March 4, 1985; David Morse, "Reviving the Mon Valley: The Campaign to Save Dorothy Six," *Nation,* September 7, 1985; "Save Dorothy 6 . . . RALLY Saturday May 18," leaflet; *Pittsburgh Press,* May 31, 1986.

56 *Pittsburgh Press,* January 31, and November 25, 1985; *McKeesport Daily News,* November 23, 1985. Also providing support for the Steel Valley Authority idea were the campaigns of "Rainbow Democrats" Delores Patrick and Bob Anderson for the Homestead City Council in spring 1985. Rainbow Democrats for Council, "Homestead Has a Future!" leaflet, n.d.; Eric Davin to Staughton Lynd, October 27, 1986. On the Steel Valley Authority, see Joseph S. Hornack and Staughton Lynd, "The Steel Valley Authority," 15 *New York University Review of Law and Social Change* (1986–87), pp. 113–35.

   The full story of the Dorothy campaign's failure is beyond the scope of this article. The campaign was funded primarily by the United Steelworkers of America, which gave the union the leverage to decide who should undertake feasibility studies to determine if the buyout was practical. The union selected the Wall Street investment firm, Lazard Fréres. Lazard Fréres, assuming that all capital would come from private rather than public sources and that it was assessing a stand-alone Duquesne Works rather than a regional reindustrialization effort, recommended against the buyout.

57 In "Remaking the American C.E.O.," the *New York Times* stated: "The new order eschews loyalty to workers, products, corporate structures, businesses, factories, communities, even the nation. All such allegiances are viewed as expendable under the new rules. With survival at stake, only market leadership, strong profits and a high stock price can be allowed to matter." *New York Times,* January 25, 1987.

58 LTV absorbed Jones & Laughlin Steel (1970), Youngstown Sheet & Tube Company (1978), and Republic Steel (1984). After 1984 the three companies were collectively known as LTV Steel. For LTV's declaration of bankruptcy, see LTV Corporation, "LTV Files to Reorganize under Chapter 11," press release, July 17, 1986.

59 William J. Witt letter to the editor, *Youngstown Vindicator,* August 10, 1986; editorial, July 23, 1986; "Congressional Delegation Investigates LTV Action," *Stripscript* (Local 2265, United Steelworkers of America), August 1986.

60 Delores Hrycyk was a "typical" activist in the Ecumenical Coalition and TriState agitations, first, in her association with the Catholic Church, and second, in her experience in local-level skirmishes both with the steel companies and with the national Steelworkers union. When her husband, Mike Hrycyk, was laid off by Republic Steel in Youngstown, Hrycyk led an effort to obtain full pension benefits for workers laid off by the Youngstown facility. See *Canton Repository,* December 14, 1986.

61 In July 1986 the estimated value of LTV's steel facilities was $1.342 billion, whereas the LTV Steel pension plan was underfunded by more than $2 billion. R. D. Smith & Co., Inc., *LTV in Bankruptcy: A Preliminary Appraisal* (New York, July 28, 1986), pp. 3, 6.

Under the federal Employee Retirement Income Security Act (ERISA), the Pension Benefit Guaranty Corporation has a claim against LTV for the amount by which the pension plan is underfunded. See Employee Retirement Income Security Act, 29 United States Code sections 1361–62.

62 *Wall Street Journal,* May 21, 1987.

63 William Serrin, "Collapse of Our Industrial Heartland," *New York Times Magazine,* June 6, 1982, pp. 42–43; "Talk of the Town," *New Yorker,* April 29, 1985, p. 28.

64 Ecumenical Coalition of the Mahoning Valley, *Religious Response to the Mahoning Valley Steel Crisis,* p. 2; National Conference of Catholic Bishops, *Economic Justice for All,* p. 12.

65 *Economic Justice for All,* p. 58.

66 *New York Times,* June 5, 1984; Barbara Doherty, *The Struggle to Save Morse Cutting Tool* (North Dartmouth, Mass., n.d.); "Contract with New Owner of Morse Continues Gains," *UE News,* June 10, 1985; "Judge, to Save Jobs, Orders Sale of Assets at Lower Bid," *Wall Street Journal,* June 9, 1987; Peter Gilmore, "Union-Community Campaign Reopens Morse Tool," *UE News,* July 20, 1987.

67 Fink, *Workingmen's Democracy,* pp. 34–35; Christopher L. Tomlins, *The State and the Unions: Labor Relations, Law, and the Organized Labor Movement in America, 1880–1960* (Cambridge: Cambridge University Press, 1985), p. 328.

68 The National Legal Services Corporation, which combines federal funding with decentralized administration in field offices managed by local workers (attorneys) and consumers (clients), has been an important model for the Youngstown and Pittsburgh movements. See Staughton Lynd, "Reindustrialization from Below," 3 *democracy* (Summer 1983), pp. 21–33; and Staughton Lynd, "Toward a Not-for-Profit Economy: Public Development Authorities for Acquisition and Operation of Industry," 22 *Harvard Civil Rights/Civil Liberties Law Review* (Winter 1987), pp. 13–41.

11. INTERNATIONALIZATION OF CAPITAL

1 Eric Leif Davin and Staughton Lynd, "Picket Line and Ballot Box: The Forgotten Legacy of the Local Labor Party Movement, 1932–1936," 22 *Radical History Review* (Winter 1979–80); Davin, "The Very Last Hurrah? The Defeat of the Labor Party Idea, 1934–1936," in *"We Are All Leaders": The Alternative Unionism of the Early 1930s,* ed. Staughton Lynd (Champaign: University of Illinois Press, 1996), chap. 5.

2 Mary Van Kleeck to Senator Robert Wagner, March 12, 1934, quoted in Cletus Daniel, *The American Civil Liberties Union and the Wagner Act: An Inquiry into the Depression-Era Crisis in American Liberalism* (Ithaca: Cornell University Press, 1980), pp. 71–73.

3 Roger Baldwin to Senator David Walsh, March 20, 1934, and to Senator Robert Wagner, April 1, 1935, in Daniel, *The American Civil Liberties Union and the Wagner Act,* pp. 75, 101–2.

4 Federated Press dispatch, April 2, 1935, Columbia University.

5 Robert R. R. Brooks, *As Steel Goes . . . : Unionism in a Basic Industry* (New Haven: Yale University Press, 1940), chap. 3.

6 See the interview with George Patterson in *Rank and File: Personal Histories by Working-Class Organizers,* ed. Alice Lynd and Staughton Lynd (New York: Monthly Review Press, 1988), pp. 83–89, and his description of what happened to the Associated Employees when they joined the United Steelworkers of America in Lizabeth Cohen, *Making a New Deal: Industrial Workers in Chicago, 1919–1939* (Cambridge: Cambridge University Press, 1990), p. 358.

7   David Montgomery, *The Fall of the House of Labor: The Workplace, the State, and American Labor Activism, 1865–1925* (Cambridge: Cambridge University Press, 1987), pp. 317–19.

8   John Sargent in *Rank and File,* ed. Lynd and Lynd, pp. 98–100.

9   Montgomery, *The Fall of the House of Labor,* p. 325.

10 See Peter Rachleff, "Organizing 'Wall to Wall': The Independent Union of All Workers, 1933–1937," in *"We Are All Leaders,"* ed. Lynd, chap. 2.

12. THE WEBBS, LENIN, ROSA LUXEMBURG

1   Karl Marx and Frederick Engels, *The Communist Manifesto* (Chicago: Charles H. Kerr, n.d.), p. 27.

2   Ibid., pp. 32–33 (emphasis added).

3   Karl Marx, *Critique of the Gotha Program* (1875), in *The Marx-Engels Reader,* ed. Robert C. Tucker (New York: W. W. Norton, 1972), p. 389, quoting the introductory words of the Rules of the First International.

4   Fifteen years later, Grover Cleveland, President of the United States at the time of the Pullman strike, sought to justify his role in an article in *McClure's Magazine.* Debs replied in Eugene V. Debs, *The Federal Government and the Chicago Strike* (Chicago: Charles H. Kerr, 1910). Debs based his passionate rebuttal on the report of the commission appointed by Cleveland to investigate the strike, which, Debs observed, included Carroll D. Wright, Commissioner of Labor, and two lawyers, but no representative of the working class. After affirming that Cleveland made all his moves in the interest of the railroads and on the advice of railroad attorneys, Debs recited the commission's findings that federal troops had been unnecessary and that strike leaders never incited violence. He concluded: "The Chicago strike was in many respects the grandest industrial battle in history, and I am prouder of my small share in it than of any other act in my life.... Had the carpenter of Nazareth been in Chicago at the time, He would have been on the side of the poor, the heavy-laden and sore at heart, and He would have denounced their oppressors and been sent to prison for contempt of court under President Cleveland's administration." Debs, *The Federal Government and the Chicago Strike,* pp. 4, 8–10, 13–14, 21, 30–31.

5   Sidney Webb and Beatrice Webb, *The History of Trade Unionism,* 2d ed. (London: Longmans, Green, 1902), chap. 3.

6   Sidney Webb and Beatrice Webb, *Industrial Democracy* (Edinburgh: R. & R. Clark, 1898), pp. 833–34.

7   Sidney Webb and Beatrice Webb, *The History of Trade Unionism, 1666–1920* (printed by the authors for the trade unionists of the United Kingdom, Christmas 1919), pp. 575 ff.

8   Allan K. Wildman, *The Making of a Workers' Revolution: Russian Social Democracy, 1891–1903* (Chicago: University of Chicago Press, 1967), pp. 38–45; Richard Pipes, *Social Democracy and the St. Petersburg Labor Movement, 1885–1897* (Cambridge: Harvard University Press, 1963), pp. 57–67.

9   Wildman, *Workers' Revolution,* pp. 47–48 (emphasis added).

10 Ibid., chap. 4. Krupskaya recalled in her memoirs that "[t]he agitational leaflets enjoyed a huge success" (quoted on p. 56). Lenin himself wrote in *What Is to Be Done?* that the leaflets roused a "passion for exposure" among the workers, that correspondence "poured in" from the plants, and that the agitation amounted to a "declaration of war" that stimulated the workers to put forward demands and to support these

demands with strikes. Lenin, *What Is to Be Done?*, in 4 *Collected Works of V. I. Lenin* (New York: International Publishers, 1929), pp. 136–38.

There was nothing specifically Russian about the success of these leaflets. Little shop newspapers or articles in the radical press made available to the workers had the same effect in the United States in the early 1930s. When Katherine Hyndman ("Catherine Ellis") posted on the bulletin board at Bauer and Black in Chicago an article she had written for the *Daily Worker* about impending layoffs at the plant, work stopped. "Somebody was standing up on the work table, everybody was gathered around, and she was reading this article. . . . [T]hey thought it was wonderful. Hooray! Somebody cares about us. Listen, it's in print." *Rank and File: Personal Histories by Working-Class Organizers*, ed. Alice Lynd and Staughton Lynd (New York: Monthly Review Press, 1988), p. 17. Similarly in metal-working shops in Brooklyn, "our procedure was to put out a little shop paper with news from several departments. . . . The fellows from the shop furnished the news for the papers but never so they could be identified with the material. . . . These little shop papers created a sensation whenever they appeared." James J. Matles, *Them and Us: Struggles of a Rank-And-File Union* (Englewood Cliffs: Prentice-Hall, 1974), pp. 25–26.

11 Wildman, *Workers' Revolution*, chaps. 2 and 3, esp. pp. 50–51, 56, 62–63.

12 Pipes, *Social Democracy*, pp. 110–11, translating passages from *Proekt i obiasnenie programmi sotsial-demokraticheskoi partii*, to be found in V. I. Lenin, 2 *Sochinenie* (Moscow, 1946), pp. 80, 96, 97, 98 (all italics are Pipes's). Pipes notes that the last sentence quoted was cited by activist M. A. Silvin as illustrating very well the attitude of Social Democrats in 1896. I have added to this paragraph as quoted by Pipes the immediately preceding sentence in my own translation.

13 B. I. Gorev, *Iz partiinago proshlago* (Leningrad, 1924), p. 37, quoted in Wildman, *Making of a Workers' Revolution*, pp. 98–99; Pipes, *Social Democracy*, pp. 77–78, 90–91, 114–15. Lenin concedes that he and other older Social Democrats argued in 1897 for an "organization of revolutionaries which should have control of all the various workers' benefit clubs." Lenin, *What Is to Be Done?* p. 118. A. F. Kostin, the Soviet author of *Lenin and the Leagues of Struggle* (Moscow: Progress Publishers, 1983), pp. 80 ff., is therefore not mistaken when he characterizes the St. Petersburg League of Struggle as "an embryo of the party of a new type." Kostin notes that a quarter of a century later Lenin wrote in *Left-Wing Communism: An Infantile Disorder:* "There have always been attacks on the 'dictatorship of leaders' in our Party. The first time I heard such attacks, I recall, was in 1895, when, officially, no party yet existed, but a central group was taking shape in St. Petersburg." This passage from *Left-Wing Communism* may be found in V. I. Lenin, *Selected Works* (Moscow: Progress Publishers, 1975), pp. 530–31.

14 Lenin, *What Is to Be Done?* p. 206.

15 After Krupskaya joined him in 1898, Lenin and his wife spent their mornings translating the Webbs. The translation was published under the title *Teoria i praktika angliiskago trediunionizma*, 2 vols. (St. Petersburg, 1900–1901). Ronald W. Clark, *Lenin* (New York: Harper & Row, 1988), pp. 50–51; Thomas Taylor Hammond, *Lenin on Trade Unions and Revolution, 1893–1917* (New York: Columbia University Press, 1957), p. 80n. Solomon M. Schwarz, a Russian Social Democratic labor organizer in the early years of this century, agrees that Lenin "must have been influenced by the views he formed while translating Sidney and Beatrice Webbs' *Industrial Democracy*." Schwarz observes, "The

· immense bibliography of the second and third editions of Lenin's *Sochineniia* contain not one major work on the subject [of trade unionism] that came out after the Webbs'." Solomon M. Schwarz, *The Russian Revolution of 1905: The Workers' Movement and the Formation of Bolshevism and Menshevism* (Chicago: University of Chicago Press, 1967), p. 326n. As Jeremy Brecher noted in 1973, Eric Hobsbawm long ago pointed out the irony that Lenin's attack on spontaneity in *What Is to Be Done?* "reflects a close and extremely critical reading of the Webbs' great defense of the 'spontaneous' British trade-union movement." Jeremy Brecher, "*Who* Advocates Spontaneity?" 7 *Radical America* (November–December 1973), p. 112 n. 20, citing Eric Hobsbawm, "The Fabians Reconsidered," in *Labouring Men: Studies in the History of Labour* (New York: Basic Books, 1964), p. 255n. See also Eric Hobsbawm, "Lenin and the 'Aristocracy of Labour'," in *Revolutionaries: Contemporary Essays* (New York: Pantheon Books, 1973), pp. 122–23.

16 Lenin, *What Is to Be Done?*, pp. 114–15, 123.

17 Ibid., p. 214, summarizing the Webbs, *Industrial Democracy*, chap. 1.

18 Lenin, *What Is to Be Done?*, p. 223n.

19 Ibid., p. 222. The quoted words forecast the relationship that the Communist Party of the United States sought to develop with the leadership of the nascent CIO after 1935.

20 For example, after the arrest of many labor movement leaders in April 1894, representatives of the principal industrial districts met for months to organize the Central Workers Group, most active members of which came from large machine shops such as the Neva shipbuilding plant, the Putilov Works, and the Obukhovsky plant. Pipes, *Social Democracy*, pp. 76–77. When the great textile strike of 1896 spontaneously broke out, "[e]ach striking factory elected representatives to maintain relations with other factories and to carry on negotiations with management. On May 17, one hundred such representatives assembled a kind of protosoviet . . . to formulate their demands. There is no evidence that the assembly was attended by any Social Democratic intellectuals" (p. 103). Also in 1894–1896, St. Petersburg workers organized a citywide Workers' Fund, "which was to become the chief organ of all the district workers' funds." Wildman, *Workers' Revolution*, pp. 94–95, quoting the memoirs of V. I. Babushkin who worked in the Neva shipbuilding plant. Again in 1899–1900, when the few socialist intellectuals to survive arrest began cautiously reassembling an organization, they discovered that during the previous summer "a Workers' Organization had come into being that had drawn up a set of bylaws and an elaborate plan of organization and action." According to the plan, citywide leadership was exercised by a committee "made up of representatives of district committees (the Obukhov, the Narva, the Vyborg, and so on), which in their turn were to represent numerous workers' *kassy* [funds] in the factories." Wildman, *Workers' Revolution*, p. 113.

21 V. I. Lenin, *The State and Revolution: The Marxist Teaching on the State and the Tasks of the Proletariat in the Revolution* (Peking: Foreign Languages Press, 1976), pp. 53, 141.

22 In 1905 the party belatedly accepted the soviets on tactical grounds as "the technical apparatus" for carrying the party's leadership to the working class. From 1905 to 1917 the soviets did not play an important role in the thinking of Lenin or the Bolshevik Party. Even in the summer of 1917 the Bolshevik attitude toward the soviets was that these bodies represented one among several possible roads to power, not that the soviets were the necessary building blocks of a new society. Thus when in July–August the Bolsheviks appeared to have lost mass support in the soviets Lenin proposed that the

factory committees would now become the insurrectionary organs, and the party withdrew the slogan "All Power to the Soviets." That slogan was revived in September–October only when the Bolsheviks gained a majority in the St. Petersburg soviet. When the party began to lose its soviet majorities in 1918, the concept of soviet authority receded rapidly. Martin Buber, *Paths in Utopia* (Boston: Beacon Press, 1966), chap. 9; Samuel Farber, *Before Stalinism: The Rise and Fall of Soviet Democracy* (London: Verso, 1990), chap. 1.

23 "Self-activity" as a term in English has its own history. See George Rawick, "Working-Class Self-Activity," 3 *Radical America* (March–April 1969), reprinted in *Workers' Struggles, Past and Present: A Radical America Reader*, ed. James Green (Philadelphia: Temple University Press, 1983), in which the wildcat strike is presented as "the new form of working-class self-activity and organization"; C. L. R. James, F. Forest (Raya Dunayevskaya), and Ria Stone (Grace Lee), *The Invading Socialist Society* (Detroit: Bewick Editions, 1972), p. 4: "Proletarian democracy is not the result of socialism. Socialism is the result of proletarian democracy.... The proletariat mobilizes itself as a self-acting force through its own committees, unions, parties and other organizations"; Peter Rachleff, "Soviets and Factory Committees in the Russian Revolution," 8 *Radical America* (November–December 1974), reprinted in *Root and Branch: The Rise of the Workers' Movements* (Greenwich, Conn.: Fawcett Books, 1975); and *Within the Shell of the Old: Essays on Workers' Self-Organization*, ed. Don Fitz and David Roediger (Chicago: Charles H. Kerr, 1990).

24 As more fully described in the text, Kollontai based her speech on behalf of the Workers' Opposition at the Bolshevik Congress in 1921 on the idea of *samodeyatelnost*. Beatrice Farnsworth, *Alexandra Kollontai: Socialism, Feminism, and the Bolshevik Revolution* (Stanford: Stanford University Press, 1980), p. 221. Kollontai later used this term to characterize the sense of independence needed by Russian working women (p. 315n). See also Barbara Evans Clements, *Bolshevik Feminist: The Life of Alexandra Kollontai* (Bloomington: Indiana University Press, 1979), pp. 151, 191, 194, 203.

Trotsky's political writing during the years 1903–1906 parallels Luxemburg's. Both were reacting, first, to Lenin's *What Is to Be Done?* (published in 1902) and to the 1903 congress of the Russian Social Democratic Party, and second, to the Russian Revolution of 1905. Trotsky argued that the basic task of revolutionaries was "the development of the self-activity [*samodeyatelnost*] of the proletariat." He warned that Lenin's methods would lead "to the Party organisation 'substituting' itself for the Party, the Central Committee substituting itself for the Party organisation, and finally the dictator substituting himself for the Central Committee." Like Luxemburg, he indignantly rejected Lenin's belief that party organization should model itself on the division of labor in a capitalist factory, and juxtaposed such passages by Lenin with *Capital*'s description of alienated labor. Leon Trotsky, *Our Political Tasks* (London: New Park Publications, [1904]), pp. 67–72, 77, 83–90.

25 "I haven't mailed you the Webbs," Luxemburg wrote to Leo Jogiches at almost the same time that Lenin and Krupskaya were translating the Webbs in Siberian exile. Rosa Luxemburg to Leo Jogiches, July 10, 1898, *Comrade and Lover: Rosa Luxemburg's Letters to Leo Jogiches*, ed. Elzbieta Ettinger (Cambridge: MIT Press, 1979), p. 57. It appears that Luxemburg read the Webbs in German translation, because in the articles published in September 1898 and later collected as *Reform or Revolution* she cited "Webb, *Theorie und Praxis der Gewerkschaften*." *Marxism and Social Democracy: The Revisionist Debate,*

1896–1898, ed. and trans. by H. Tudor and J. M. Tudor (Cambridge: Cambridge University Press, 1988), p. 275.

26 Rosa Luxemburg, *The Russian Revolution and Leninism or Marxism?* ed. Bertram D. Wolfe (Ann Arbor: University of Michigan Press, 1970), p. 83.

27 Ibid., pp. 84–85.

28 Ibid., p. 86.

29 Ibid., pp. 84, 86.

30 Ibid., pp. 87, 88, 89.

31 Ibid., pp. 89–90.

32 Ibid., pp. 91–92. Richard Pipes and Allan Wildman generally confirm Luxemburg's assertion that the strikes she describes were "spontaneous" rather than planned by Social Democrats. Thus the textile strike of 1896 in St. Petersburg "was without question spontaneous in the sense that it was neither instigated nor managed by any outside group," and the Social Democratic Union of Struggle was likewise "caught unprepared by a second great textile strike, which took place at the beginning of January 1897." Pipes, *Social Democracy,* pp. 103, 112. Most Social Democrats were "taken by surprise" by the upheaval of 1901. In Rostov in 1902, the Social Democratic Committee was "caught napping," and at precisely the time general strikes sprang up across southern Russia in 1903 "the cream of *Iskra*'s 'professional revolutionaries' were wending their way via secret routes to Brussels for the Second [RSDP] Congress." Wildman, *Workers' Revolution,* pp. 136n, 246–48.

33 Luxemburg, *The Russian Revolution,* pp. 92–93.

34 Ibid., p. 94.

35 Ibid., pp. 95, 108.

36 Rosa Luxemburg taught in the Social Democratic party school from 1907 until the beginning of World War I. In contrast to the typical Germanic pedagogic style of lecturing to a passive audience, she "took trouble with each one of the students and was prepared if necessary to carry on individual tuition after hours." J. P. Nettl, 1 *Rosa Luxemburg* (London: Oxford University Press, 1966), pp. 390–91, basing himself in part on the memories of Rosi Wolffstein Frölich, who was a pupil at the school in 1912–1913. Rosa Luxemburg was contemptuous of the "miserably slapdash" training offered by trade union educational programs as compared to the education of the party school. Her student Wilhelm Pieck told the 1908 party congress that the trade unions wanted "a mass of members instructed just sufficiently to be able to follow them, but not enough to enable them to think systematically for themselves" (pp. 393–95). In her last major speech, in December 1918, Luxemburg continued to criticize a pedantic model of "workers' education": "Fortunately, we have gone beyond the days when it was proposed to 'educate' the workers socialistically.... To educate the proletarian masses meant to deliver lectures to them, to circulate leaflets and pamphlets among them. No, the school of the socialist proletariat doesn't need all this. The workers will learn in the school of action." "Our Program and the Political Situation," in *Selected Political Writings of Rosa Luxemburg,* ed. Dick Howard (New York: Monthly Review Press, 1971), p. 406.

37 Rosa Luxemburg, *Reform or Revolution,* in *Rosa Luxemburg Speaks,* ed. Mary-Alice Waters (New York: Pathfinder Press, 1970), pp. 48–51, 71–72. The reference to Sisyphus is on page 71.

38 Nettl, 1 *Luxemburg,* pp. 168–69 (discussion at 1899 party congress), 223 (the phrase "gave great offense"), 300–301 (1905 trade union congress).

39 Quoted in Richard Abraham, *Rosa Luxemburg: A Life for the International* (Oxford: St. Martin's Press, 1989), p. 61.

40 Nettl, 1 *Luxemburg,* p. 362.

41 Ibid., pp. 315, 346, 357.

42 Rosa Luxemburg, *The Mass Strike, the Political Party and the Trade Unions,* in *Rosa Luxemburg Speaks,* ed. Waters, pp. 160–61. Again the historical record appears to support Luxemburg's assessment of the relative roles of worker self-activity and vanguard leadership. The nationwide general strike of October 1905 took "by surprise the leaders of the Socialist underground," very much including the Bolsheviks, who also initially opposed the institution of the soviet "as a rival to the party." Isaac Deutscher, *The Prophet Armed: Trotsky, 1879–1921* (New York: Oxford University Press, 1954), p. 125.

43 Luxemburg, *The Mass Strike,* p. 163.

44 Ibid., pp. 164–65.

45 Ibid., pp. 165–66.

46 Ibid., pp. 166–68.

47 Ibid., pp. 173–75.

48 Ibid., pp. 176–79.

49 Ibid., p. 179. This event is confirmed by Laura Engelstein, *Moscow, 1905: Working-Class Organization and Political Conflict* (Stanford: Stanford University Press, 1982), p. 167: "During the last week in October, workers in many St. Petersburg factories began a campaign to institute the eight-hour workday by direct action. They did so simply by walking off the job after eight hours of work."

50 Rosa Luxemburg to Karl and Luise Kautsky, February 5, 1906, in *The Letters of Rosa Luxemburg,* ed. Stephen Eric Bronner (Boulder: Westview, 1978), p. 114.

51 Rosa Luxemburg, "The Two Methods of Trade-Union Policy," 1 *Die Neue Zeit* (October 24, 1906), in *Rosa Luxemburg: Selected Political Writings,* ed. Robert Looker (New York: Grove Press, 1974), pp. 145–46. Engelstein describes a list of demands by Moscow printers similar in many ways to the agreement quoted by Luxemburg. *Moscow, 1905,* p. 77.

52 Luxemburg, *The Mass Strike,* p. 190.

53 Ibid., pp. 190–95 ("Lessons of the Working-Class Movement in Russia Applicable to Germany").

54 Ibid., pp. 195–200 ("Cooperation of Organized and Unorganized Workers Necessary for Victory").

55 Ibid., pp. 214–18.

56 "Bernstein . . . says that capitalist development does not lead to a general economic collapse. He does not reject merely a certain form of the collapse. He rejects the very possibility of collapse" (Luxemburg, *Reform or Revolution,* p. 39). "[O]ur view [is] that capitalist society is caught in insoluble contradictions which will ultimately necessitate an explosion, a collapse" (speech of October 3, 1898, to the Stuttgart Congress [1898], in *Selected Political Writings,* ed. Howard, p. 39). "Those comrades . . . just snip the concept of a breakdown, of a social catastrophe, out of the pattern of evolution as Marx and Engels conceive it, and get a nice comfy notion of evolution: just what an [Academic Socialist like] Herr Bernstein would want. If we want to learn from history, we see that all previous class struggles have gone as follows: through legal reforms and small steps

forward, the rising class grew stronger within the limits of the old society, until it was strong enough to cast off its old shackles *by means of a social and political catastrophe*" (speech of October 11, 1899, to the Hanover Congress [1899], in *Selected Political Writings,* ed. Howard, p. 48).

57 Rosa Luxemburg, "Women's Suffrage and Class Struggle," speech at the Second Social Democratic Women's Rally, Stuttgart, May 12, 1912, in *Selected Political Writings,* ed. Howard, p. 219.

58 Nettl, 2 *Luxemburg,* p. 481.

59 Ibid., pp. 483–485; Abraham, *Rosa Luxemburg,* p. 113.

60 "Why Was the German Proletariat Silent during the July Days," *Selected Writings of Alexandra Kollontai,* ed. Alix Holt (New York: W. W. Norton, 1977), p. 100.

61 Alexandra Kollontai, *The Autobiography of a Sexually Emancipated Woman* (New York: Schocken Books, 1975), p. 89; Clements, *Kollontai,* p. 85.

62 Nettl, 2 *Luxemburg,* p. 610; Farnsworth, *Kollontai,* p. 44.

63 Nettl, 2 *Luxemburg,* p. 618. The Hague conference was attended by, among others, Jane Addams from the United States. Jane Addams, *Peace and Bread in Time of War* (Boston: G. K. Hall, 1960). Both Nettl and Elzbieta Ettinger see a slight softening of Luxemburg's attitude toward the women's movement during the war. Ettinger, Introduction to Luxemburg's *Letters to Jogiches,* pp. xxviii–xxix.

64 Angelica Balabanoff, *My Life as a Rebel* (New York: Harper, 1938), pp. 130–33. See Richard Stites, *The Women's Liberation Movement in Russia: Feminism, Nihilism, and Bolshevism, 1860–1930* (Princeton: Princeton University Press, 1938), pp. 284–85; Farnsworth, *Kollontai,* pp. 52–55.

65 Rosa Luxemburg to Hans Diefenbach, March 30, 1917, in *Letters,* ed. Bronner, p. 190. See also Luxemburg to Sonja Liebknecht, May 2, 1917 (defending dung beetle from ants that were eating it alive), July 20, 1917 (walking carefully in the prison garden so as not to crush the "underground apartments" of wild bees and wasps), mid-December 1917 (watching the beating of a water buffalo: "tears were running from my eyes—they were *his* tears"), in *Letters,* ed. Bronner, pp. 202–3, 219, 240–41.

66 Nettl, 1 *Luxemburg,* p. 334. See Luxemburg, *The Mass Strike,* e.g., pp. 186, 202.

67 Tsuyoshi Hasegawa, *The February Revolution: Petrograd, 1917* (Seattle: University of Washington Press, 1981), chaps. 12–13, especially pp. 216–17, 230–31, 234; L. D. Trotsky, 1 *The History of the Russian Revolution,* trans. Max Eastman (Ann Arbor: University of Michigan Press, 1964), p. 109.

68 Luxemburg, "A Duty of Honour," *Die Rote Fahne,* November 18, 1918, in *Selected Political Writings,* ed. Looker, pp. 258, 259, 261. Luxemburg's position contrasts with that of future Bolsheviks and Mensheviks alike at the 1903 congress of the Russian Social Democratic Party. When Plekhanov urged "that the revolutionary government should not abolish capital punishment—it might need it in order to destroy the Tsar," his views "evoked one single protest from an obscure delegate and gave rise to a feeble doubt in a few others, but they were generally received with acclamation." Deutscher, *The Prophet Armed,* p. 77.

69 Luxemburg, "What Does the Spartacus League Want?" *Die Rote Fahne,* December 14, 1918, in *Selected Political Writings,* ed. Howard, p. 370.

70 Luxemburg, "Our Program and the Political Situation," in *Selected Political Writings,* ed. Howard, pp. 380–84. As Howard points out, at 383 n. 6, Luxemburg said this without

knowing that German Social Democrats who solicited Engels's thoughts for a new preface to an 1895 edition of Marx's *Class Struggles in France* eliminated all passages that they considered too radical and deliberately created the false impression that Engels advocated the use of only parliamentary methods in the transition to socialism. "Engels protested, but died before any changes could be made."

[71] Luxemburg, *Selected Political Writings,* ed. Howard, pp. 396–97, 403.

[72] Luxemburg, *The Russian Revolution and Leninism or Marxism?* ed. Wolfe, p. 69. It seems that the paragraph of Luxemburg's manuscript with the words "Freiheit ist immer Freiheit der Andersdenkenden" is in the margin, with an insertion mark at the end but with no corresponding insertion mark in the text. Paul Levi made the passage an integral part of the text as first published, a practice that has been followed by most subsequent editors. Eric D. Weitz, "'Rosa Luxemburg Belongs to Us!': German Communism and the Luxemburg Legacy," 27 *Central European History* (1994), p. 28n.

[73] Luxemburg, *The Russian Revolution,* pp. 68, 71, 76–78.

[74] Ibid., pp. 70–71.

[75] Ibid., p. 71.

[76] Clements, *Kollontai,* p. 123.

[77] Ibid., p. 127. According to Louise Bryant, the Countess Panina who had held office under Kerensky commented, "This absurd Madame Kollontay invites the servants to come and sit in armchairs at her meetings." Louise Bryant, *Six Months in Russia* (London: Heinemann, 1919), p. 125, quoted in *Selected Writings of Alexandra Kollontai,* p. 117.

[78] "The Workers' Opposition," in *Selected Writings of Alexandra Kollontai,* pp. 178, 188. Angelica Balabanoff memorably describes Lenin's anger at Kollontai for her part in the Workers' Opposition. His personal attack included references to her sexual life that drew laughter from delegates to the Party Congress. Thereafter, Kollontai's portrait was removed from the walls of party offices. Balabanoff was herself offered the opportunity to fill Party positions previously held by Alexandra Kollontai, which she indignantly rejected. Angelica Balabanoff, *Impressions of Lenin* (Ann Arbor: University of Michigan Press, 1964), pp. 97–99.

[79] Kollontai, "The Workers' Opposition," in *Selected Writings,* pp. 189, 190, 192, 193, 199.

[80] Nettl, 2 *Luxemburg,* p. 767; Paul Frölich, *Rosa Luxemburg* (New York: Monthly Review Press, 1972), pp. 289–90.

[81] Luxemburg, "What Does the Spartacus League Want?" in *Selected Political Writings,* ed. Looker, p. 284; Luxemburg, "Our Program and the Political Situation," in *Selected Political Writings,* ed. Howard, pp. 375–76. A reference to Golgotha also occurs in "The Spirit of Russian Literature: Life of Korolenko," which Luxemburg wrote in prison in 1918 as a preface to Korolenko's autobiography. In this remarkable essay Luxemburg ascribes to the masters of Russian literature an "aching sympathy," a "brooding over the problems of society," which well describe herself. *Rosa Luxemburg Speaks,* ed. Waters, p. 346. In chronicling Korolenko's response to the Russian famine of the early 1890s, Luxemburg refers to "the entire Golgotha of the Russian village with its begging children, silent mothers, steeped in misery, wailing old men, sickness and hopelessness," as well as to "the Samaritans, those self-sacrificing men and women who were heroically rushed to the stricken areas to nurse the sick" (p. 357). The following pages describe Korolenko's impassioned opposition to the death penalty. One is led to wonder if one of the many books that Luxemburg reread in prison, perhaps without mentioning it to

her comrades, was the Bible. Throughout her life, Rosa Luxemburg's approach to religion was not to condemn it as an opiate of the people, but rather to present socialism as the fulfillment of the social ideals of the early Christians.

> Did not Jesus Christ . . . teach that "it is easier for a camel to pass through the eye of a needle than for a rich man to enter the Kingdom of Heaven"? . . . If the clergy really desire that the principle "Love thy neighbor as thyself" be applied to real life, why do they not welcome keenly the propaganda of the social democrats? . . . [T]he clergy should bless the social democrats, for did not he whom they serve, Jesus Christ, say, "That you do for the poor, you do for me"?

"Socialism and the Churches," in *Rosa Luxemburg Speaks*, ed. Waters, p. 133. The last quotation is that rendered in Matthew 25:40 of the King James version as, "Inasmuch as ye have done it unto one of the least of these my brethren, ye have done it unto me."

82 For example, Elizabeth Faue, *Community of Suffering and Struggle: Women, Men, and the Labor Movement in Minneapolis, 1915–1945* (Chapel Hill: University of North Carolina Press, 1991); the activity of Anna Walentynowicz and Alina Pienkowska in the the strike at the Gdansk shipyards that led to the creation of Polish Solidarity, Staughton Lynd, *Solidarity Unionism: Rebuilding the Labor Movement from Below* (Chicago: Charles H. Kerr, 1992), pp. 34–35; Barbara Kingsolver, *Holding the Line: Women in the Great Arizona Mine Strike of 1983* (Ithaca, N.Y.: ILR Press, 1989); and Toni Gilpin, Gary Isaac, Dan Letwin, and Jack McKivigan, *On Strike for Respect: The Yale Strike of 1984–1985* (Chicago: Charles H. Kerr, 1988).

Glossary

Bolshevik The name given to a supposed majority of the Russian Social Democratic Party after its 1903 congress. The word "bolshe" in Russian means "more" or "greater." Led by Lenin, the Bolsheviks organized the November 1917 revolution in Russia that established the Soviet Union.

Bourgeoisie A synonym for "middle class." Analogously, Marx and others refer to the "petty bourgeoisie," meaning "lower middle class."

Capitalism An economic system in which means of production (large factories, etc.) are held as private property, and in which those without property sell their labor power to survive. From the standpoint of the large property owners or capitalists, the purpose of production in a capitalist economy is to maximize profit.

Communism Refers to (1) a political movement and (2) an imagined future society. The movement is made up of Communist parties. They were formed after World War I, during which most socialist parties supported their respective national governments. The imagined future society is described by Marx and Lenin as one in which each person would work "according to his [or her] ability" but would receive goods or services "according to his [or her] need," and in which the state as a repressive institution would wither away.

Company union A trade union, usually in a single workplace, dominated, interfered with, financed, or otherwise supported by the boss. Corporations started company unions on a large scale in the early 1930s in an effort to head off the formation of truly independent unions.

Direct action First used by anarchists such as Emma Goldman in the late nineteenth century, the term connotes personal protest activity such as refusal to pay taxes, picketing, sit-downs and sit-ins, and strikes. "Direct action" is considered by its advocates to be more effective than voting for candidates chosen by and from the ruling class.

Draft resistance Refusal to be conscripted for war. Draft resistance during the Vietnam War took a variety of forms, ranging from refusal to register for the draft through draft card burning to refusal of induction.

Dual union   Labor law in the United States provides for the selection of a single union to be the exclusive representative of all workers in an appropriate bargaining unit. Where such a recognized representative exists, any effort to initiate autonomous rank-and-file activity may be attacked as a disguised attempt to form a competing or "dual" union.

Dues checkoff   An arrangement whereby management deducts union dues from a worker's paycheck, and then sends the money directly to the union. Dues checkoff came into general use in CIO unions during and after World War II. It replaced the practice of shop stewards collecting dues from individual workers on the shop floor.

Eminent domain   A legal process whereby a public entity acquires private property from an owner unwilling to give it up. An eminent domain taking must be for a public purpose, and the private owner must be paid the fair market value of the property taken.

General strike   A strike of all workers in a particular community or nation at the same time. Examples mentioned in the text are the general strike of Russian workers during the Russian Revolution of 1905, and local general strikes in Minneapolis, San Francisco, and Toledo in 1934.

Imperialism   In general, "imperialism" is the conquest of one country by another, as when Italy invaded Ethiopia in the 1930s. Lenin used the term to refer to the investment of capital in relatively undeveloped, low-wage societies by corporations headquartered in mature capitalist economies. He believed that imperialism would be the "last stage of capitalism."

International union   A term referring to a nationwide trade union based in the United States that has Canadian members.

Leninism (or Marxism-Leninism)   The doctrines and practices associated with the Russian socialist Lenin. Lenin played a leading role in founding the Bolshevik Party and organizing the Russian Revolution of 1917. His doctrines and practices included (1) the conviction that a Marxist revolutionary party must be a highly centralized organization made up of full-time revolutionaries that will provide political instruction to the working class, and (2) the belief that mature capitalist economies are characterized by "imperialism," that is, by corporate investment of capital in relatively undeveloped, low-wage societies.

Management prerogatives   Management's right to take unilateral action with respect to shop rules, work schedules, and details of plant management, and with respect to the investment decisions that affect the overall future of a firm: what products or services to offer, where to locate a facility, whether or not to shut down a facility, etc. Unions may try to limit management prerogatives through collective bargaining, and government may regulate or abolish management prerogatives by legislation.

Mississippi Summer Project   During the summer of 1964, hundreds of white middle-class students came to Mississippi at the invitation of black civil rights activists. Some of the volunteers worked as teachers in improvised summer high schools for black teenagers known as "freedom schools." Others assisted in voter registration and in the creation of the Mississippi Freedom Democratic Party (MFDP), which conducted "freedom votes" for blacks not permitted to take part in the official electoral process. The MFDP unsuccessfully sought to have its own delegates seated at the Democratic Party convention in Atlantic City in August 1964.

National Industrial Recovery Act (NIRA)   A federal labor law enacted in 1933, section 7a of which proclaimed the right of workers to organize unions of their own choosing. The NIRA was administered, ineffectively, by the National Recovery Administration (NRA).

New Left   Term used by student radicals of the 1960s to distinguish themselves from the Communists and Trotskyists of the "Old Left." In the United States the principal organizations of the New Left were Students for a Democratic Society (SDS) and the Student Nonviolent Coordinating Committee (SNCC).

Norris-Laguardia Act   A federal labor law enacted in 1932, which restricted federal judges in issuing court orders (injunctions) in labor disputes.

Old Left   Term used by student radicals of the 1960s to describe the older Communists and Trotskyists who adhered to traditional Marxism. "Old Left" radicals played a major role in the labor organizing of the 1930s.

Paris Commune   Brief uprising of the Parisian working class in 1871 at the end of the Franco-Prussian War. Marx and Engels viewed the Paris Commune as the first proletarian revolution. They found especially instructive the fact that the Communards did not attempt to use the machinery of the bourgeois state, but instead governed through newly created committees, combining legislative and administrative functions.

Participatory democracy   A phrase that appeared in the Port Huron Statement of the Students for a Democratic Society in 1962. In contrast to representative democracy, in which voters choose representatives who make decisions for them, participatory democracy would give citizens an opportunity to take part personally in decision making.

Port Huron Statement Pamphlet stating the political perspective of Students for a Democratic Society (SDS). Drafted by Tom Hayden, it was adopted by a gathering at Port Huron, Michigan, in 1962.

Proletariat Synonym for "working class." A proletarian is one who, having no property of his or her own, can live only by selling labor power to the owners of capital.

Quakers Formally, the Religious Society of Friends. A small Protestant grouping that originated in England during the Civil War of the 1640s. Originally composed of farmers and artisans, the Quakers became more affluent and respectable. They have steadfastly witnessed against war and slavery, for the equality of men and women and of members of all races, and for better treatment of Native Americans, prisoners, and the mentally disturbed.

Second International The worldwide network of Social Democratic parties that existed from the 1880s until the outbreak of World War I in 1914. The word "second" refers to the fact that there existed in the 1860s and 1870s a much smaller network of anarchist and socialist groups in which Karl Marx played a leading role, known as the "First International."

Sit-downs (and Sit-ins) "Sit-down" strikes, in which workers did not leave the factory or office but occupied it instead, were widespread in the United States in the years 1935–1937. "Sit-ins," in which black students sat at lunch counters that refused to serve them and stayed until arrested, began in February 1960 and led to the creation of the Student Nonviolent Coordinating Committee (SNCC).

Socialism Like Communism, both a political movement and an imagined future society. Socialism as a political movement, sometimes called Social Democracy, is typified by mass socialist parties closely allied with the trade union movements of their respective countries. Marx envisioned socialism as a society intermediate between capitalism and Communism in which persons would be compensated on the basis of their work, rather than (as in Communism) on the basis of their need. Many socialists believe that while the means of production (large factories, etc.) must be owned by the people, they should be administered in a decentralized, participatorily democratic manner.

Soviet In form, soviets resembled the central labor bodies of capitalist societies: all sectors of the working class in a given community sent delegates to meetings of the "soviet." Soviets were spontaneously created by Russian workers during the Russian revolutions of 1905 and 1917. After the Bolsheviks came to power in November 1917 the soviets were suppressed.

Stalinism   The doctrines and practices associated with Russian socialist Joseph Stalin. Stalin took part in the Russian Revolution of 1917; in the 1920s, after Lenin's death, he became the leader of Communism both in the Soviet Union and worldwide. "Stalinism" has come to signify the ruthless way in which Stalin imprisoned and executed old comrades, and the undemocratic way in which he sought to impose his will on the working-class movement.

Students for a Democratic Society (SDS)   The principal organization of white student radicals during the 1960s. SDS promulgated a position statement in 1962 known as the Port Huron Statement, remembered particularly for its advocacy of "participatory democracy." SDS also organized the first march on Washington against the Vietnam War in April 1965.

Student Nonviolent Coordinating Committee (SNCC)   The principal organization of black student activists during the 1960s. SNCC grew out of sit-ins early in 1960 and declared its existence at a conference in April of that year. SNCC sent full-time staff representatives into dangerous areas of the Deep South to assist blacks to register and vote.

Taylorism   Frederick W. Taylor advised corporations in the first quarter of the twentieth century how to make production more efficient. He initiated time-and-motion studies as a result of which workers were directed what motions to perform, and how long each motion should take. Where Taylorism was applied, the work to be done, the tools to be used, and the duration and speed of work, were no longer determined by the worker but by the owner of the means of production.

Third International (or Comintern)   The organization of Communist parties worldwide. In practice, the political line of the Third International was dictated by the Bolshevik Party of the Soviet Union and its perception of Soviet interests. During the years 1929 to 1934 or 1935, the Comintern and its constituent parties pursued a so-called Third Period strategy that characterized other socialists as "social fascists" and sought to create new trade unions led by Communists.

Trotskyism   The doctrines and practices associated with Russian socialist Leon Trotsky, especially the belief that socialism could not be built in a single country but could only come into being through worldwide "permanent revolution." Trotsky directed the Red Army during the civil war that followed the Russian Revolution of 1917. After Lenin's death, he lost out in a power struggle with Stalin and went into exile. The principal Trotskyist organization in the United States is the Socialist Workers Party.

Union shop   A union shop is a workplace in which any one who is hired must join the existing union at that workplace. The Taft-Hartley Act of 1947 permitted individual states to ban the union shop, and many states (known as "right to work" states) have done so.

Wagner Act   The federal labor law enacted in 1935, formally known as the National Labor Relations Act (NLRA). Amended by the Taft-Hartley Act in 1947 and by the Landrum-Griffin Act in 1959, the Wagner Act as amended is usually referred to as the Labor Management Relations Act (LMRA).

Wildcat strike   A strike in violation of a no-strike clause in a collective bargaining agreement and/or without authorization by higher union bodies.

Index